FIGHT ME

TINI HOWARD
WRITER

JACOPO CAMAGNI (#6) & GERMÁN PERALTA (#7-9)
ARTISTS

GURU-eFX
COLOR ARTIST

VC's JOE SABINO
LETTERER

JUAN JOSÉ RYP & MATTHEW WILSON (#6-8)
AND DAN MORA & NOLAN WOODARD (#9)
COVER ART

JAY BOWEN
LOGO DESIGN

SARAH BRUNSTAD
ASSOCIATE EDITOR

WIL MOSS
EDITOR

COLLECTION EDITOR **JENNIFER GRÜNWALD**   VP PRODUCTION & SPECIAL PROJECTS **JEFF YOUNGQUIST**
ASSISTANT MANAGING EDITOR **MAIA LOY**   BOOK DESIGNER **JAY BOWEN**
ASSISTANT MANAGING EDITOR **LISA MONTALBANO**   SVP PRINT, SALES & MARKETING **DAVID GABRIEL**
EDITOR, SPECIAL PROJECTS **MARK D. BEAZLEY**   EDITOR IN CHIEF **C.B. CEBULSKI**

STRIKEFORCE VOL. 2: FIGHT ME. Contains material originally published in magazine form as STRIKEFORCE (2019) #6-9 and WAR OF THE REALMS STRIKEFORCE: THE DARK ELF REALM (2019) #1. First printing 2020. ISBN 978-1-302-92010-4. Published by MARVEL WORLDWIDE, INC., a subsidiary of MARVEL ENTERTAINMENT, LLC. OFFICE OF PUBLICATION: 1290 Avenue of the Americas, New York, NY 10104. © 2020 MARVEL. No similarity between any of the names, characters, persons, and/or institutions in this magazine with those of any living or dead person or institution is intended, and any such similarity which may exist is purely coincidental. **Printed in Canada.** KEVIN FEIGE, Chief Creative Officer; DAN BUCKLEY, President, Marvel Entertainment; JOHN NEE, Publisher; JOE QUESADA, EVP & Creative Director; TOM BREVOORT, SVP of Publishing; DAVID BOGART, Associate Publisher & SVP of Talent Affairs; Publishing & Partnership; DAVID GABRIEL, VP of Print & Digital Publishing; JEFF YOUNGQUIST, VP of Production & Special Projects; DAN CARR, Executive Director of Publishing Technology; ALEX MORALES, Director of Publishing Operations; DAN EDINGTON, Managing Editor; RICKEY PURDIN, Director of Talent Relations; SUSAN CRESPI, Production Manager; STAN LEE, Chairman Emeritus. For information regarding advertising in Marvel Comics or on Marvel.com, please contact Vit DeBellis, Custom Solutions & Integrated Advertising Manager, at vdebellis@marvel.com. For Marvel subscription inquiries, please call 888-511-5480. **Manufactured between 10/2/2020 and 11/3/2020 by SOLISCO PRINTERS, SCOTT, QC, CANADA.**

10 9 8 7 6 5 4 3 2 1

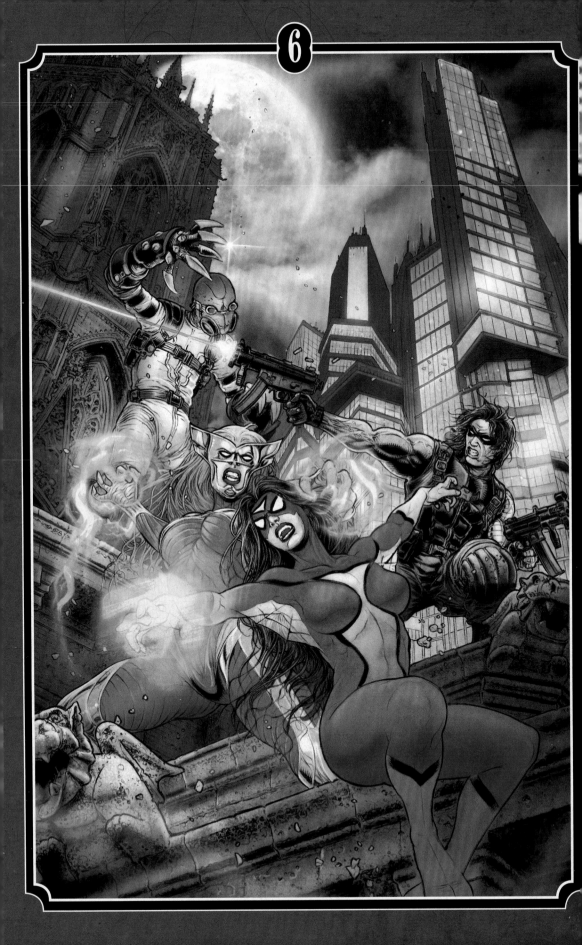

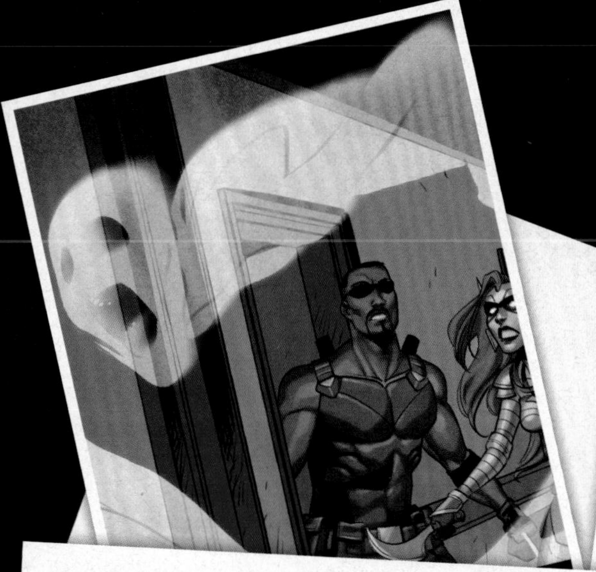

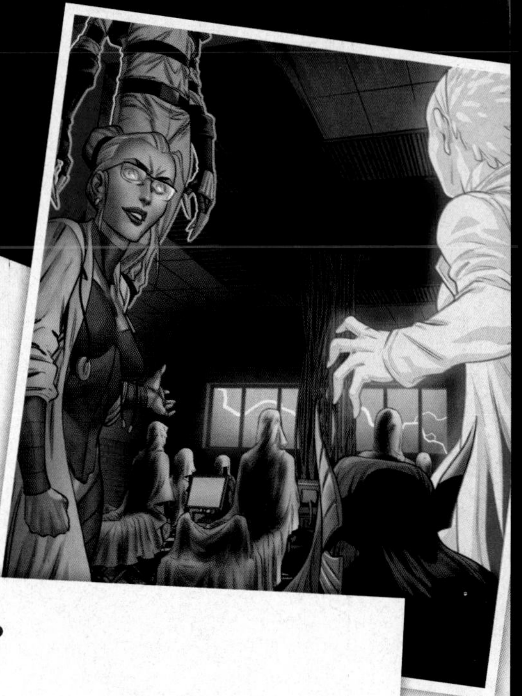

6

MISSION REPORT:

A horde of shape-shifting fae called the Vridai invaded Midgard in the wake of the War of the Realms, kidnapping a seemingly random group of heroes and using their forms to steal a batch of deadly diseases.

The Avengers caught the "rogue heroes," and when Blade recognized the fae from a previous encounter, he took the lead, asking the other Avengers to steer clear. Knowledge of the Vridai is itself a poison, one he's determined to keep from spreading.

After the new covert team seemingly defeated the Vridai, Monica began having strange energy-infused seizures apparently linked to an illegal experiment called the Aaru Project. Leaving Daimon and Wiccan behind with a captive (and comatose) Vridai, the team tracked the energy to a hospital in the middle of nowhere.

They found the place full of ghosts — not only the E.M.P. projections of murdered patients, but also the super villain Ghost, who lured the team here at the behest of crazy former psychologist Karla Sofen...

...A.K.A. Moonstone! Sofen hopes to use Monica's powers to stabilize her experiment, and she's already enacted the first stage: raising the dead!

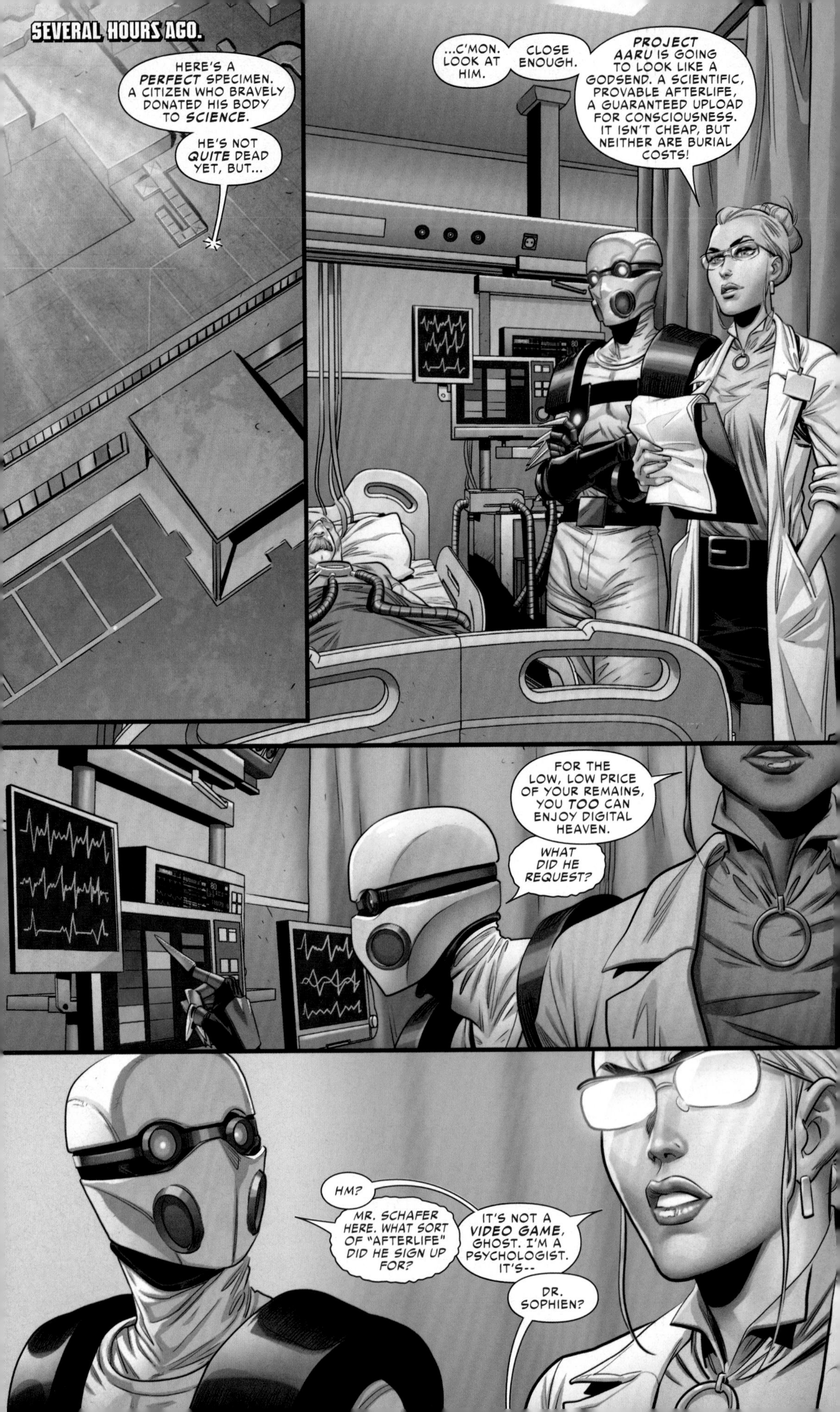
SEVERAL HOURS AGO.
HERE'S A *PERFECT* SPECIMEN. A CITIZEN WHO BRAVELY DONATED HIS BODY TO *SCIENCE*.
HE'S NOT *QUITE* DEAD YET, BUT...
...C'MON. LOOK AT HIM.
CLOSE ENOUGH.
PROJECT AARU IS GOING TO LOOK LIKE A GODSEND. A SCIENTIFIC, PROVABLE AFTERLIFE, A GUARANTEED UPLOAD FOR CONSCIOUSNESS. IT ISN'T CHEAP, BUT NEITHER ARE BURIAL COSTS!
FOR THE LOW, LOW PRICE OF YOUR REMAINS, YOU *TOO* CAN ENJOY DIGITAL HEAVEN.
WHAT DID HE REQUEST?
HM?
MR. SCHAFER HERE. WHAT SORT OF "AFTERLIFE" DID HE SIGN UP FOR?
IT'S NOT A *VIDEO GAME*, GHOST. I'M A PSYCHOLOGIST. IT'S--
DR. SOPHIEN?

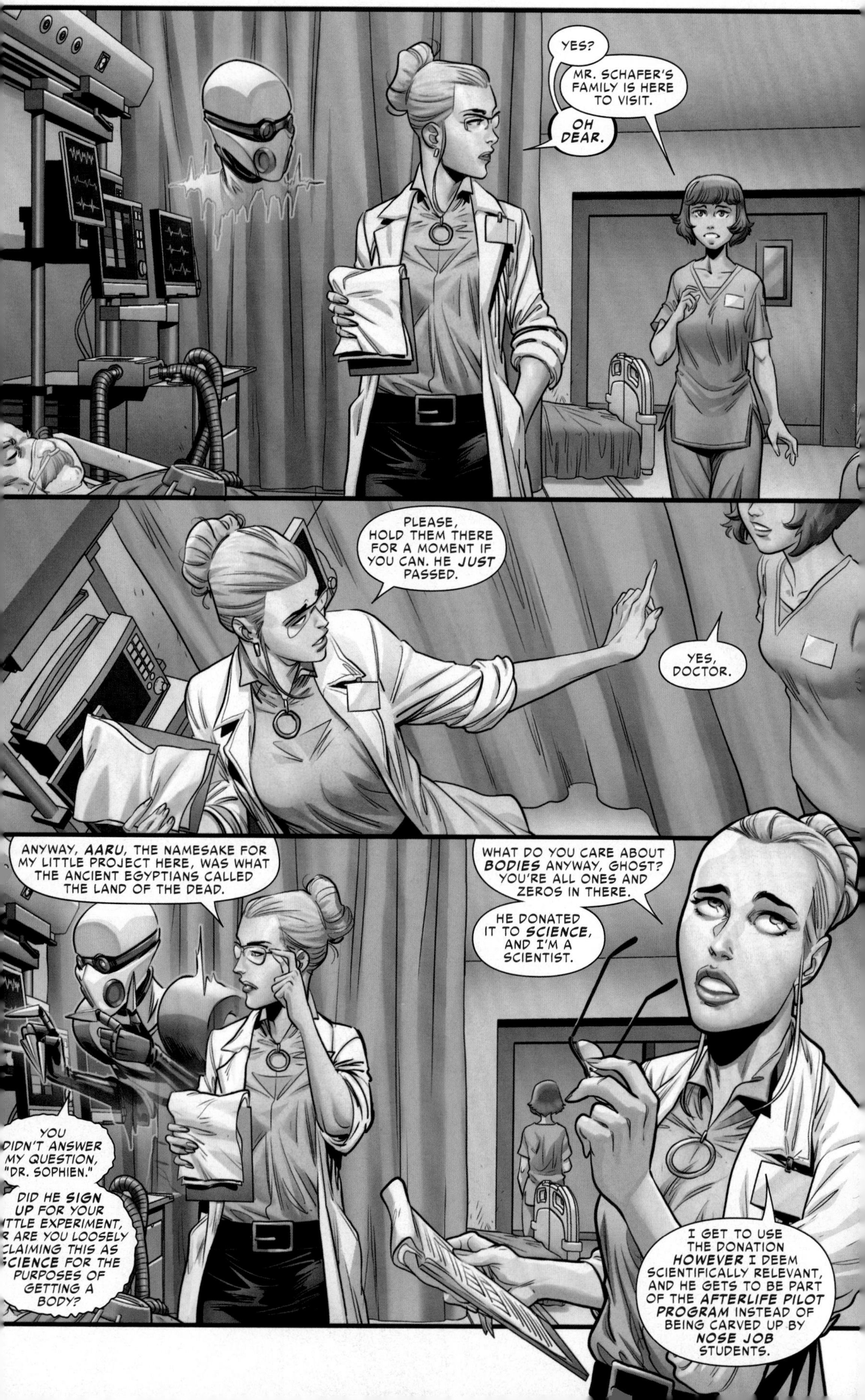
YES?
MR. SCHAFER'S FAMILY IS HERE TO VISIT.
OH DEAR.
PLEASE, HOLD THEM THERE FOR A MOMENT IF YOU CAN. HE JUST PASSED.
YES, DOCTOR.
ANYWAY, AARU, THE NAMESAKE FOR MY LITTLE PROJECT HERE, WAS WHAT THE ANCIENT EGYPTIANS CALLED THE LAND OF THE DEAD.
YOU DIDN'T ANSWER MY QUESTION, "DR. SOPHIEN."
DID HE SIGN UP FOR YOUR LITTLE EXPERIMENT, OR ARE YOU LOOSELY CLAIMING THIS AS SCIENCE FOR THE PURPOSES OF GETTING A BODY?
WHAT DO YOU CARE ABOUT BODIES ANYWAY, GHOST? YOU'RE ALL ONES AND ZEROS IN THERE.
HE DONATED IT TO SCIENCE, AND I'M A SCIENTIST.
I GET TO USE THE DONATION HOWEVER I DEEM SCIENTIFICALLY RELEVANT, AND HE GETS TO BE PART OF THE AFTERLIFE PILOT PROGRAM INSTEAD OF BEING CARVED UP BY NOSE JOB STUDENTS.

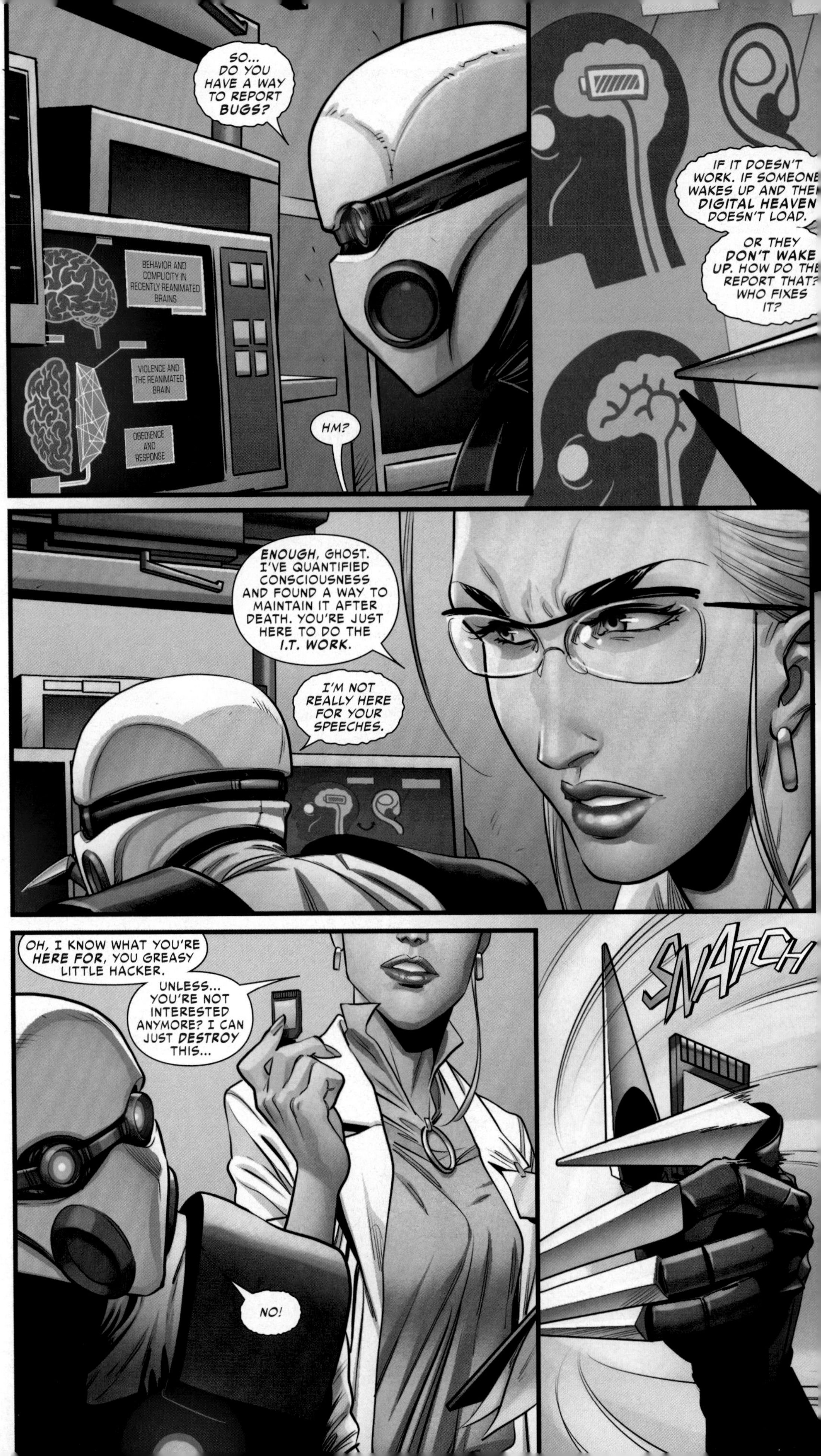
SO... DO YOU HAVE A WAY TO REPORT BUGS?
BEHAVIOR AND COMPLICITY IN RECENTLY REANIMATED BRAINS
VIOLENCE AND THE REANIMATED BRAIN
OBEDIENCE AND RESPONSE
HM?
IF IT DOESN'T WORK. IF SOMEONE WAKES UP AND THEI DIGITAL HEAVEN DOESN'T LOAD.
OR THEY DON'T WAKE UP. HOW DO THE REPORT THAT? WHO FIXES IT?
ENOUGH, GHOST. I'VE QUANTIFIED CONSCIOUSNESS AND FOUND A WAY TO MAINTAIN IT AFTER DEATH. YOU'RE JUST HERE TO DO THE I.T. WORK.
I'M NOT REALLY HERE FOR YOUR SPEECHES.
OH, I KNOW WHAT YOU'RE HERE FOR, YOU GREASY LITTLE HACKER.
UNLESS... YOU'RE NOT INTERESTED ANYMORE? I CAN JUST DESTROY THIS...
NO!
SNATCH

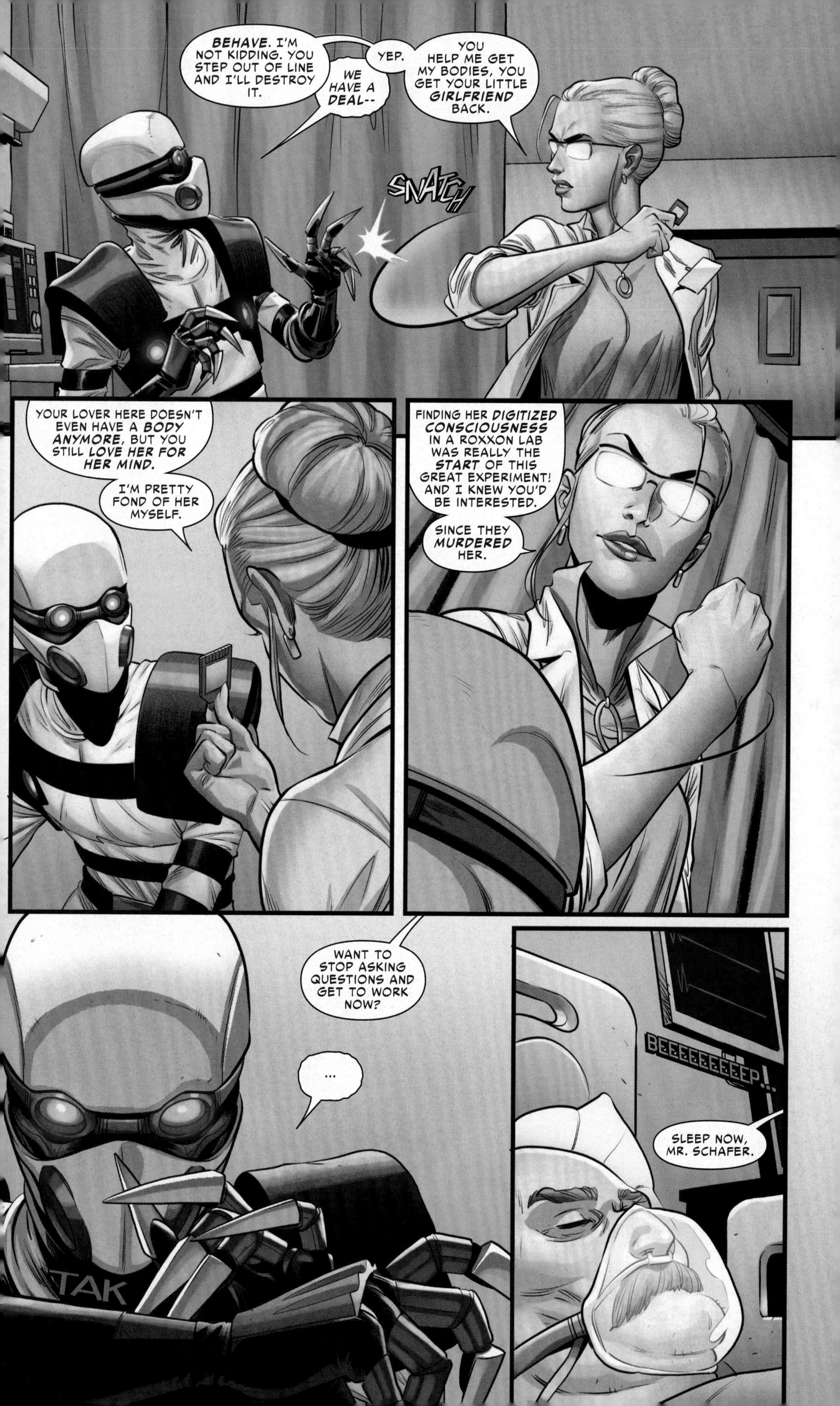

BEHAVE. I'M NOT KIDDING. YOU STEP OUT OF LINE AND I'LL DESTROY IT.
YEP.
WE HAVE A DEAL--
YOU HELP ME GET MY BODIES, YOU GET YOUR LITTLE GIRLFRIEND BACK.
SNATCH
YOUR LOVER HERE DOESN'T EVEN HAVE A BODY ANYMORE, BUT YOU STILL LOVE HER FOR HER MIND.
I'M PRETTY FOND OF HER MYSELF.
FINDING HER DIGITIZED CONSCIOUSNESS IN A ROXXON LAB WAS REALLY THE START OF THIS GREAT EXPERIMENT! AND I KNEW YOU'D BE INTERESTED.
SINCE THEY MURDERED HER.
WANT TO STOP ASKING QUESTIONS AND GET TO WORK NOW?
...
BEEEEEEEEEP...
SLEEP NOW, MR. SCHAFER.

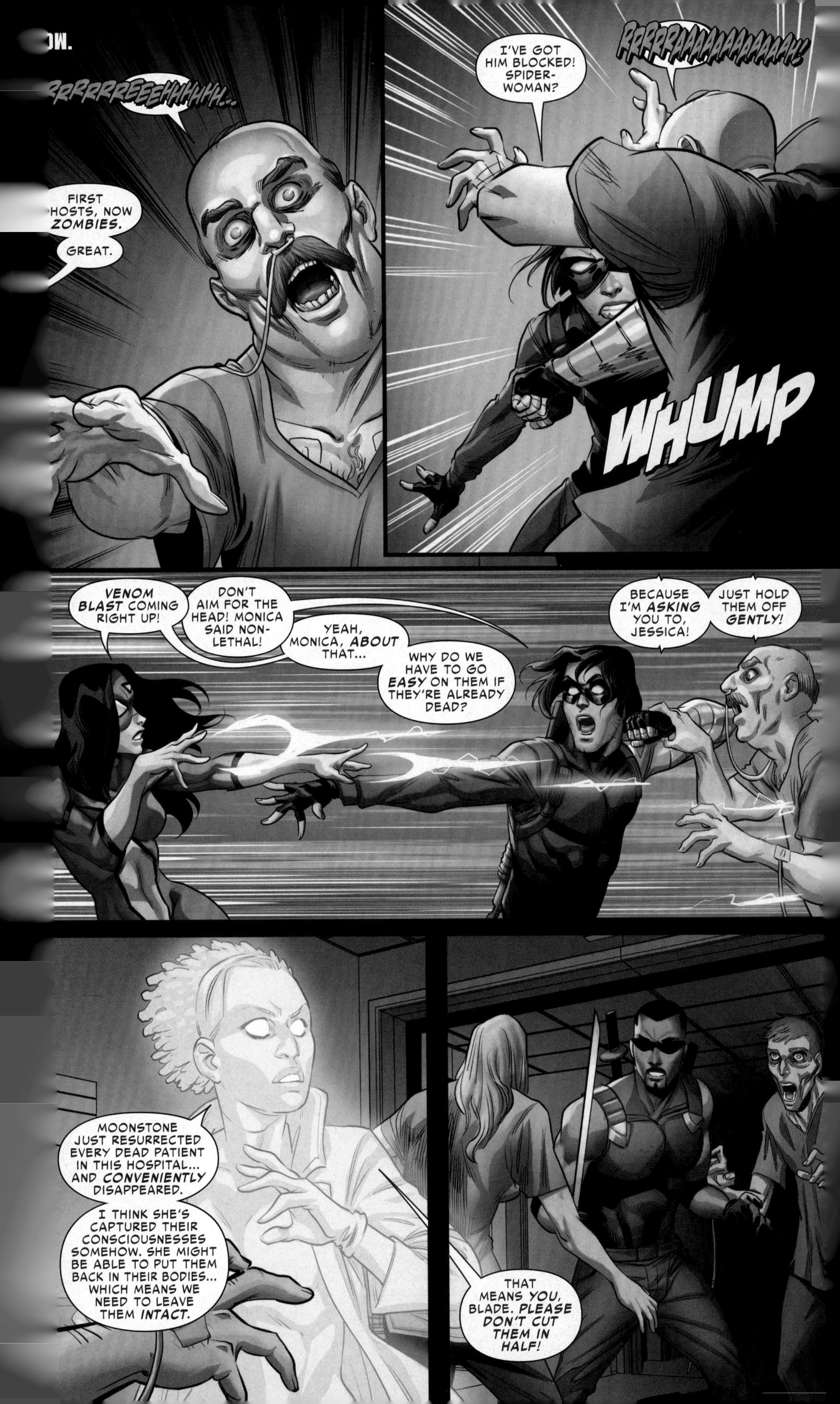

OW.
RRRRRRREEEHHHHH...
FIRST HOSTS, NOW ZOMBIES.
GREAT.
I'VE GOT HIM BLOCKED! SPIDER-WOMAN?
RRRRAAAAAAAAAAAH!
WHUMP
VENOM BLAST COMING RIGHT UP!
DON'T AIM FOR THE HEAD! MONICA SAID NON-LETHAL!
YEAH, MONICA, ABOUT THAT...
WHY DO WE HAVE TO GO EASY ON THEM IF THEY'RE ALREADY DEAD?
BECAUSE I'M ASKING YOU TO, JESSICA!
JUST HOLD THEM OFF GENTLY!
MOONSTONE JUST RESURRECTED EVERY DEAD PATIENT IN THIS HOSPITAL... AND CONVENIENTLY DISAPPEARED.
I THINK SHE'S CAPTURED THEIR CONSCIOUSNESSES SOMEHOW. SHE MIGHT BE ABLE TO PUT THEM BACK IN THEIR BODIES... WHICH MEANS WE NEED TO LEAVE THEM INTACT.
THAT MEANS YOU, BLADE. PLEASE DON'T CUT THEM IN HALF!

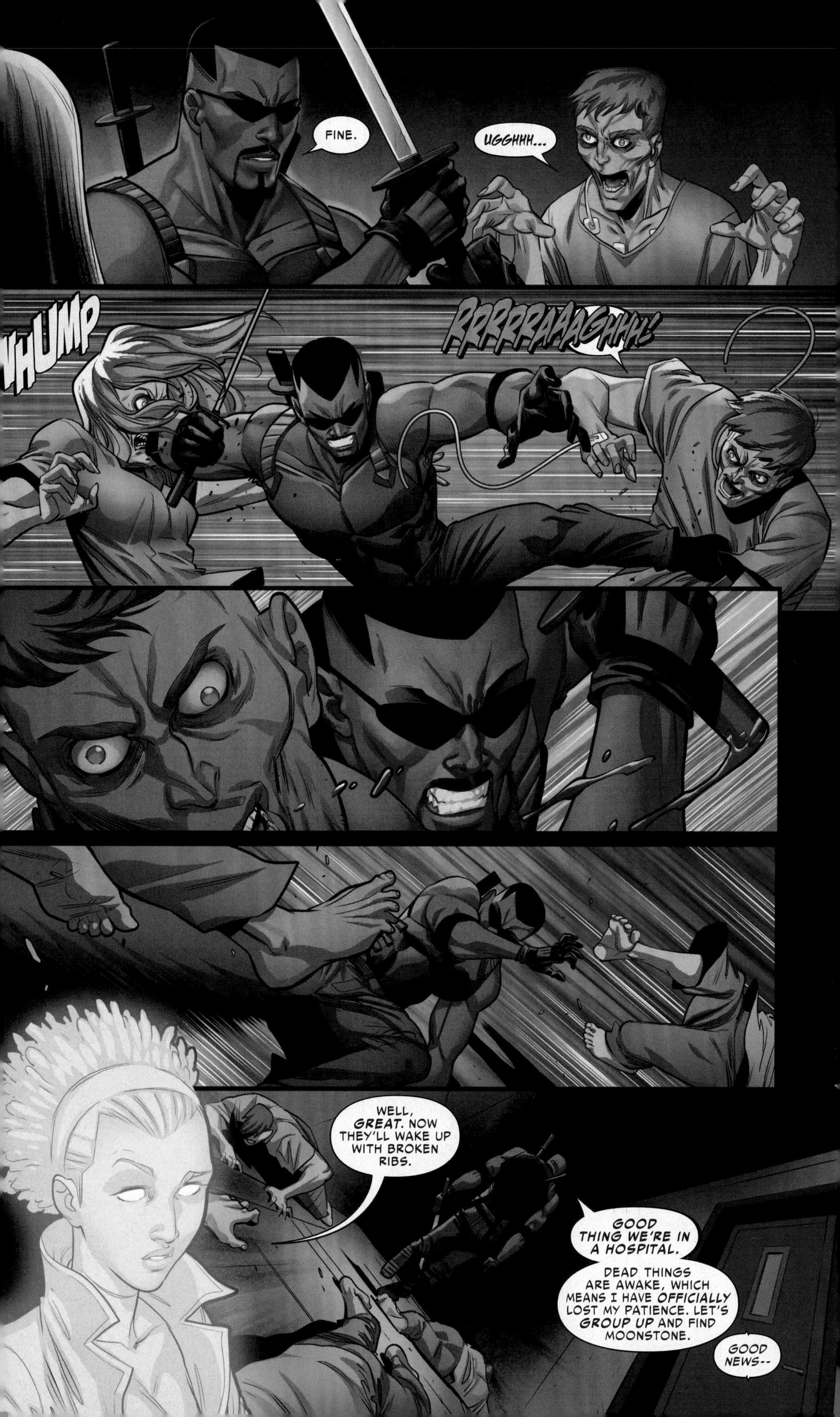
FINE.
UGGHHH...
WHUMP
RRRRRAAAGHHH!
WELL, GREAT. NOW THEY'LL WAKE UP WITH BROKEN RIBS.
GOOD THING WE'RE IN A HOSPITAL.
DEAD THINGS ARE AWAKE, WHICH MEANS I HAVE OFFICIALLY LOST MY PATIENCE. LET'S GROUP UP AND FIND MOONSTONE.
GOOD NEWS--

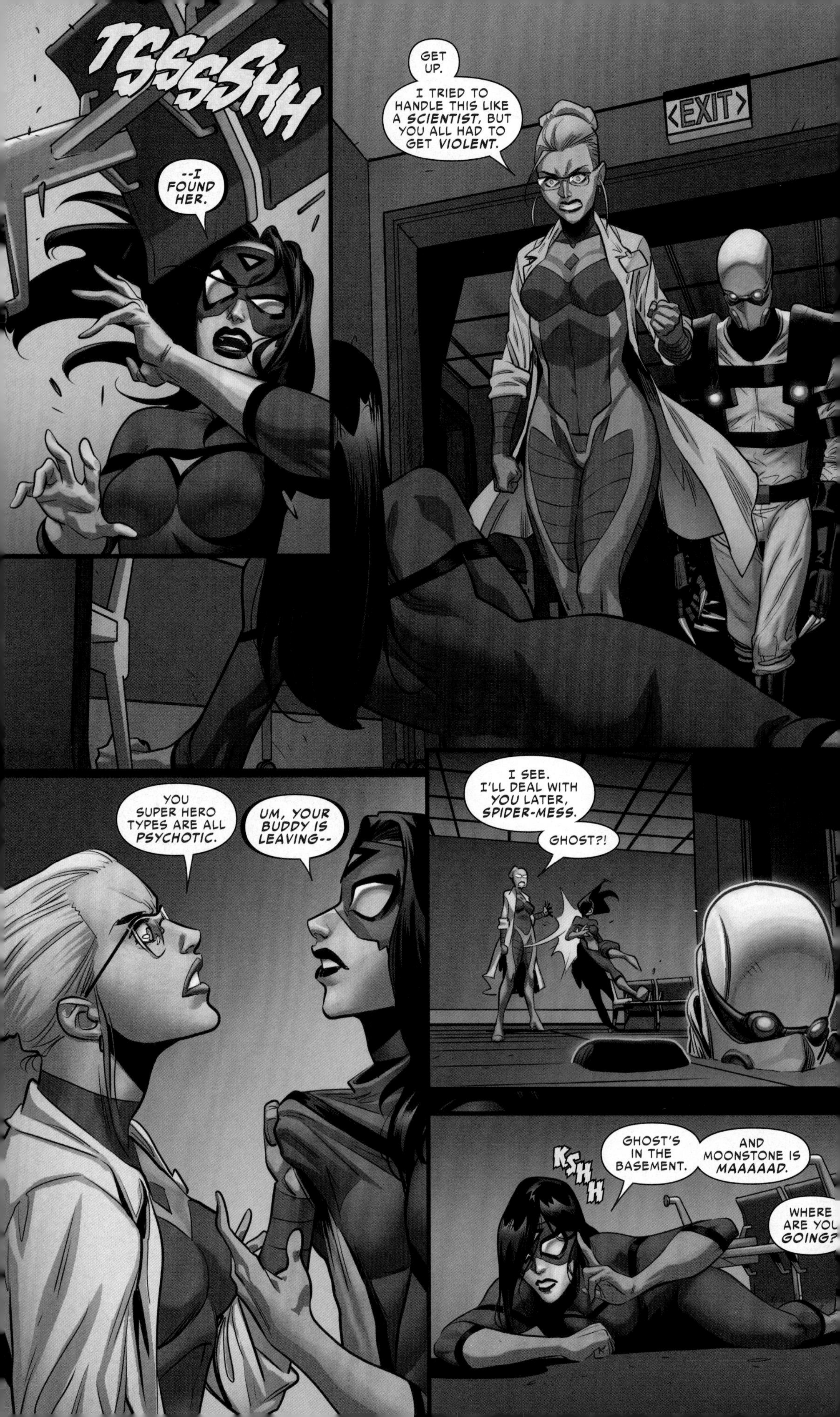
TSSSSHH
--I FOUND HER.
GET UP.
I TRIED TO HANDLE THIS LIKE A SCIENTIST, BUT YOU ALL HAD TO GET VIOLENT.
EXIT
YOU SUPER HERO TYPES ARE ALL PSYCHOTIC.
UM, YOUR BUDDY IS LEAVING--
I SEE. I'LL DEAL WITH YOU LATER, SPIDER-MESS.
GHOST?!
KSHH
GHOST'S IN THE BASEMENT.
AND MOONSTONE IS MAAAAAD.
WHERE ARE YOU GOING?

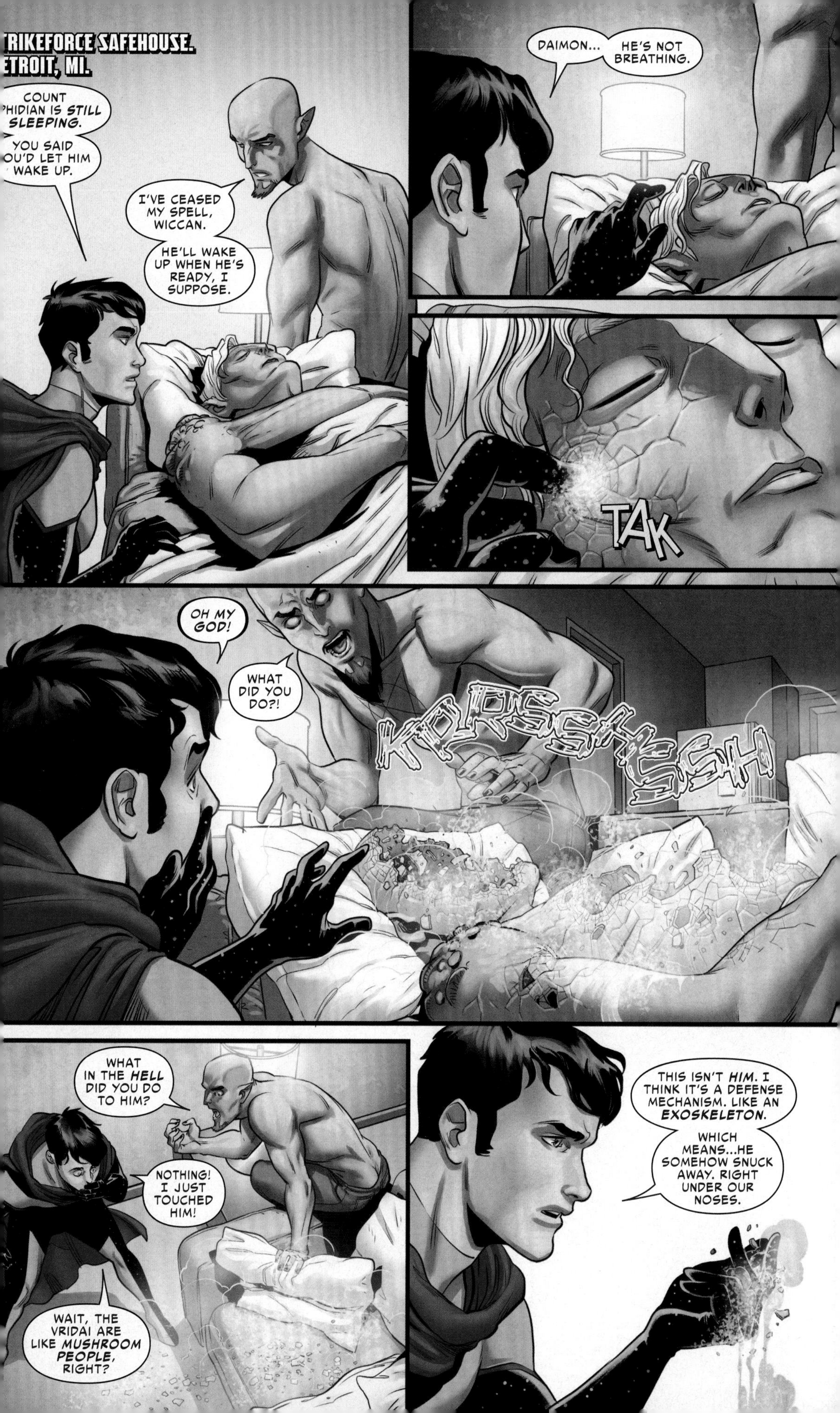
TRIKEFORCE SAFEHOUSE.
ETROIT, MI.
COUNT PHIDIAN IS STILL SLEEPING.
YOU SAID YOU'D LET HIM WAKE UP.
I'VE CEASED MY SPELL, WICCAN.
HE'LL WAKE UP WHEN HE'S READY, I SUPPOSE.
DAIMON...
HE'S NOT BREATHING.
TAK
OH MY GOD!
WHAT DID YOU DO?!
KRRSSHHSSH
WHAT IN THE HELL DID YOU DO TO HIM?
NOTHING! I JUST TOUCHED HIM!
WAIT, THE VRIDAI ARE LIKE MUSHROOM PEOPLE, RIGHT?
THIS ISN'T HIM. I THINK IT'S A DEFENSE MECHANISM. LIKE AN EXOSKELETON.
WHICH MEANS...HE SOMEHOW SNUCK AWAY. RIGHT UNDER OUR NOSES.

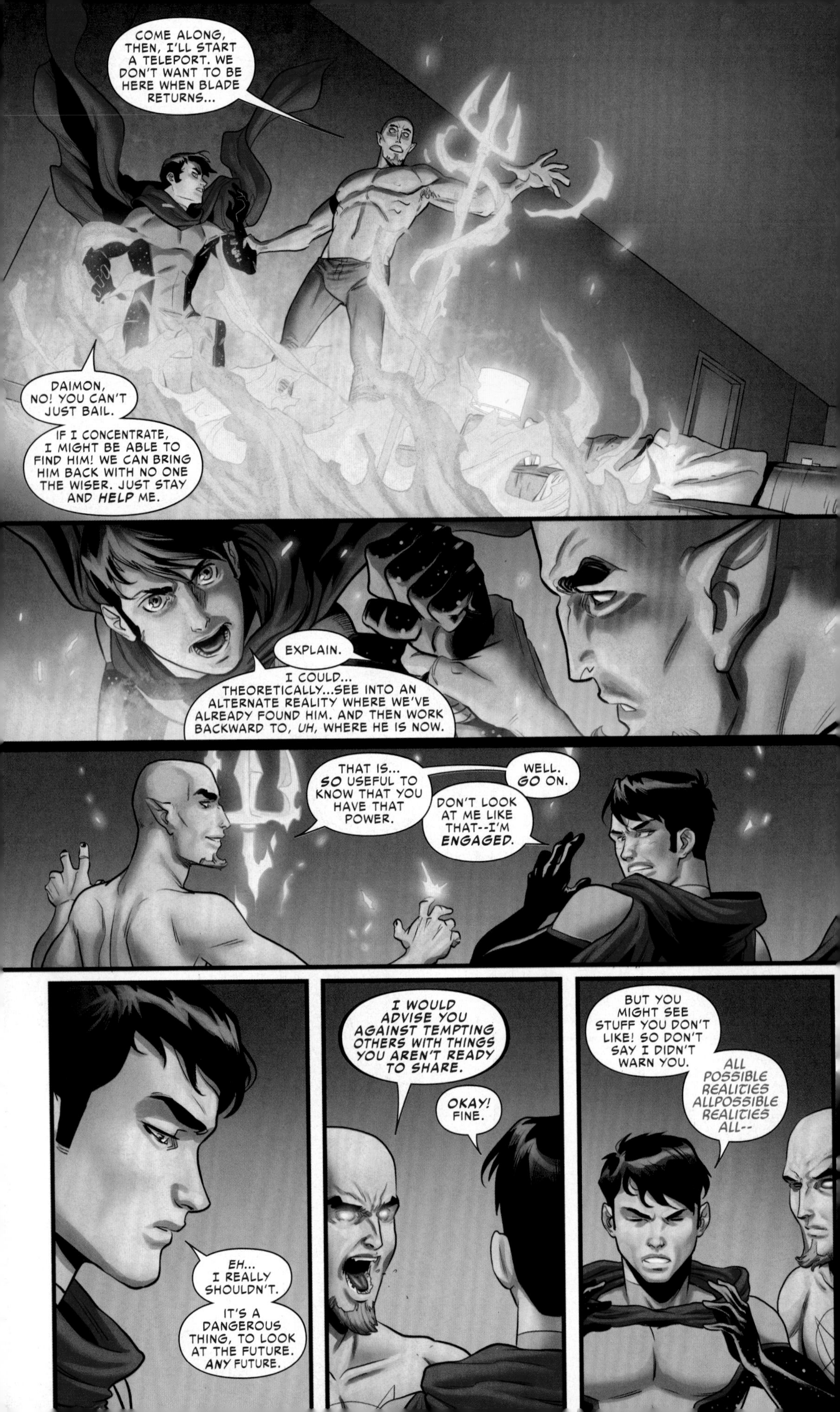
COME ALONG, THEN, I'LL START A TELEPORT. WE DON'T WANT TO BE HERE WHEN BLADE RETURNS...
DAIMON, NO! YOU CAN'T JUST BAIL.
IF I CONCENTRATE, I MIGHT BE ABLE TO FIND HIM! WE CAN BRING HIM BACK WITH NO ONE THE WISER. JUST STAY AND HELP ME.
EXPLAIN.
I COULD... THEORETICALLY...SEE INTO AN ALTERNATE REALITY WHERE WE'VE ALREADY FOUND HIM. AND THEN WORK BACKWARD TO, UH, WHERE HE IS NOW.
THAT IS... SO USEFUL TO KNOW THAT YOU HAVE THAT POWER.
WELL. GO ON.
DON'T LOOK AT ME LIKE THAT--I'M ENGAGED.
EH... I REALLY SHOULDN'T.
IT'S A DANGEROUS THING, TO LOOK AT THE FUTURE. ANY FUTURE.
I WOULD ADVISE YOU AGAINST TEMPTING OTHERS WITH THINGS YOU AREN'T READY TO SHARE.
OKAY! FINE.
BUT YOU MIGHT SEE STUFF YOU DON'T LIKE! SO DON'T SAY I DIDN'T WARN YOU.
ALL POSSIBLE REALITIES ALLPOSSIBLE REALITIES ALL--

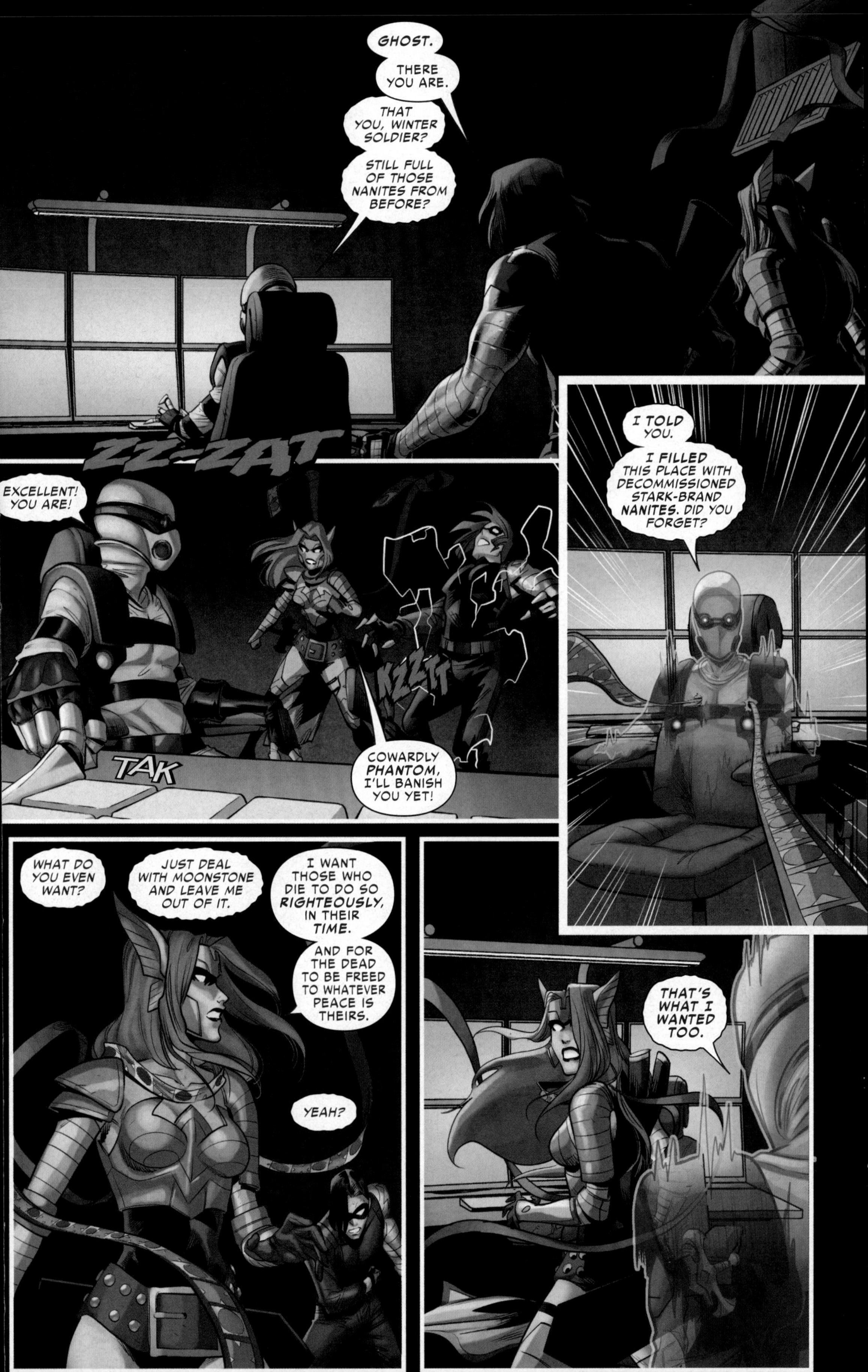
GHOST.
THERE YOU ARE.
THAT YOU, WINTER SOLDIER?
STILL FULL OF THOSE NANITES FROM BEFORE?
ZZ-ZAT
EXCELLENT! YOU ARE!
KZZTT
TAK
COWARDLY PHANTOM, I'LL BANISH YOU YET!
I TOLD YOU.
I FILLED THIS PLACE WITH DECOMMISSIONED STARK-BRAND NANITES. DID YOU FORGET?
WHAT DO YOU EVEN WANT?
JUST DEAL WITH MOONSTONE AND LEAVE ME OUT OF IT.
I WANT THOSE WHO DIE TO DO SO RIGHTEOUSLY, IN THEIR TIME.
AND FOR THE DEAD TO BE FREED TO WHATEVER PEACE IS THEIRS.
YEAH?
THAT'S WHAT I WANTED TOO.

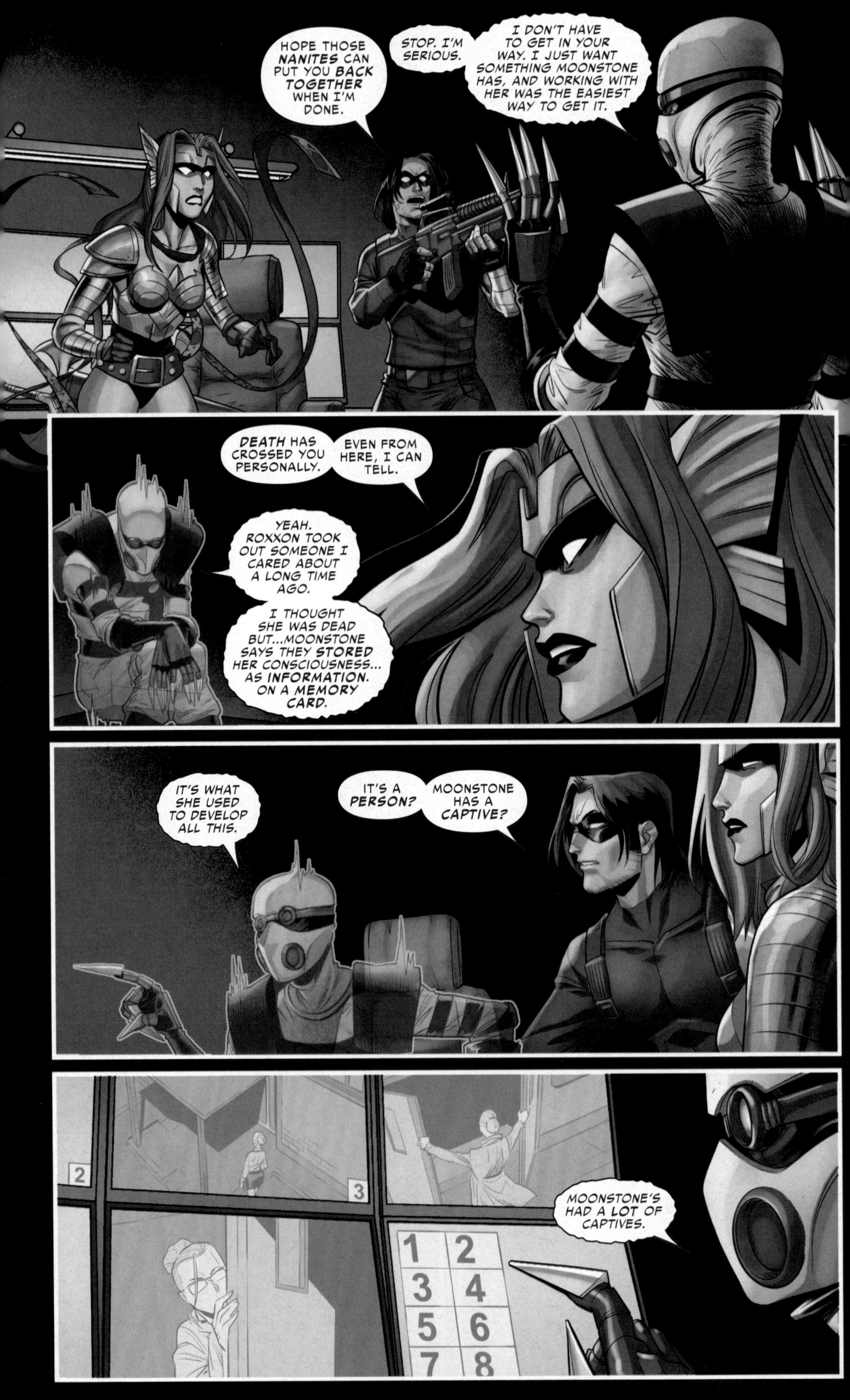
HOPE THOSE NANITES CAN PUT YOU BACK TOGETHER WHEN I'M DONE.
STOP. I'M SERIOUS.
I DON'T HAVE TO GET IN YOUR WAY. I JUST WANT SOMETHING MOONSTONE HAS, AND WORKING WITH HER WAS THE EASIEST WAY TO GET IT.
DEATH HAS CROSSED YOU PERSONALLY.
EVEN FROM HERE, I CAN TELL.
YEAH. ROXXON TOOK OUT SOMEONE I CARED ABOUT A LONG TIME AGO.
I THOUGHT SHE WAS DEAD BUT...MOONSTONE SAYS THEY STORED HER CONSCIOUSNESS... AS INFORMATION. ON A MEMORY CARD.
IT'S WHAT SHE USED TO DEVELOP ALL THIS.
IT'S A PERSON?
MOONSTONE HAS A CAPTIVE?
2
3
MOONSTONE'S HAD A LOT OF CAPTIVES.
1 2
3 4
5 6
7 8

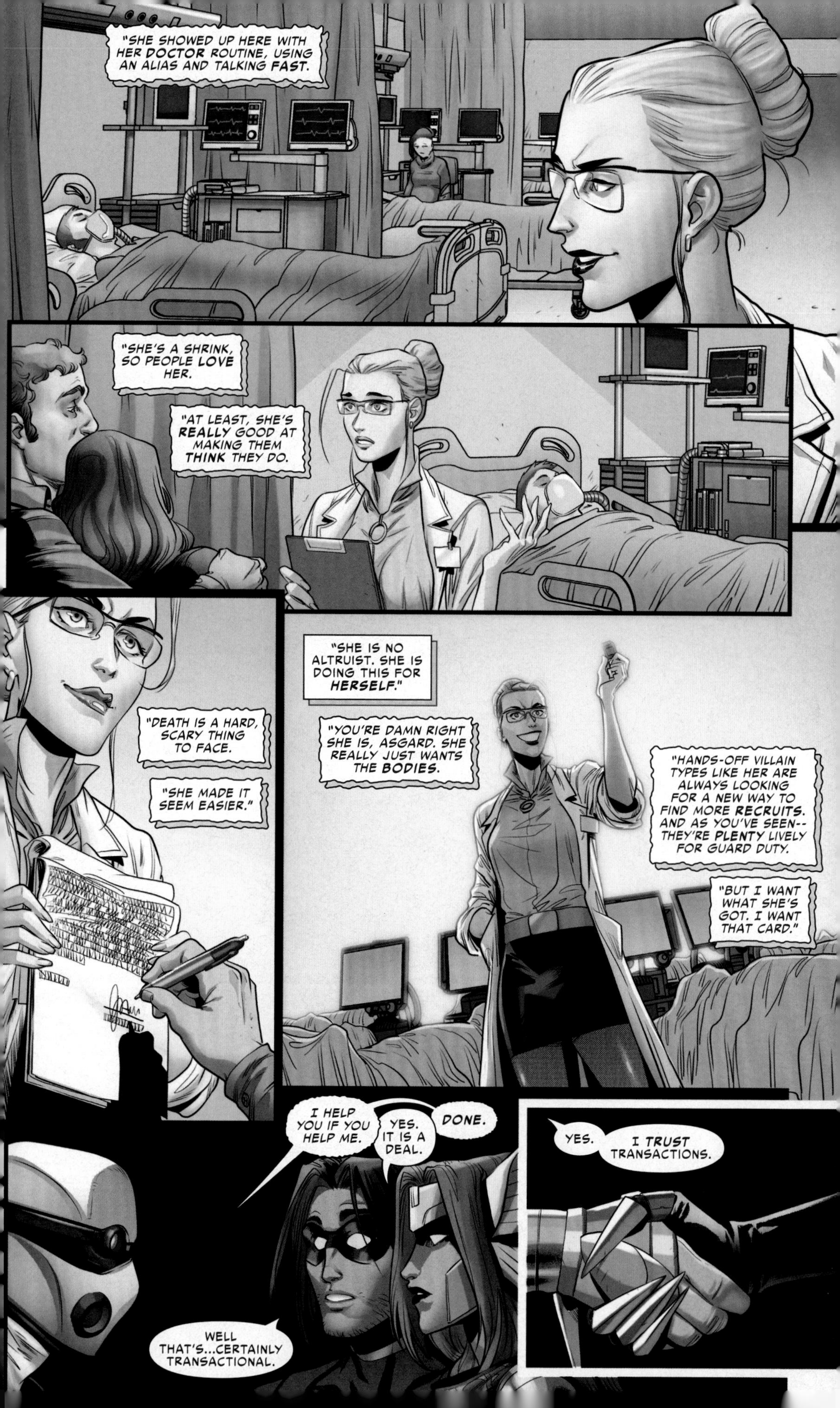
"SHE SHOWED UP HERE WITH HER DOCTOR ROUTINE, USING AN ALIAS AND TALKING FAST.
"SHE'S A SHRINK, SO PEOPLE LOVE HER.
"AT LEAST, SHE'S REALLY GOOD AT MAKING THEM THINK THEY DO.
"DEATH IS A HARD, SCARY THING TO FACE.
"SHE MADE IT SEEM EASIER."
"SHE IS NO ALTRUIST. SHE IS DOING THIS FOR HERSELF."
"YOU'RE DAMN RIGHT SHE IS, ASGARD. SHE REALLY JUST WANTS THE BODIES.
"HANDS-OFF VILLAIN TYPES LIKE HER ARE ALWAYS LOOKING FOR A NEW WAY TO FIND MORE RECRUITS. AND AS YOU'VE SEEN-- THEY'RE PLENTY LIVELY FOR GUARD DUTY.
"BUT I WANT WHAT SHE'S GOT. I WANT THAT CARD."
I HELP YOU IF YOU HELP ME.
YES. IT IS A DEAL.
DONE.
WELL THAT'S...CERTAINLY TRANSACTIONAL.
YES.
I TRUST TRANSACTIONS.

"DAIMON, I FOUND HIM!"

AAAAUUUGGGHHH!

OH, I FEEL REALLY SILLY NOW-- HE'S IN THE BUILDING.

WHAT IN THE HELL WAS THAT?!

EH? SORRY IF YOU SAW SOMETHING BAD, I DON'T HAVE A LOT OF PRECISION.

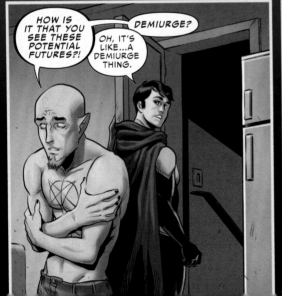

HOW IS IT THAT YOU SEE THESE POTENTIAL FUTURES?!

DEMIURGE?

OH, IT'S LIKE...A DEMIURGE THING.

I ONLY KNOW THAT WORD AS IT REFERS TO THE EXTRAPLANAR DOMINUS OF ALL REALITY--

YEAH, THAT. THAT'S ME. NOT YET, BUT GETTING THERE.

NOW C'MON, I'M NOT GOING INTO THIS GROSS BASEMENT ALONE.

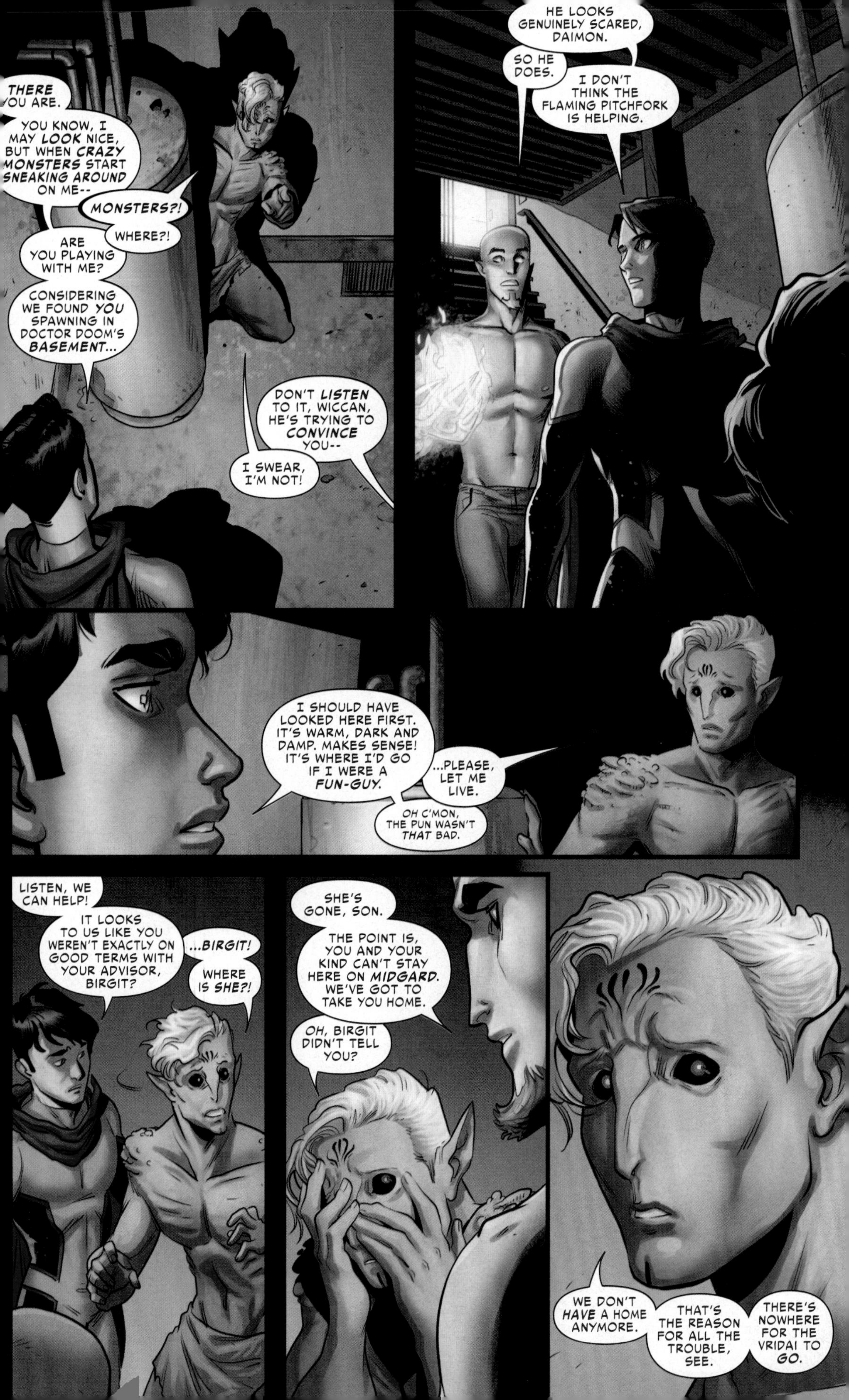
THERE YOU ARE.
YOU KNOW, I MAY LOOK NICE, BUT WHEN CRAZY MONSTERS START SNEAKING AROUND ON ME--
MONSTERS?!
WHERE?!
ARE YOU PLAYING WITH ME?
CONSIDERING WE FOUND YOU SPAWNING IN DOCTOR DOOM'S BASEMENT...
DON'T LISTEN TO IT, WICCAN, HE'S TRYING TO CONVINCE YOU--
I SWEAR, I'M NOT!
HE LOOKS GENUINELY SCARED, DAIMON.
SO HE DOES.
I DON'T THINK THE FLAMING PITCHFORK IS HELPING.
I SHOULD HAVE LOOKED HERE FIRST. IT'S WARM, DARK AND DAMP. MAKES SENSE! IT'S WHERE I'D GO IF I WERE A FUN-GUY.
...PLEASE, LET ME LIVE.
OH C'MON, THE PUN WASN'T THAT BAD.
LISTEN, WE CAN HELP!
IT LOOKS TO US LIKE YOU WEREN'T EXACTLY ON GOOD TERMS WITH YOUR ADVISOR, BIRGIT?
...BIRGIT!
WHERE IS SHE?!
SHE'S GONE, SON.
THE POINT IS, YOU AND YOUR KIND CAN'T STAY HERE ON MIDGARD. WE'VE GOT TO TAKE YOU HOME.
OH, BIRGIT DIDN'T TELL YOU?
WE DON'T HAVE A HOME ANYMORE.
THAT'S THE REASON FOR ALL THE TROUBLE, SEE.
THERE'S NOWHERE FOR THE VRIDAI TO GO.

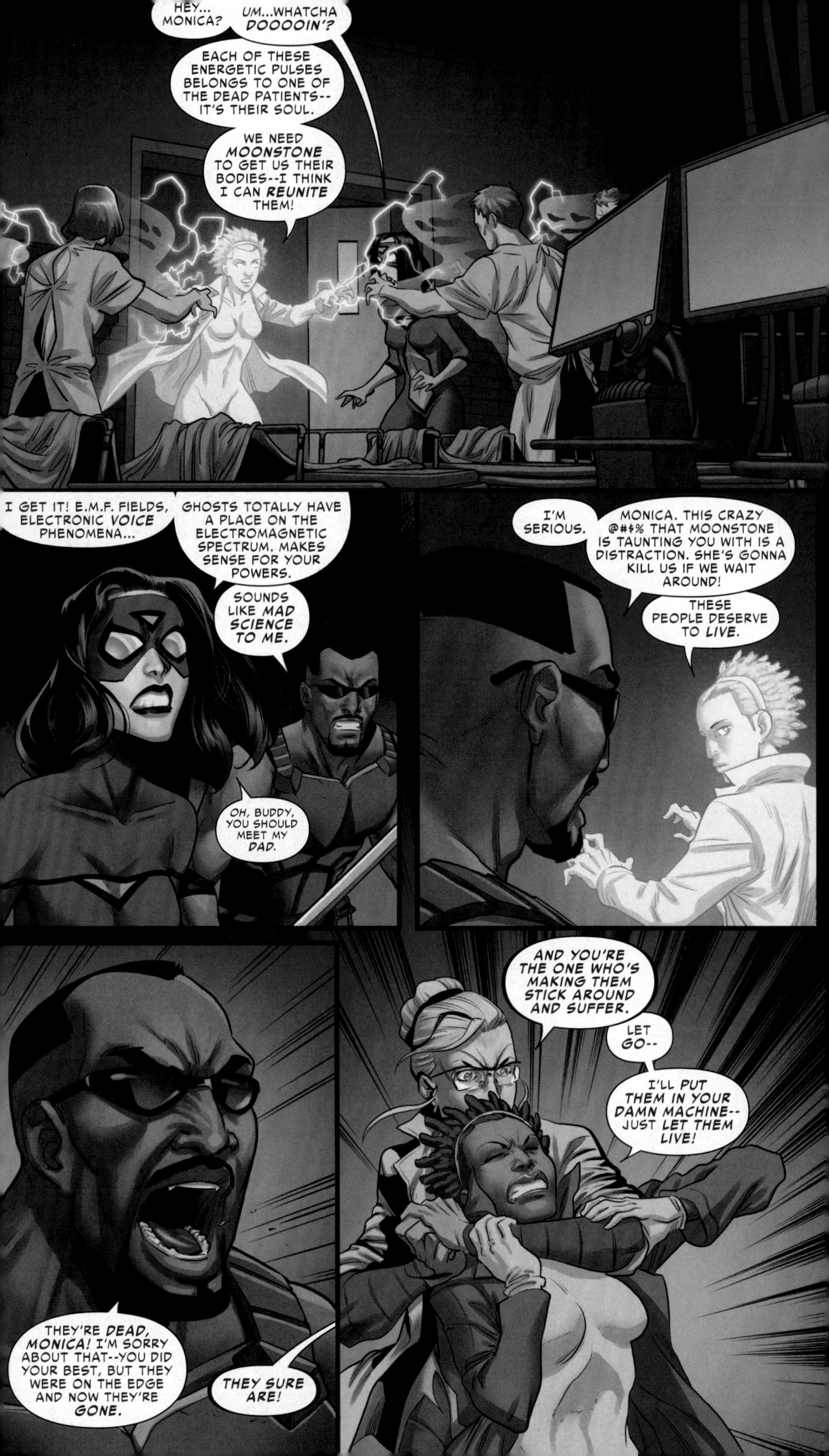
HEY... MONICA?
UM...WHATCHA DOOOOIN'?
EACH OF THESE ENERGETIC PULSES BELONGS TO ONE OF THE DEAD PATIENTS-- IT'S THEIR SOUL.
WE NEED MOONSTONE TO GET US THEIR BODIES--I THINK I CAN REUNITE THEM!
I GET IT! E.M.F. FIELDS, ELECTRONIC VOICE PHENOMENA...
GHOSTS TOTALLY HAVE A PLACE ON THE ELECTROMAGNETIC SPECTRUM. MAKES SENSE FOR YOUR POWERS.
SOUNDS LIKE MAD SCIENCE TO ME.
OH, BUDDY, YOU SHOULD MEET MY DAD.
I'M SERIOUS.
MONICA. THIS CRAZY @#$% THAT MOONSTONE IS TAUNTING YOU WITH IS A DISTRACTION. SHE'S GONNA KILL US IF WE WAIT AROUND!
THESE PEOPLE DESERVE TO LIVE.
THEY'RE DEAD, MONICA! I'M SORRY ABOUT THAT--YOU DID YOUR BEST, BUT THEY WERE ON THE EDGE AND NOW THEY'RE GONE.
THEY SURE ARE!
AND YOU'RE THE ONE WHO'S MAKING THEM STICK AROUND AND SUFFER.
LET GO--
I'LL PUT THEM IN YOUR DAMN MACHINE-- JUST LET THEM LIVE!

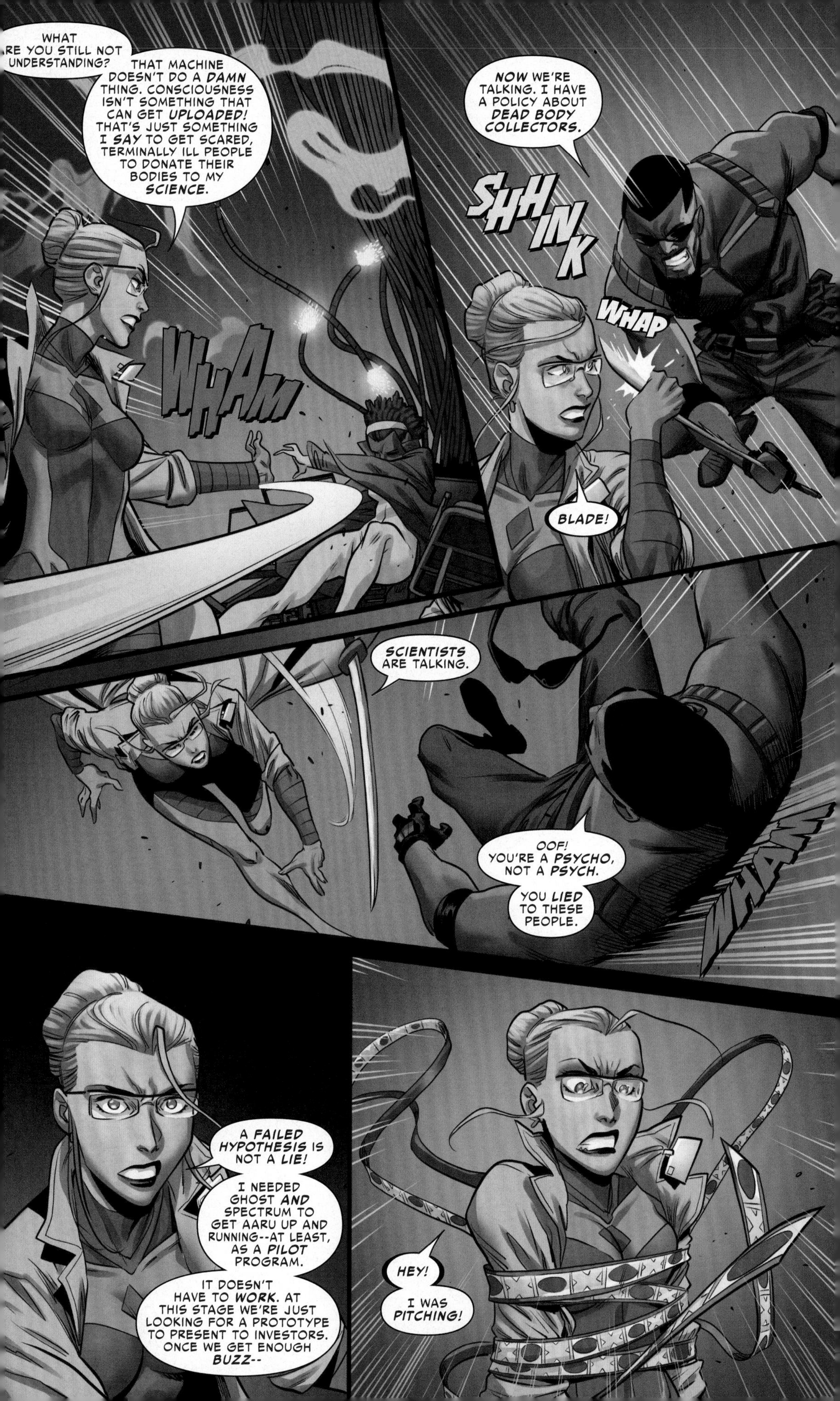
WHAT ARE YOU STILL NOT UNDERSTANDING?
THAT MACHINE DOESN'T DO A DAMN THING. CONSCIOUSNESS ISN'T SOMETHING THAT CAN GET UPLOADED! THAT'S JUST SOMETHING I SAY TO GET SCARED, TERMINALLY ILL PEOPLE TO DONATE THEIR BODIES TO MY SCIENCE.
WHAM
NOW WE'RE TALKING. I HAVE A POLICY ABOUT DEAD BODY COLLECTORS.
SHHINK
WHAP
BLADE!
SCIENTISTS ARE TALKING.
OOF! YOU'RE A PSYCHO, NOT A PSYCH.
YOU LIED TO THESE PEOPLE.
WHAM
A FAILED HYPOTHESIS IS NOT A LIE!
I NEEDED GHOST AND SPECTRUM TO GET AARU UP AND RUNNING--AT LEAST, AS A PILOT PROGRAM.
IT DOESN'T HAVE TO WORK. AT THIS STAGE WE'RE JUST LOOKING FOR A PROTOTYPE TO PRESENT TO INVESTORS. ONCE WE GET ENOUGH BUZZ--
HEY!
I WAS PITCHING!

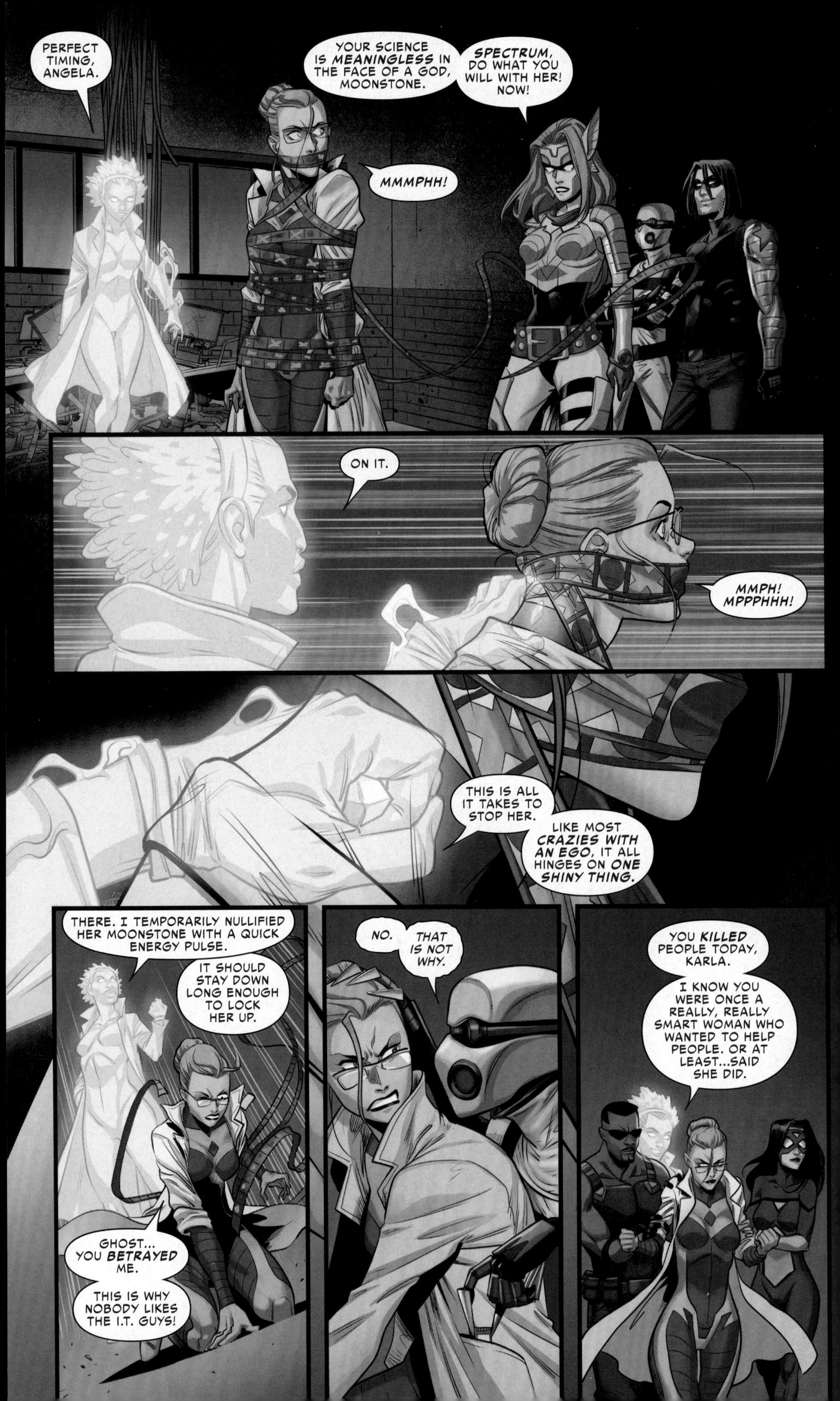
PERFECT TIMING, ANGELA.
YOUR SCIENCE IS MEANINGLESS IN THE FACE OF A GOD, MOONSTONE.
SPECTRUM, DO WHAT YOU WILL WITH HER! NOW!
MMMPHH!
ON IT.
MMPH! MPPPHHH!
THIS IS ALL IT TAKES TO STOP HER.
LIKE MOST CRAZIES WITH AN EGO, IT ALL HINGES ON ONE SHINY THING.
THERE. I TEMPORARILY NULLIFIED HER MOONSTONE WITH A QUICK ENERGY PULSE.
IT SHOULD STAY DOWN LONG ENOUGH TO LOCK HER UP.
GHOST... YOU BETRAYED ME.
THIS IS WHY NOBODY LIKES THE I.T. GUYS!
NO.
THAT IS NOT WHY.
YOU KILLED PEOPLE TODAY, KARLA.
I KNOW YOU WERE ONCE A REALLY, REALLY SMART WOMAN WHO WANTED TO HELP PEOPLE. OR AT LEAST...SAID SHE DID.

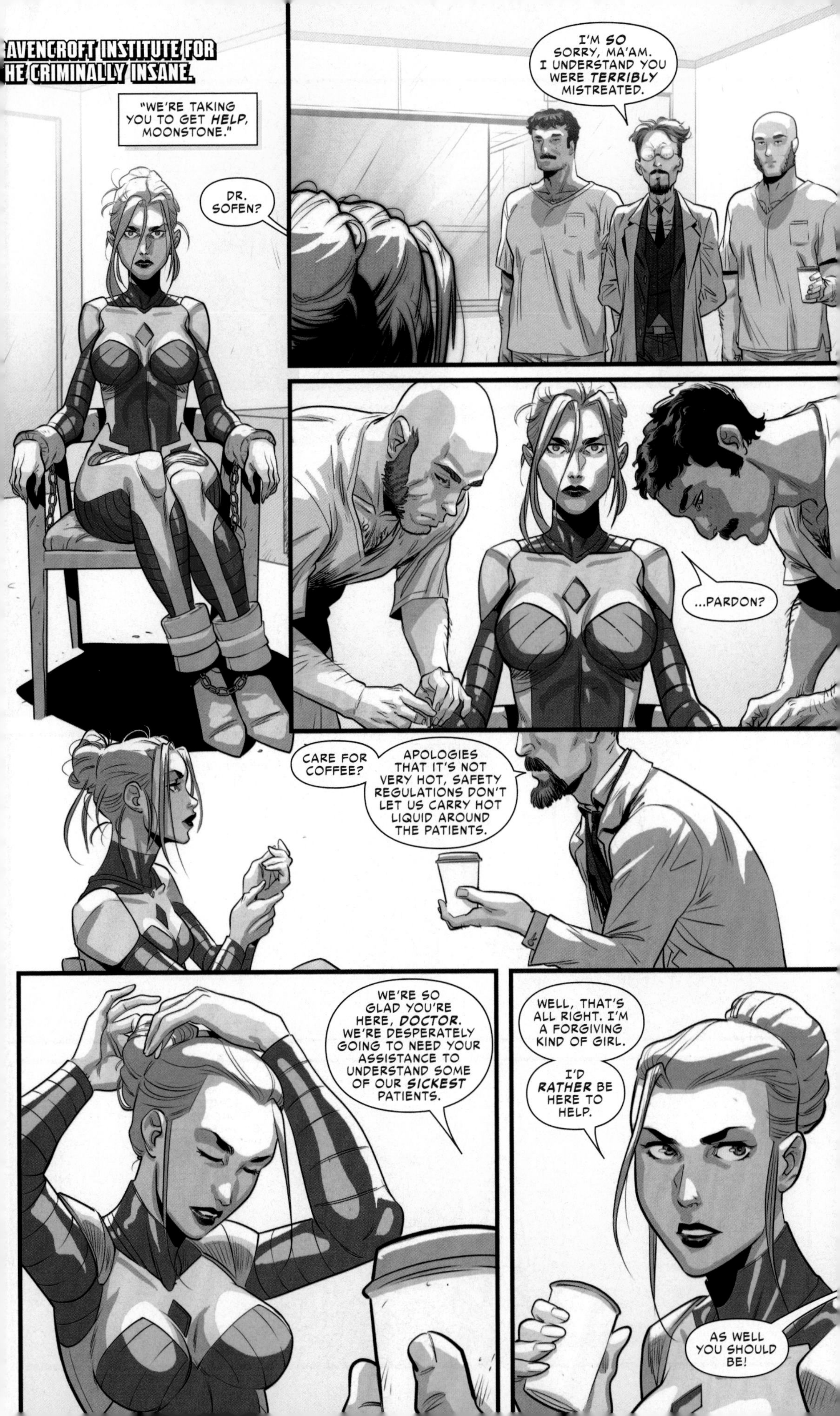
AVENCROFT INSTITUTE FOR
HE CRIMINALLY INSANE.
"WE'RE TAKING YOU TO GET HELP, MOONSTONE."
DR. SOFEN?
I'M SO SORRY, MA'AM. I UNDERSTAND YOU WERE TERRIBLY MISTREATED.
...PARDON?
CARE FOR COFFEE?
APOLOGIES THAT IT'S NOT VERY HOT, SAFETY REGULATIONS DON'T LET US CARRY HOT LIQUID AROUND THE PATIENTS.
WE'RE SO GLAD YOU'RE HERE, DOCTOR. WE'RE DESPERATELY GOING TO NEED YOUR ASSISTANCE TO UNDERSTAND SOME OF OUR SICKEST PATIENTS.
WELL, THAT'S ALL RIGHT. I'M A FORGIVING KIND OF GIRL.
I'D RATHER BE HERE TO HELP.
AS WELL YOU SHOULD BE!

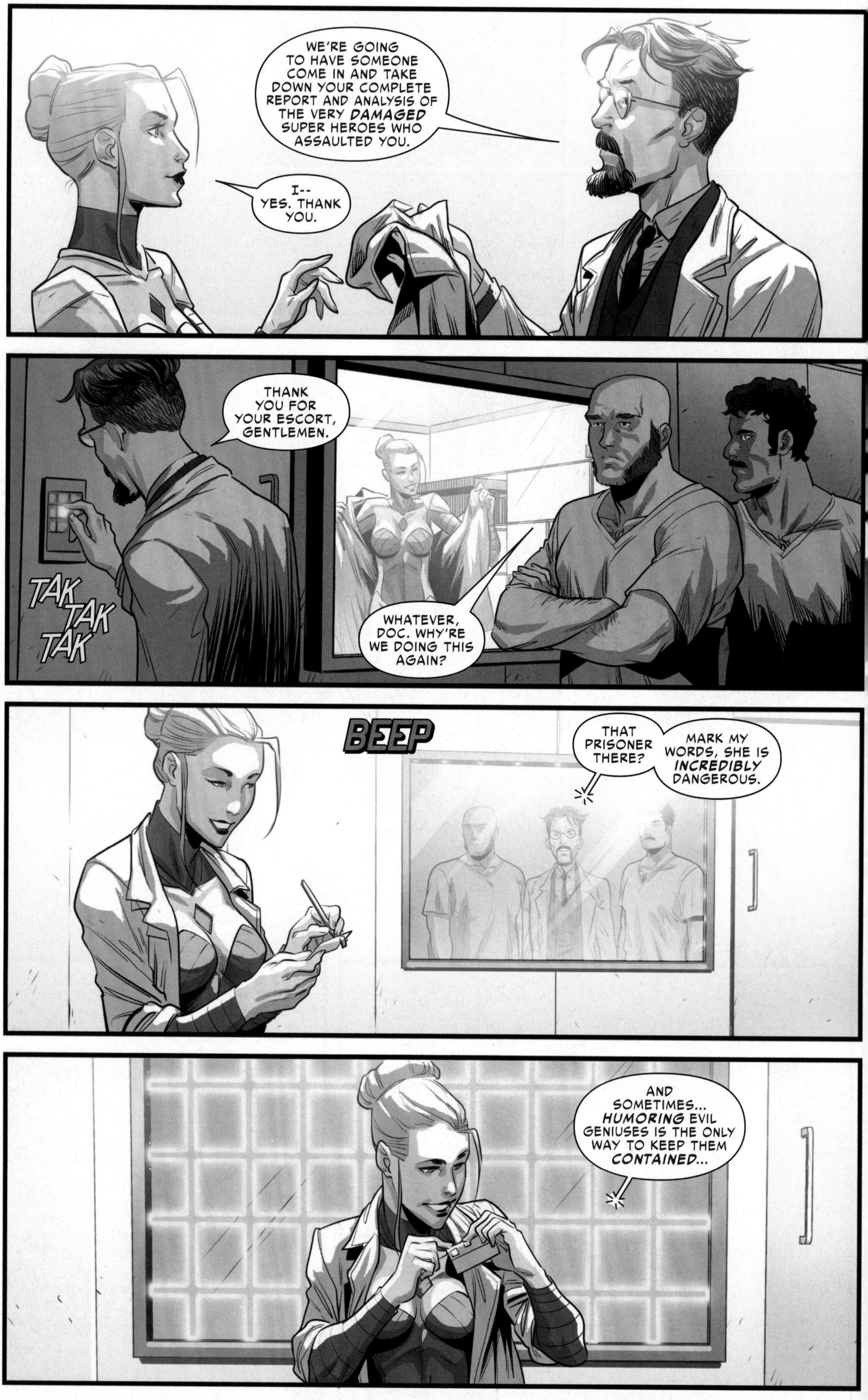
WE'RE GOING TO HAVE SOMEONE COME IN AND TAKE DOWN YOUR COMPLETE REPORT AND ANALYSIS OF THE VERY DAMAGED SUPER HEROES WHO ASSAULTED YOU.
I-- YES. THANK YOU.
THANK YOU FOR YOUR ESCORT, GENTLEMEN.
TAK TAK TAK
WHATEVER, DOC. WHY'RE WE DOING THIS AGAIN?
BEEP
THAT PRISONER THERE?
MARK MY WORDS, SHE IS INCREDIBLY DANGEROUS.
AND SOMETIMES... HUMORING EVIL GENIUSES IS THE ONLY WAY TO KEEP THEM CONTAINED...

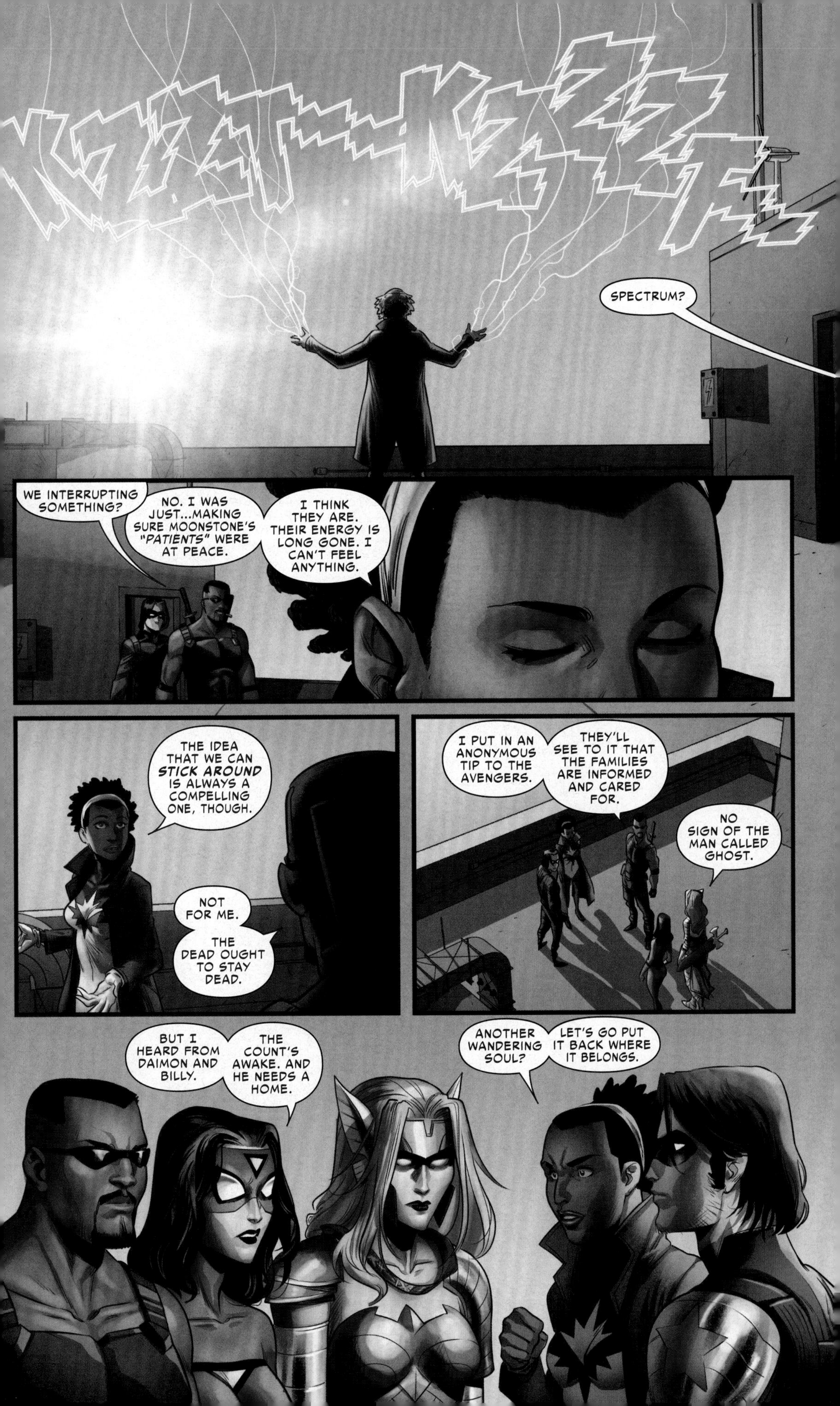
SPECTRUM?
WE INTERRUPTING SOMETHING?
NO. I WAS JUST...MAKING SURE MOONSTONE'S "PATIENTS" WERE AT PEACE.
I THINK THEY ARE. THEIR ENERGY IS LONG GONE. I CAN'T FEEL ANYTHING.
THE IDEA THAT WE CAN STICK AROUND IS ALWAYS A COMPELLING ONE, THOUGH.
NOT FOR ME.
THE DEAD OUGHT TO STAY DEAD.
I PUT IN AN ANONYMOUS TIP TO THE AVENGERS.
THEY'LL SEE TO IT THAT THE FAMILIES ARE INFORMED AND CARED FOR.
NO SIGN OF THE MAN CALLED GHOST.
BUT I HEARD FROM DAIMON AND BILLY.
THE COUNT'S AWAKE. AND HE NEEDS A HOME.
ANOTHER WANDERING SOUL?
LET'S GO PUT IT BACK WHERE IT BELONGS.

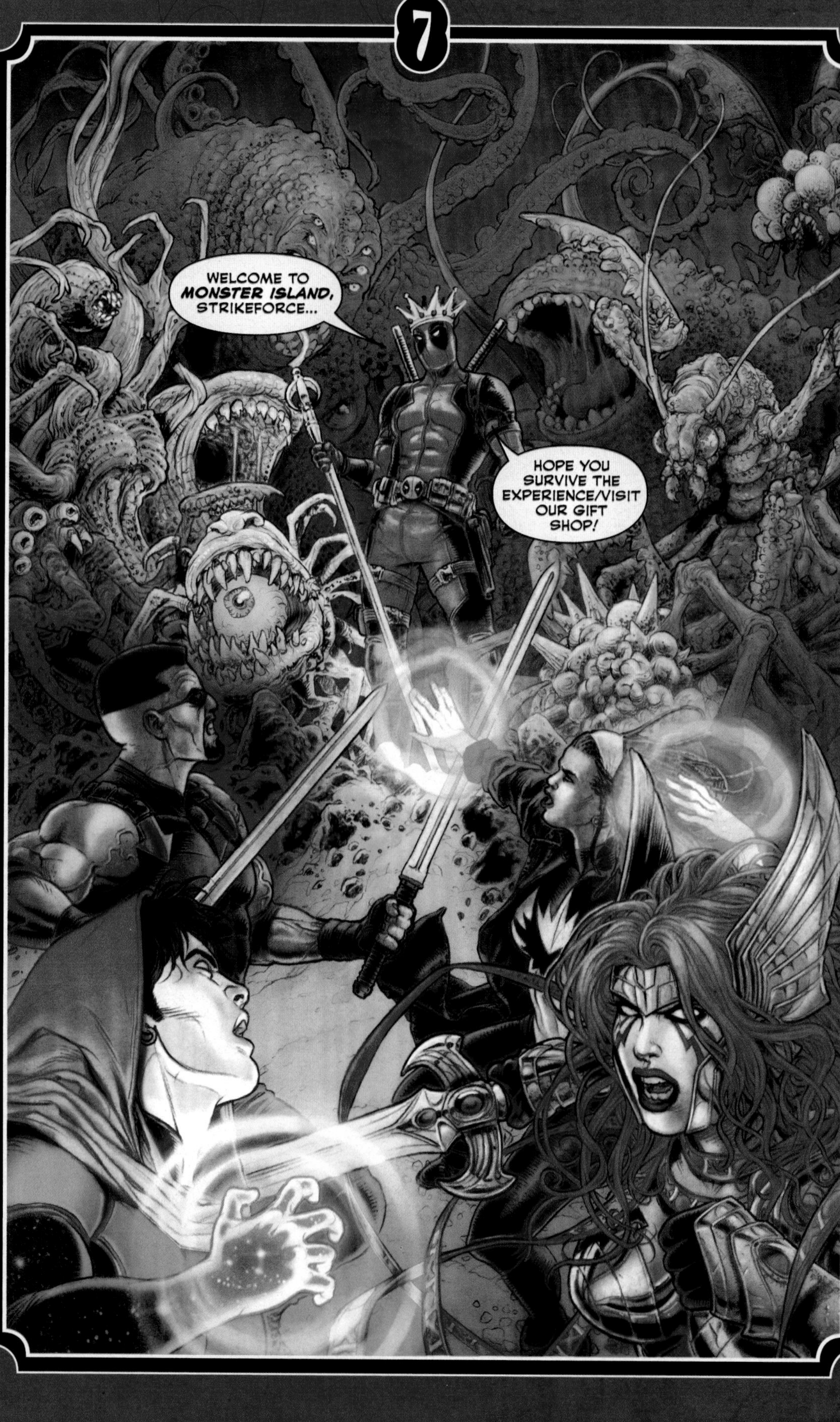
7
WELCOME TO MONSTER ISLAND, STRIKEFORCE...
HOPE YOU SURVIVE THE EXPERIENCE/VISIT OUR GIFT SHOP!

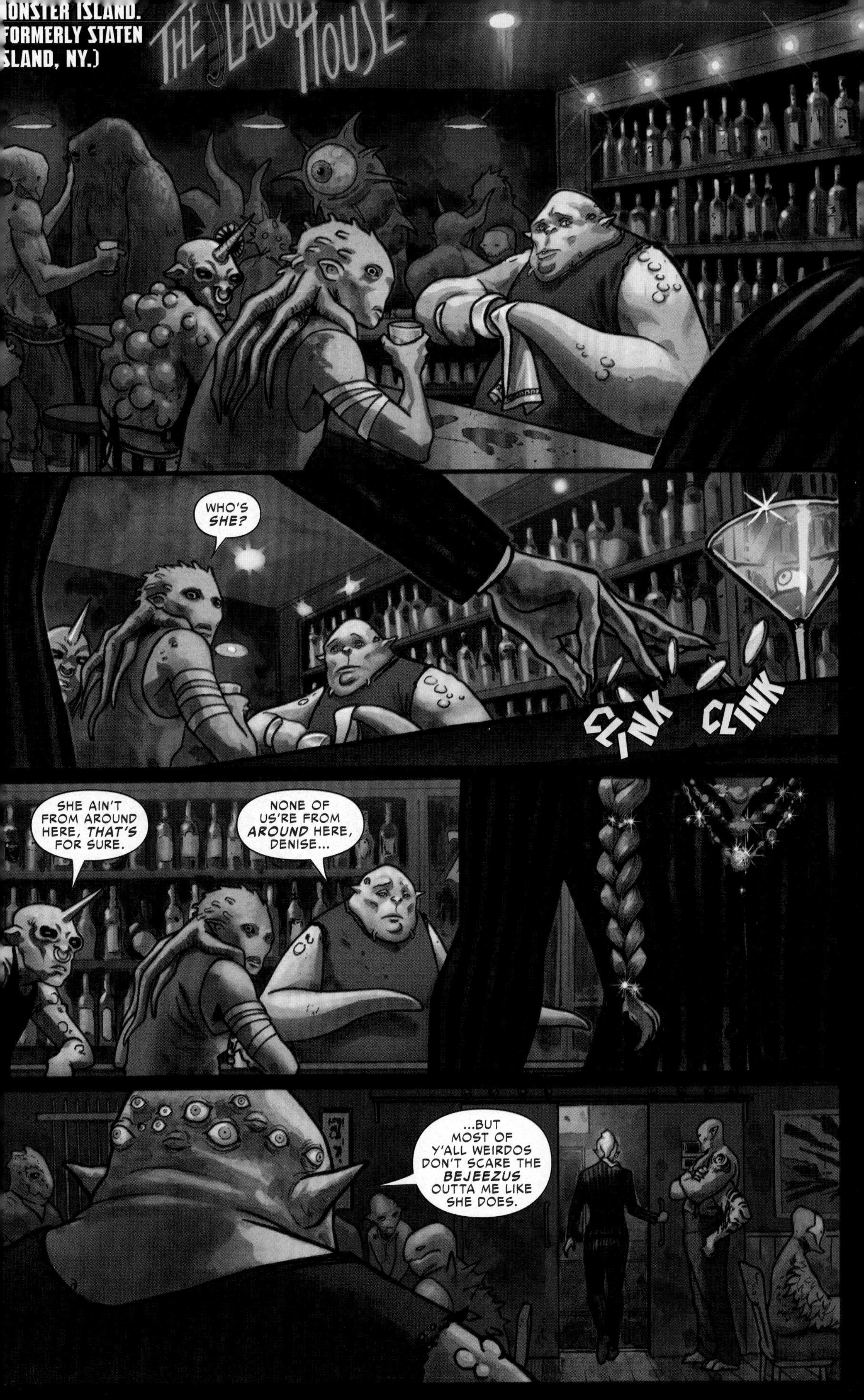

ONSTER ISLAND.
FORMERLY STATEN
SLAND, NY.)
WHO'S SHE?
CLINK
CLINK
SHE AIN'T FROM AROUND HERE, THAT'S FOR SURE.
NONE OF US'RE FROM AROUND HERE, DENISE...
...BUT MOST OF Y'ALL WEIRDOS DON'T SCARE THE BEJEEZUS OUTTA ME LIKE SHE DOES.

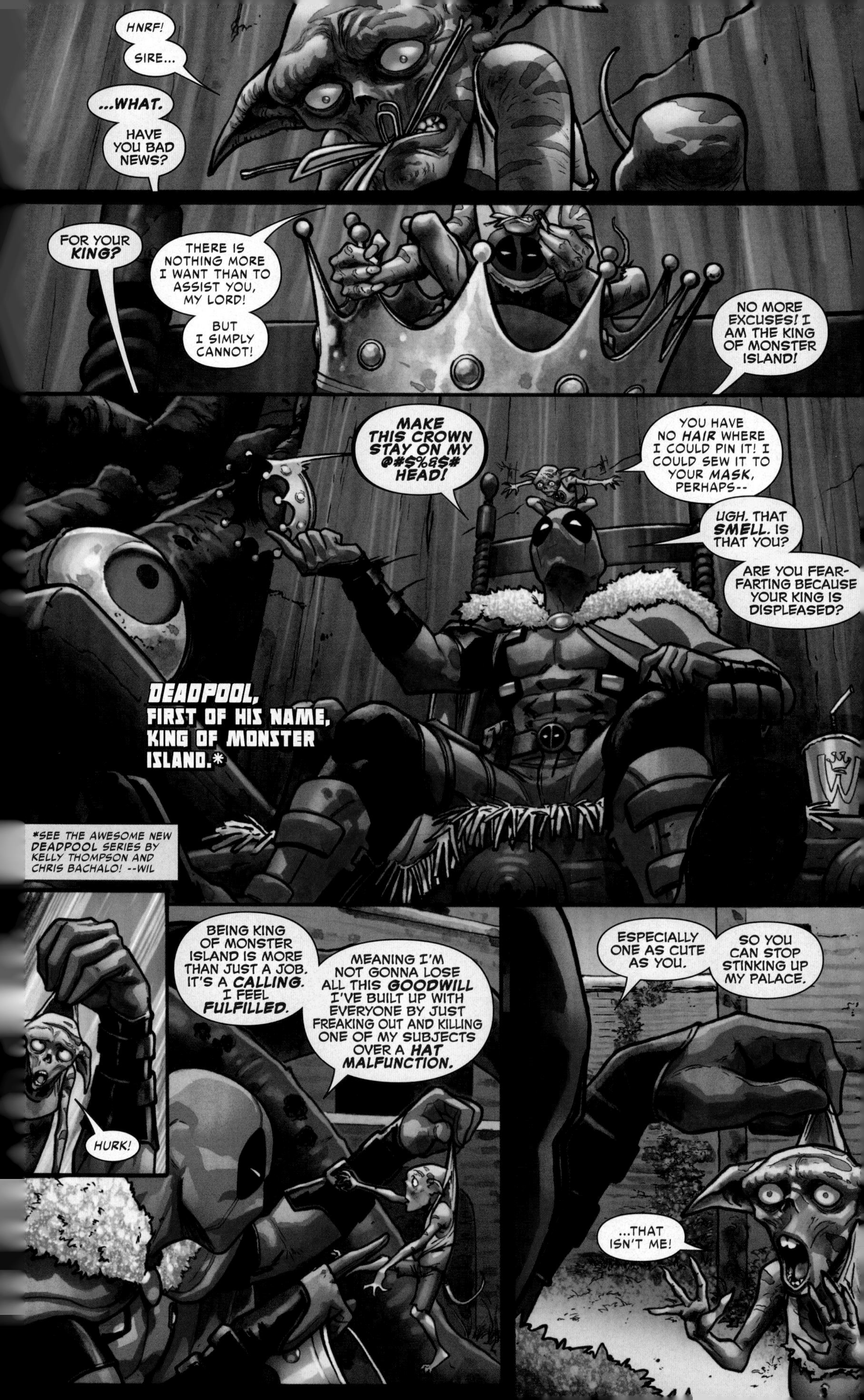
HNRF!
SIRE...
...WHAT.
HAVE YOU BAD NEWS?
FOR YOUR KING?
THERE IS NOTHING MORE I WANT THAN TO ASSIST YOU, MY LORD!
BUT I SIMPLY CANNOT!
NO MORE EXCUSES! I AM THE KING OF MONSTER ISLAND!
MAKE THIS CROWN STAY ON MY @#$%&$# HEAD!
YOU HAVE NO HAIR WHERE I COULD PIN IT! I COULD SEW IT TO YOUR MASK, PERHAPS--
UGH. THAT SMELL. IS THAT YOU?
ARE YOU FEAR-FARTING BECAUSE YOUR KING IS DISPLEASED?
DEADPOOL, FIRST OF HIS NAME, KING OF MONSTER ISLAND.*
*SEE THE AWESOME NEW DEADPOOL SERIES BY KELLY THOMPSON AND CHRIS BACHALO! --WIL
HURK!
BEING KING OF MONSTER ISLAND IS MORE THAN JUST A JOB. IT'S A CALLING. I FEEL FULFILLED.
MEANING I'M NOT GONNA LOSE ALL THIS GOODWILL I'VE BUILT UP WITH EVERYONE BY JUST FREAKING OUT AND KILLING ONE OF MY SUBJECTS OVER A HAT MALFUNCTION.
ESPECIALLY ONE AS CUTE AS YOU.
SO YOU CAN STOP STINKING UP MY PALACE.
...THAT ISN'T ME!

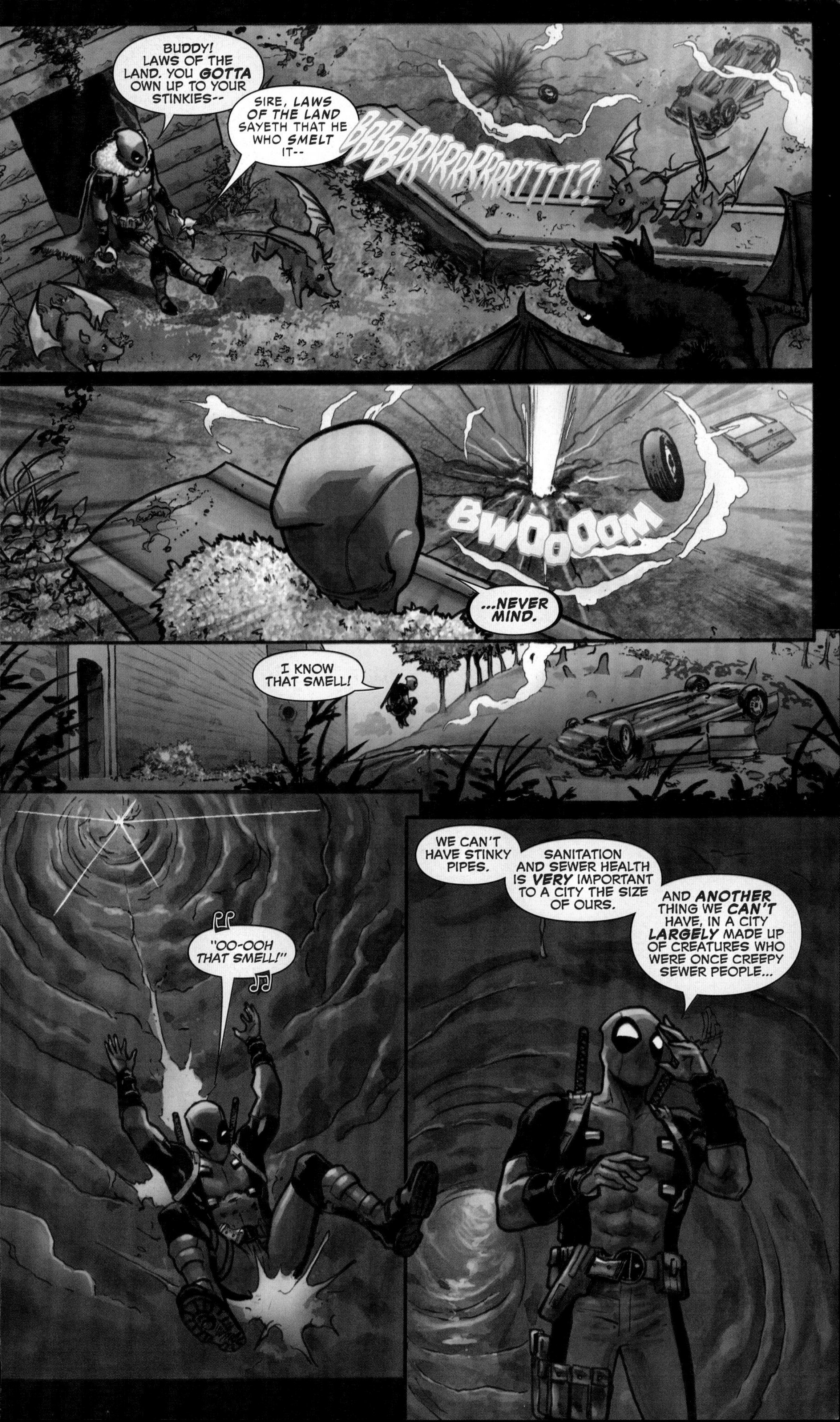
BUDDY! LAWS OF THE LAND. YOU GOTTA OWN UP TO YOUR STINKIES--
SIRE, LAWS OF THE LAND SAYETH THAT HE WHO SMELT IT--
BBBBBRRRRRRRRRRRITTTT!?!
BWOOOOM
...NEVER MIND.
I KNOW THAT SMELL!
"OO-OOH THAT SMELL!"
WE CAN'T HAVE STINKY PIPES.
SANITATION AND SEWER HEALTH IS VERY IMPORTANT TO A CITY THE SIZE OF OURS.
AND ANOTHER THING WE CAN'T HAVE, IN A CITY LARGELY MADE UP OF CREATURES WHO WERE ONCE CREEPY SEWER PEOPLE...

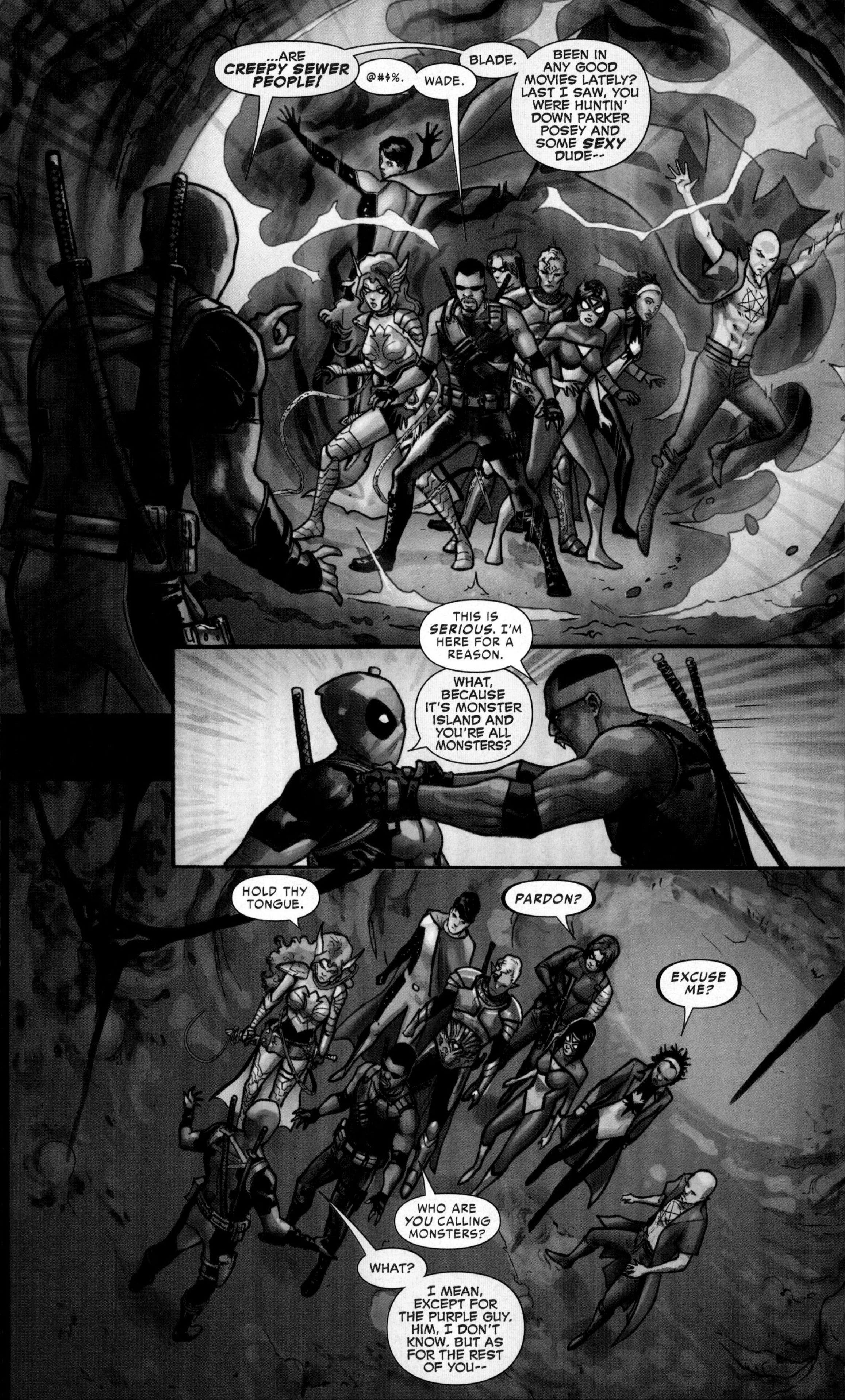
...ARE CREEPY SEWER PEOPLE!
@#$%.
WADE.
BLADE.
BEEN IN ANY GOOD MOVIES LATELY? LAST I SAW, YOU WERE HUNTIN' DOWN PARKER POSEY AND SOME SEXY DUDE--
THIS IS SERIOUS. I'M HERE FOR A REASON.
WHAT, BECAUSE IT'S MONSTER ISLAND AND YOU'RE ALL MONSTERS?
HOLD THY TONGUE.
PARDON?
EXCUSE ME?
WHO ARE YOU CALLING MONSTERS?
WHAT?
I MEAN, EXCEPT FOR THE PURPLE GUY. HIM, I DON'T KNOW. BUT AS FOR THE REST OF YOU--

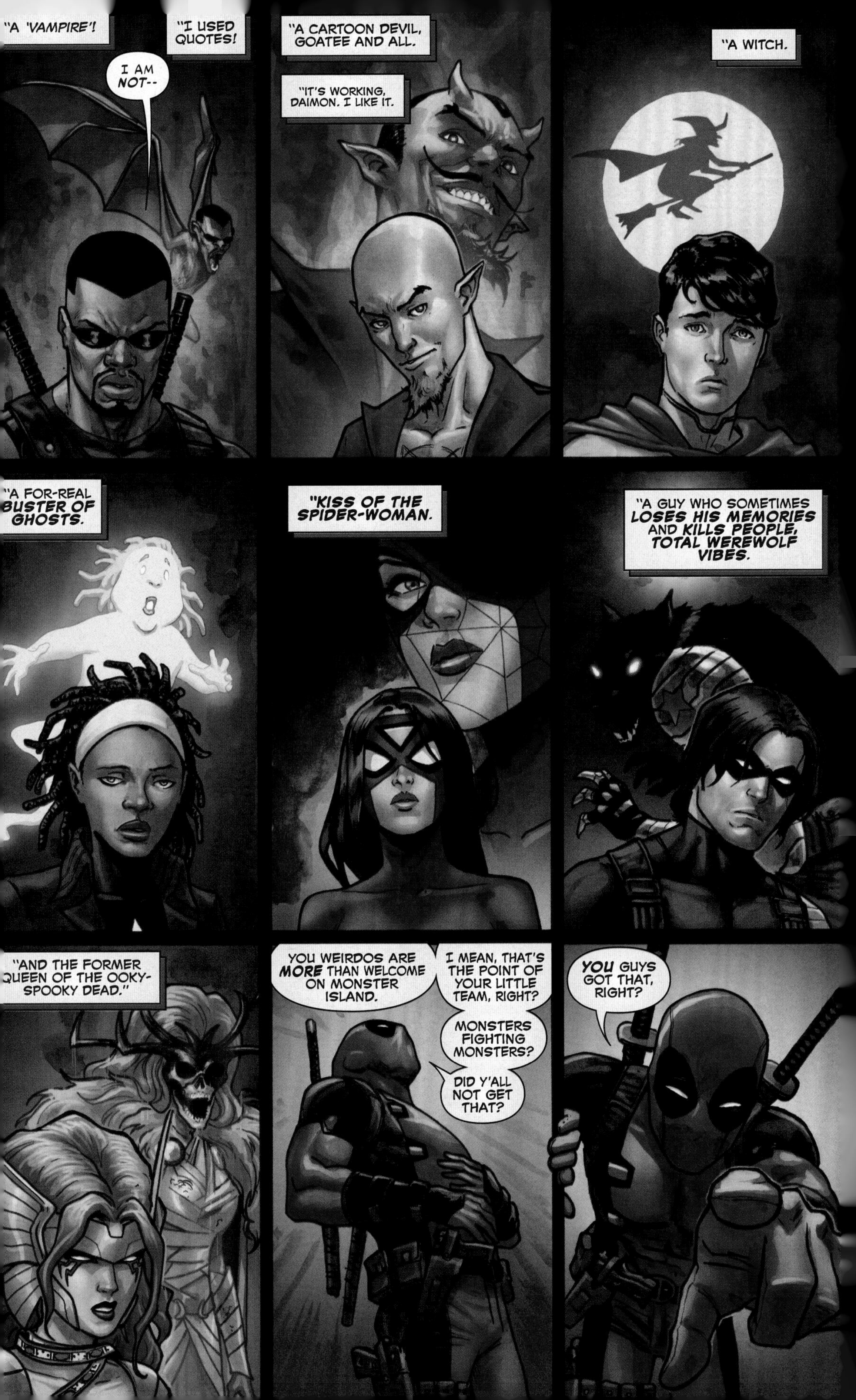
"A 'VAMPIRE'!
"I USED QUOTES!
I AM NOT--
"A CARTOON DEVIL, GOATEE AND ALL.
"IT'S WORKING, DAIMON. I LIKE IT.
"A WITCH.
"A FOR-REAL BUSTER OF GHOSTS.
"KISS OF THE SPIDER-WOMAN.
"A GUY WHO SOMETIMES LOSES HIS MEMORIES AND KILLS PEOPLE. TOTAL WEREWOLF VIBES.
"AND THE FORMER QUEEN OF THE OOKY-SPOOKY DEAD."
YOU WEIRDOS ARE MORE THAN WELCOME ON MONSTER ISLAND.
I MEAN, THAT'S THE POINT OF YOUR LITTLE TEAM, RIGHT?
MONSTERS FIGHTING MONSTERS?
DID Y'ALL NOT GET THAT?
YOU GUYS GOT THAT, RIGHT?

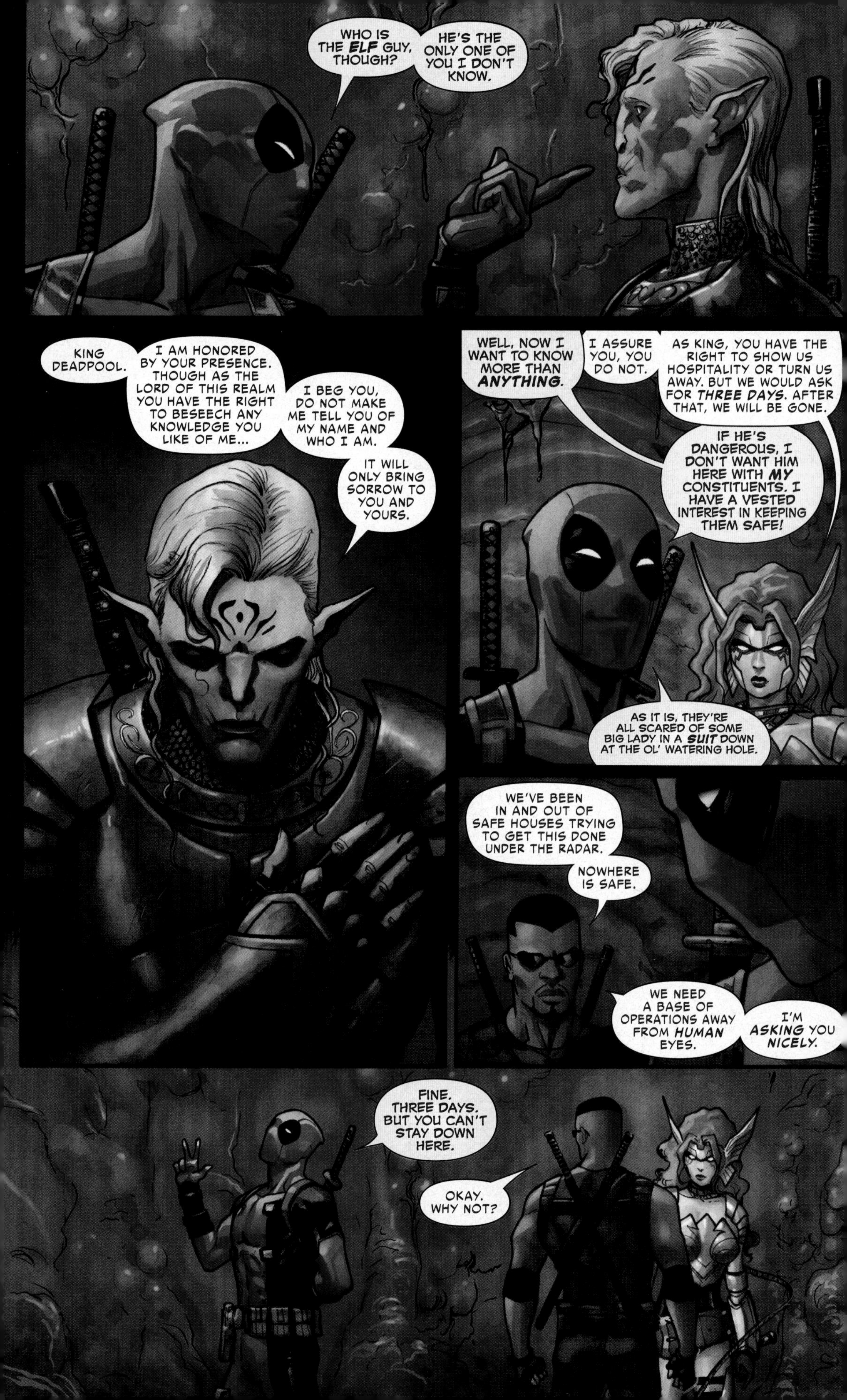
WHO IS THE ELF GUY, THOUGH?
HE'S THE ONLY ONE OF YOU I DON'T KNOW.
KING DEADPOOL.
I AM HONORED BY YOUR PRESENCE. THOUGH AS THE LORD OF THIS REALM YOU HAVE THE RIGHT TO BESEECH ANY KNOWLEDGE YOU LIKE OF ME...
I BEG YOU, DO NOT MAKE ME TELL YOU OF MY NAME AND WHO I AM.
IT WILL ONLY BRING SORROW TO YOU AND YOURS.
WELL, NOW I WANT TO KNOW MORE THAN ANYTHING.
I ASSURE YOU, YOU DO NOT.
AS KING, YOU HAVE THE RIGHT TO SHOW US HOSPITALITY OR TURN US AWAY. BUT WE WOULD ASK FOR THREE DAYS. AFTER THAT, WE WILL BE GONE.
IF HE'S DANGEROUS, I DON'T WANT HIM HERE WITH MY CONSTITUENTS. I HAVE A VESTED INTEREST IN KEEPING THEM SAFE!
AS IT IS, THEY'RE ALL SCARED OF SOME BIG LADY IN A SUIT DOWN AT THE OL' WATERING HOLE.
WE'VE BEEN IN AND OUT OF SAFE HOUSES TRYING TO GET THIS DONE UNDER THE RADAR.
NOWHERE IS SAFE.
WE NEED A BASE OF OPERATIONS AWAY FROM HUMAN EYES.
I'M ASKING YOU NICELY.
FINE. THREE DAYS. BUT YOU CAN'T STAY DOWN HERE.
OKAY. WHY NOT?

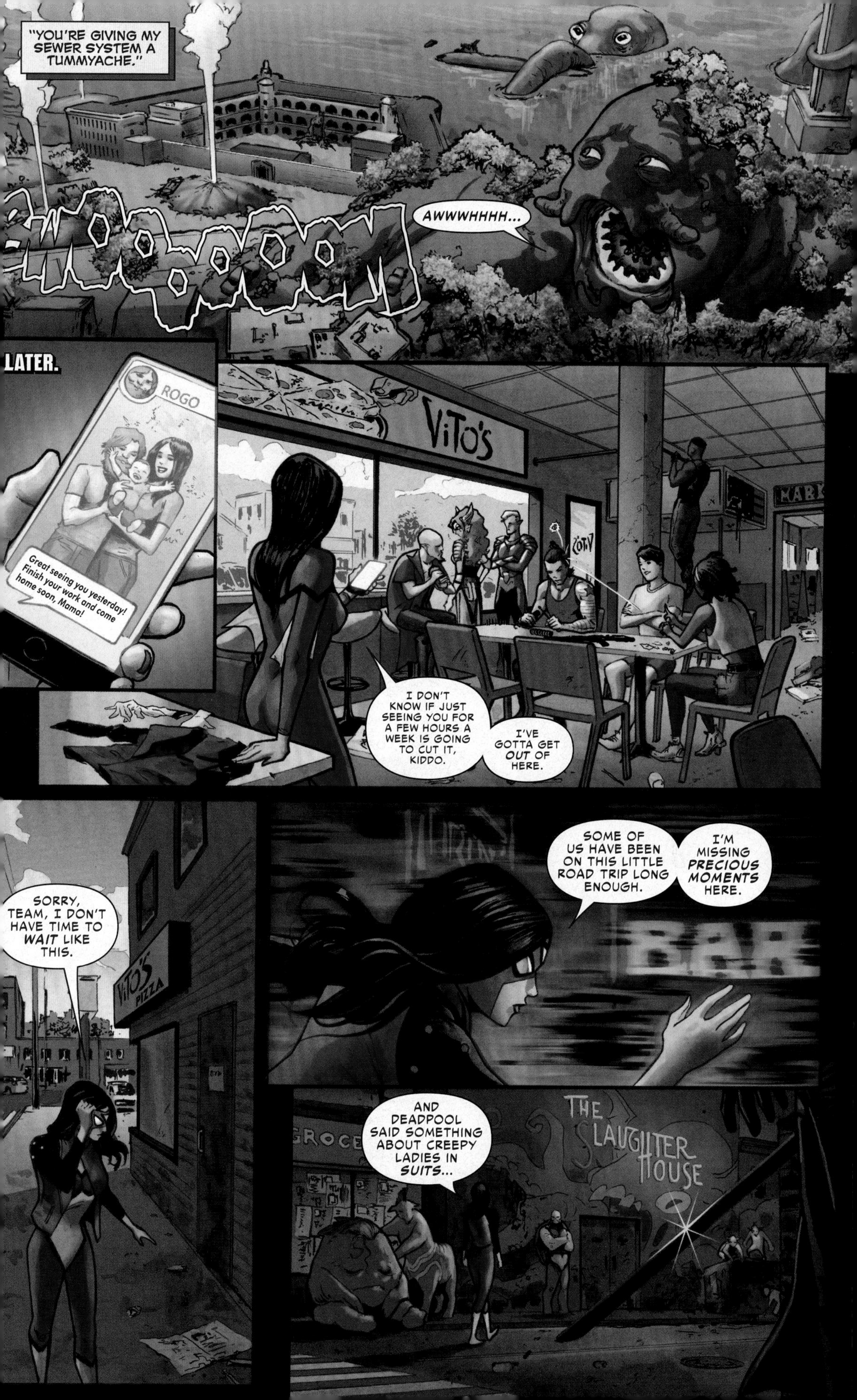
"YOU'RE GIVING MY SEWER SYSTEM A TUMMYACHE."
AWWWHHHH...
LATER.
ROGO
Great seeing you yesterday! Finish your work and come home soon, Mama!
VITO'S
I DON'T KNOW IF JUST SEEING YOU FOR A FEW HOURS A WEEK IS GOING TO CUT IT, KIDDO.
I'VE GOTTA GET OUT OF HERE.
SORRY, TEAM, I DON'T HAVE TIME TO WAIT LIKE THIS.
VITO'S PIZZA
SOME OF US HAVE BEEN ON THIS LITTLE ROAD TRIP LONG ENOUGH.
I'M MISSING PRECIOUS MOMENTS HERE.
AND DEADPOOL SAID SOMETHING ABOUT CREEPY LADIES IN SUITS...
THE SLAUGHTER HOUSE

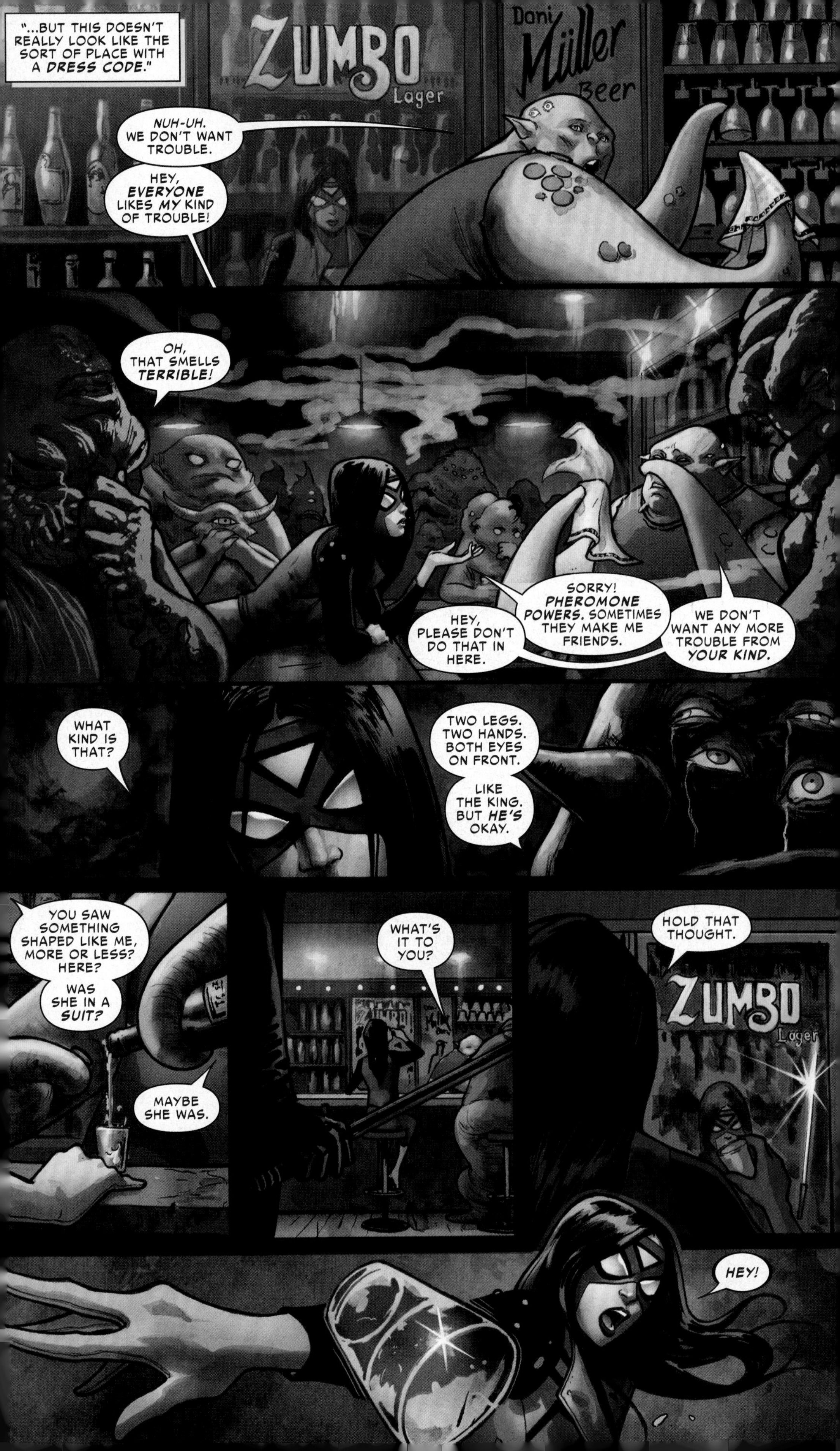
"...BUT THIS DOESN'T REALLY LOOK LIKE THE SORT OF PLACE WITH A DRESS CODE."
ZUMBO Lager
Dani Müller Beer
NUH-UH. WE DON'T WANT TROUBLE.
HEY, EVERYONE LIKES MY KIND OF TROUBLE!
OH, THAT SMELLS TERRIBLE!
HEY, PLEASE DON'T DO THAT IN HERE.
SORRY! PHEROMONE POWERS. SOMETIMES THEY MAKE ME FRIENDS.
WE DON'T WANT ANY MORE TROUBLE FROM YOUR KIND.
WHAT KIND IS THAT?
TWO LEGS. TWO HANDS. BOTH EYES ON FRONT.
LIKE THE KING. BUT HE'S OKAY.
YOU SAW SOMETHING SHAPED LIKE ME, MORE OR LESS? HERE?
WAS SHE IN A SUIT?
MAYBE SHE WAS.
WHAT'S IT TO YOU?
HOLD THAT THOUGHT.
ZUMBO Lager
HEY!

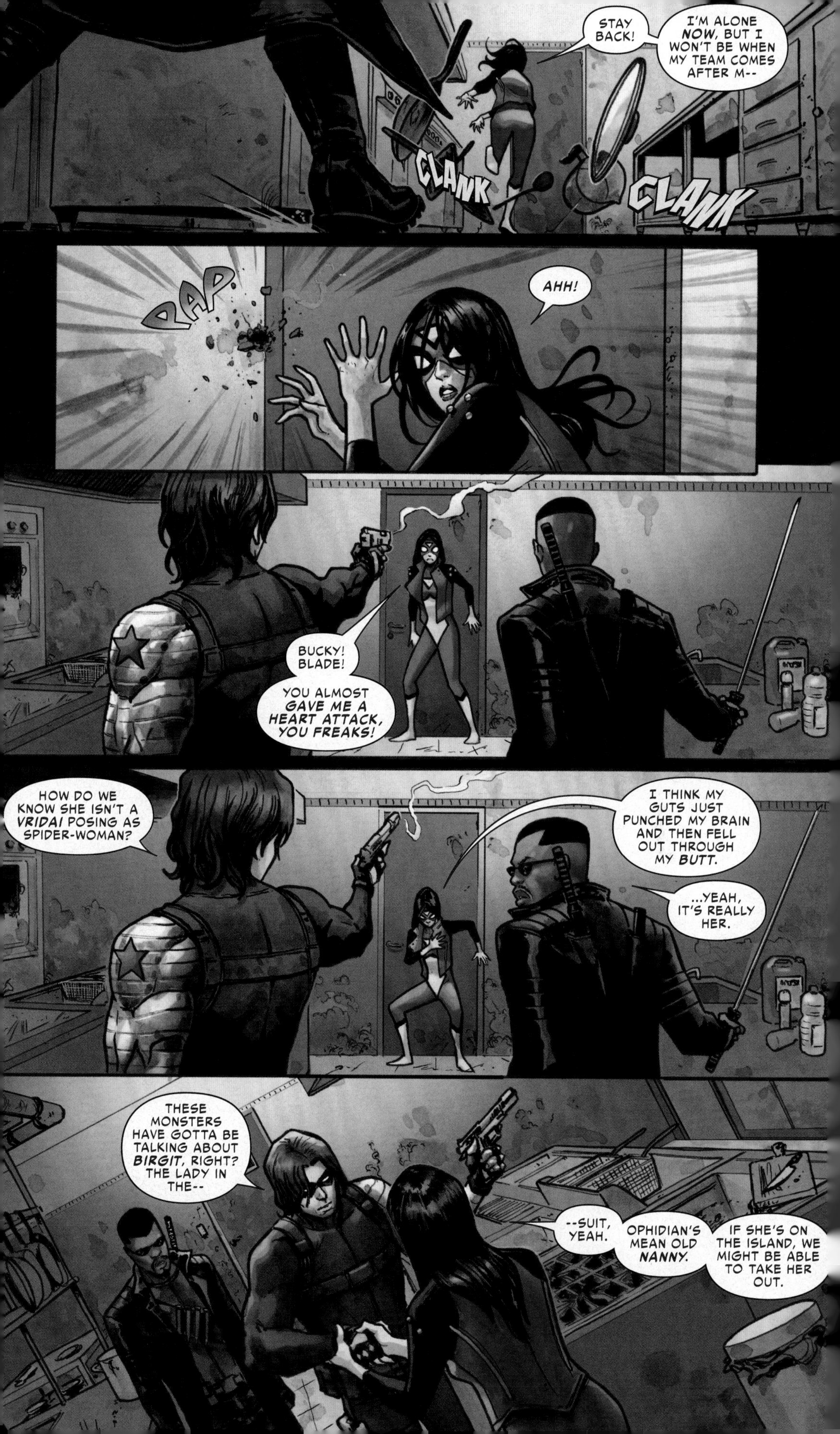
STAY BACK!
I'M ALONE NOW, BUT I WON'T BE WHEN MY TEAM COMES AFTER M--
CLANK
CLANK
RAP
AHH!
BUCKY! BLADE!
YOU ALMOST GAVE ME A HEART ATTACK, YOU FREAKS!
HOW DO WE KNOW SHE ISN'T A VRIDAI POSING AS SPIDER-WOMAN?
I THINK MY GUTS JUST PUNCHED MY BRAIN AND THEN FELL OUT THROUGH MY BUTT.
...YEAH, IT'S REALLY HER.
THESE MONSTERS HAVE GOTTA BE TALKING ABOUT BIRGIT, RIGHT? THE LADY IN THE--
--SUIT, YEAH.
OPHIDIAN'S MEAN OLD NANNY.
IF SHE'S ON THE ISLAND, WE MIGHT BE ABLE TO TAKE HER OUT.

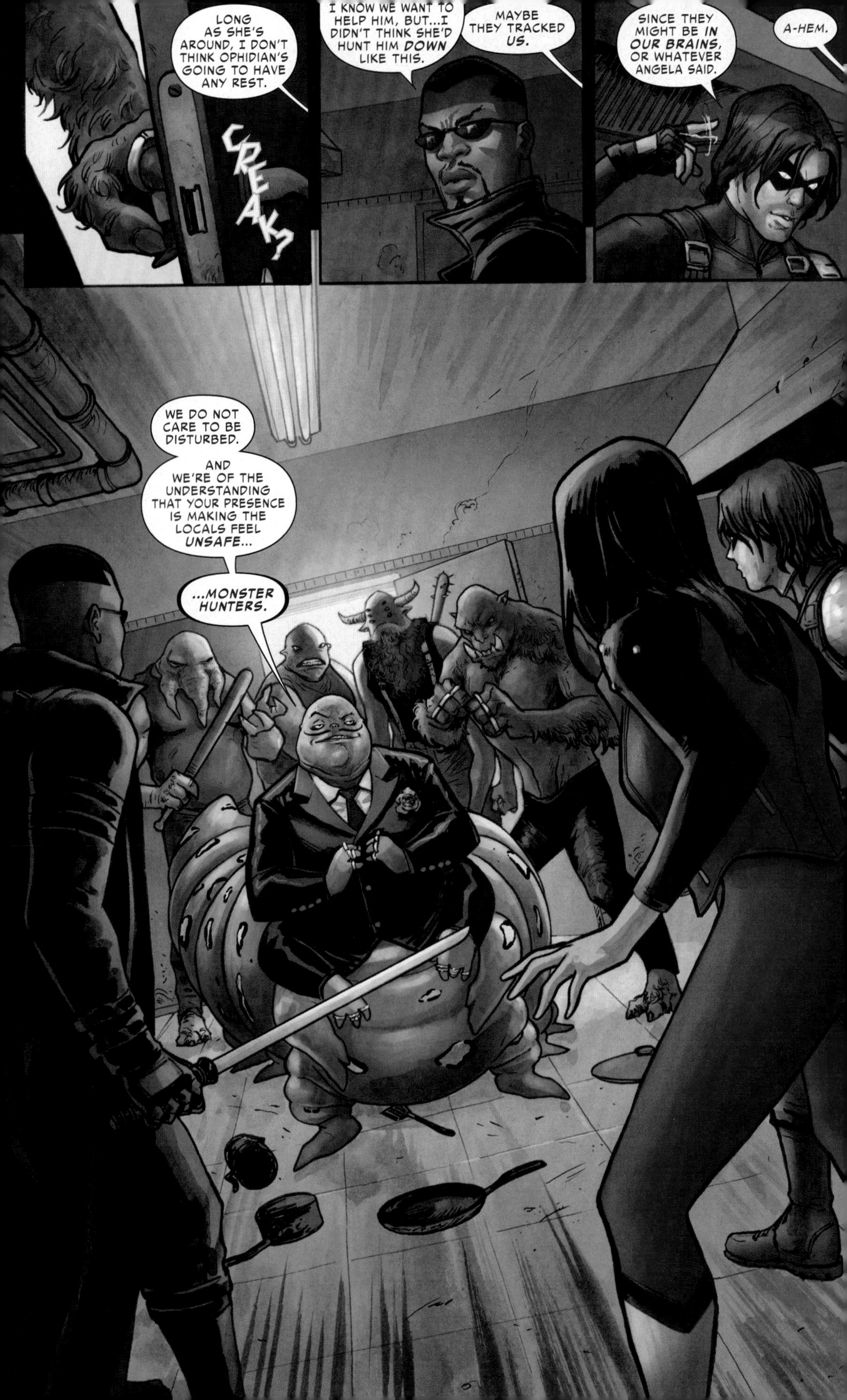

LONG AS SHE'S AROUND, I DON'T THINK OPHIDIAN'S GOING TO HAVE ANY REST.
CREAK?
I KNOW WE WANT TO HELP HIM, BUT...I DIDN'T THINK SHE'D HUNT HIM DOWN LIKE THIS.
MAYBE THEY TRACKED US.
SINCE THEY MIGHT BE IN OUR BRAINS, OR WHATEVER ANGELA SAID.
A-HEM.
WE DO NOT CARE TO BE DISTURBED.
AND WE'RE OF THE UNDERSTANDING THAT YOUR PRESENCE IS MAKING THE LOCALS FEEL UNSAFE...
...MONSTER HUNTERS.

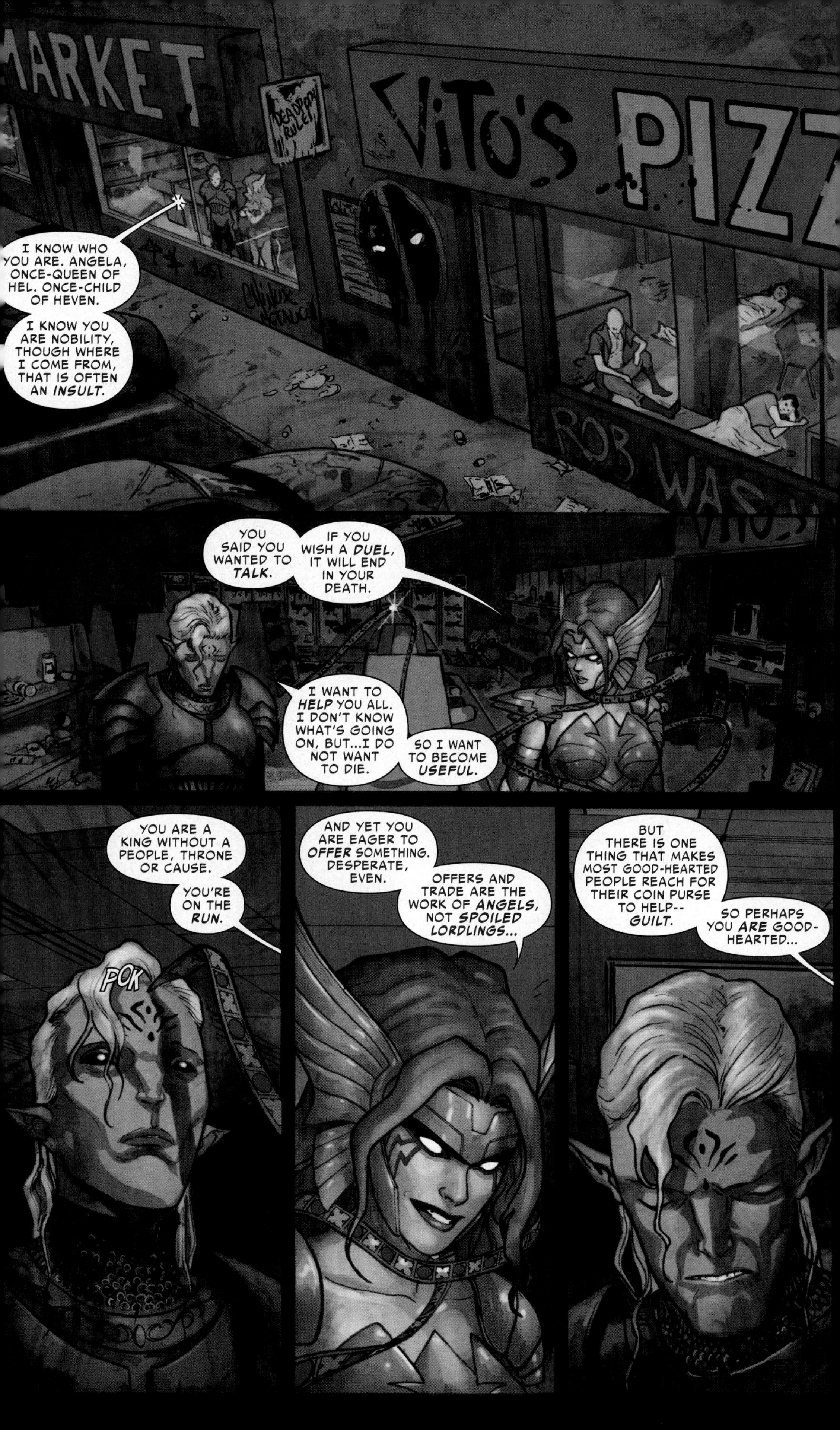
MARKET
DEADPOOL RULEZ!
VITO'S PIZZ
I KNOW WHO YOU ARE. ANGELA, ONCE-QUEEN OF HEL. ONCE-CHILD OF HEVEN.
I KNOW YOU ARE NOBILITY, THOUGH WHERE I COME FROM, THAT IS OFTEN AN *INSULT*.
ROB WAS
YOU SAID YOU WANTED TO *TALK*.
IF YOU WISH A *DUEL*, IT WILL END IN YOUR DEATH.
I WANT TO *HELP* YOU ALL. I DON'T KNOW WHAT'S GOING ON, BUT...I DO NOT WANT TO DIE.
SO I WANT TO BECOME *USEFUL*.
YOU ARE A KING WITHOUT A PEOPLE, THRONE OR CAUSE.
YOU'RE ON THE *RUN*.
POK
AND YET YOU ARE EAGER TO *OFFER* SOMETHING. DESPERATE, EVEN.
OFFERS AND TRADE ARE THE WORK OF *ANGELS*, NOT *SPOILED LORDLINGS*...
BUT THERE IS ONE THING THAT MAKES MOST GOOD-HEARTED PEOPLE REACH FOR THEIR COIN PURSE TO HELP-- *GUILT*.
SO PERHAPS YOU *ARE* GOOD-HEARTED...

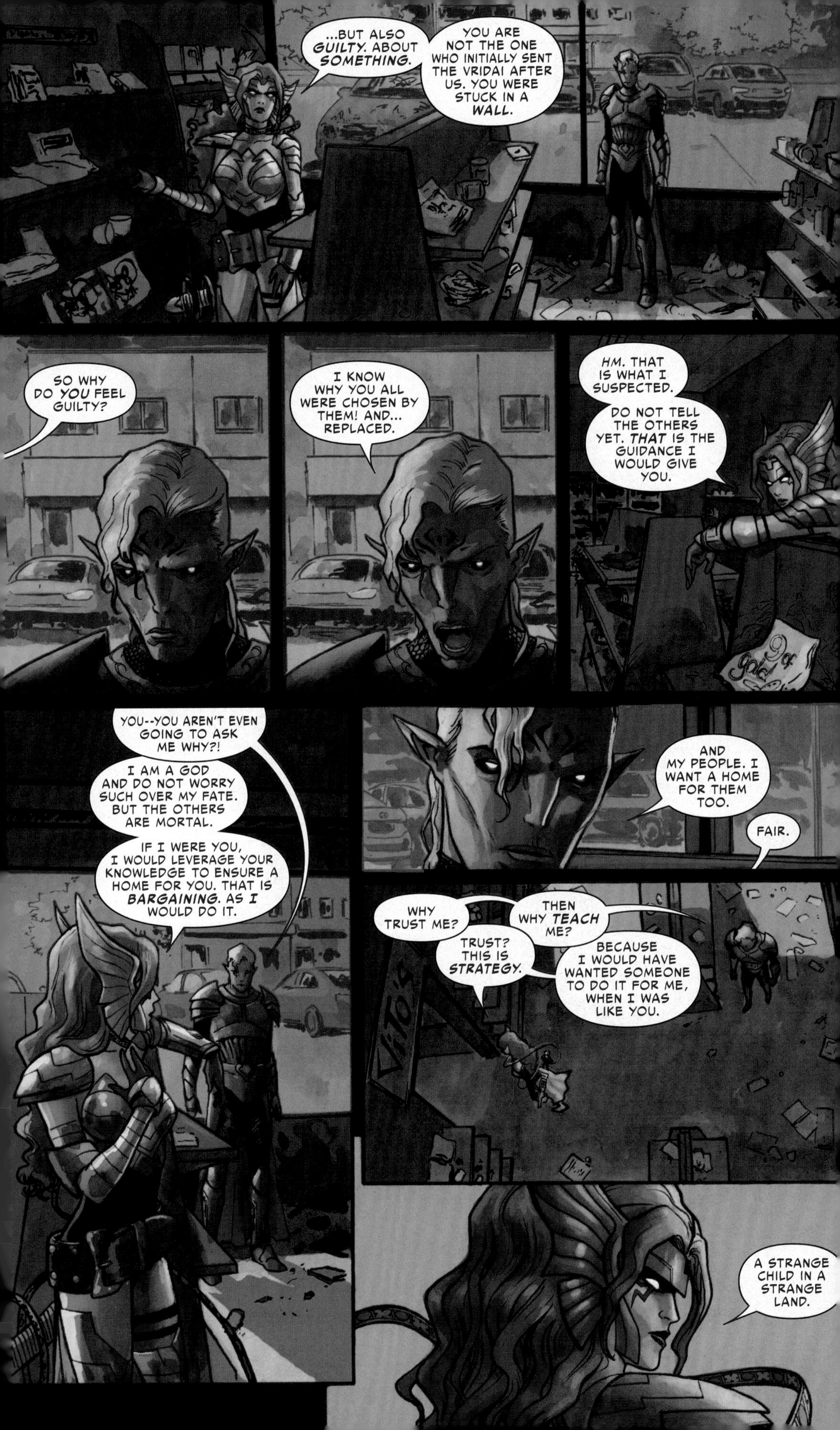
...BUT ALSO GUILTY. ABOUT SOMETHING.
YOU ARE NOT THE ONE WHO INITIALLY SENT THE VRIDAI AFTER US. YOU WERE STUCK IN A WALL.
SO WHY DO YOU FEEL GUILTY?
I KNOW WHY YOU ALL WERE CHOSEN BY THEM! AND... REPLACED.
HM. THAT IS WHAT I SUSPECTED.
DO NOT TELL THE OTHERS YET. THAT IS THE GUIDANCE I WOULD GIVE YOU.
9 of gold
YOU--YOU AREN'T EVEN GOING TO ASK ME WHY?!
I AM A GOD AND DO NOT WORRY SUCH OVER MY FATE. BUT THE OTHERS ARE MORTAL.
IF I WERE YOU, I WOULD LEVERAGE YOUR KNOWLEDGE TO ENSURE A HOME FOR YOU. THAT IS BARGAINING. AS I WOULD DO IT.
AND MY PEOPLE. I WANT A HOME FOR THEM TOO.
FAIR.
WHY TRUST ME?
THEN WHY TEACH ME?
TRUST? THIS IS STRATEGY.
BECAUSE I WOULD HAVE WANTED SOMEONE TO DO IT FOR ME, WHEN I WAS LIKE YOU.
A STRANGE CHILD IN A STRANGE LAND.

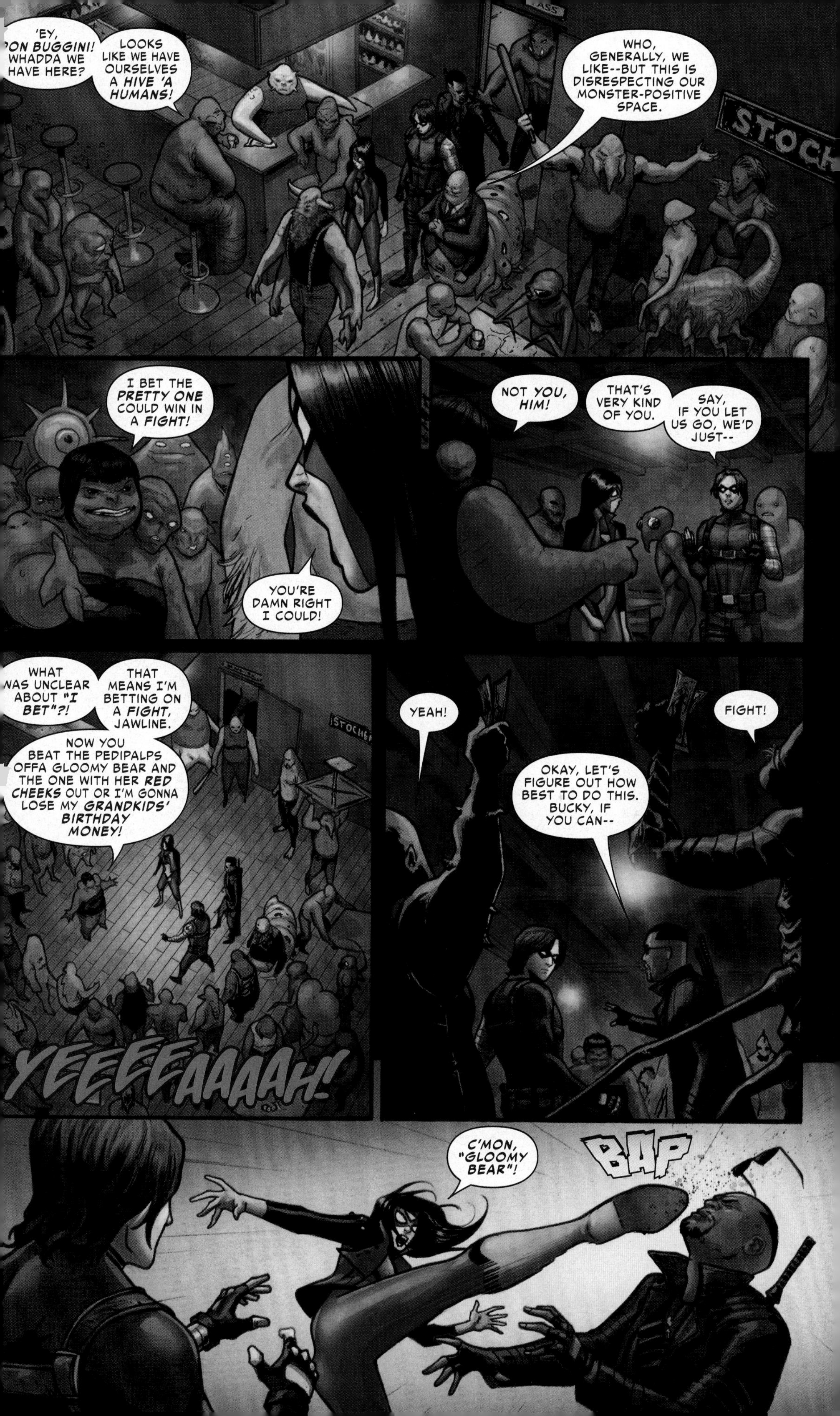

'EY, DON BUGGINI! WHADDA WE HAVE HERE?
LOOKS LIKE WE HAVE OURSELVES A HIVE 'A HUMANS!
WHO, GENERALLY, WE LIKE--BUT THIS IS DISRESPECTING OUR MONSTER-POSITIVE SPACE.
STOCH
I BET THE PRETTY ONE COULD WIN IN A FIGHT!
YOU'RE DAMN RIGHT I COULD!
NOT YOU, HIM!
THAT'S VERY KIND OF YOU.
SAY, IF YOU LET US GO, WE'D JUST--
WHAT WAS UNCLEAR ABOUT "I BET"?!
THAT MEANS I'M BETTING ON A FIGHT, JAWLINE.
NOW YOU BEAT THE PEDIPALPS OFFA GLOOMY BEAR AND THE ONE WITH HER RED CHEEKS OUT OR I'M GONNA LOSE MY GRANDKIDS' BIRTHDAY MONEY!
STOCHE
YEEEEAAAAAH!
YEAH!
FIGHT!
OKAY, LET'S FIGURE OUT HOW BEST TO DO THIS. BUCKY, IF YOU CAN--
C'MON, "GLOOMY BEAR"!
BAP

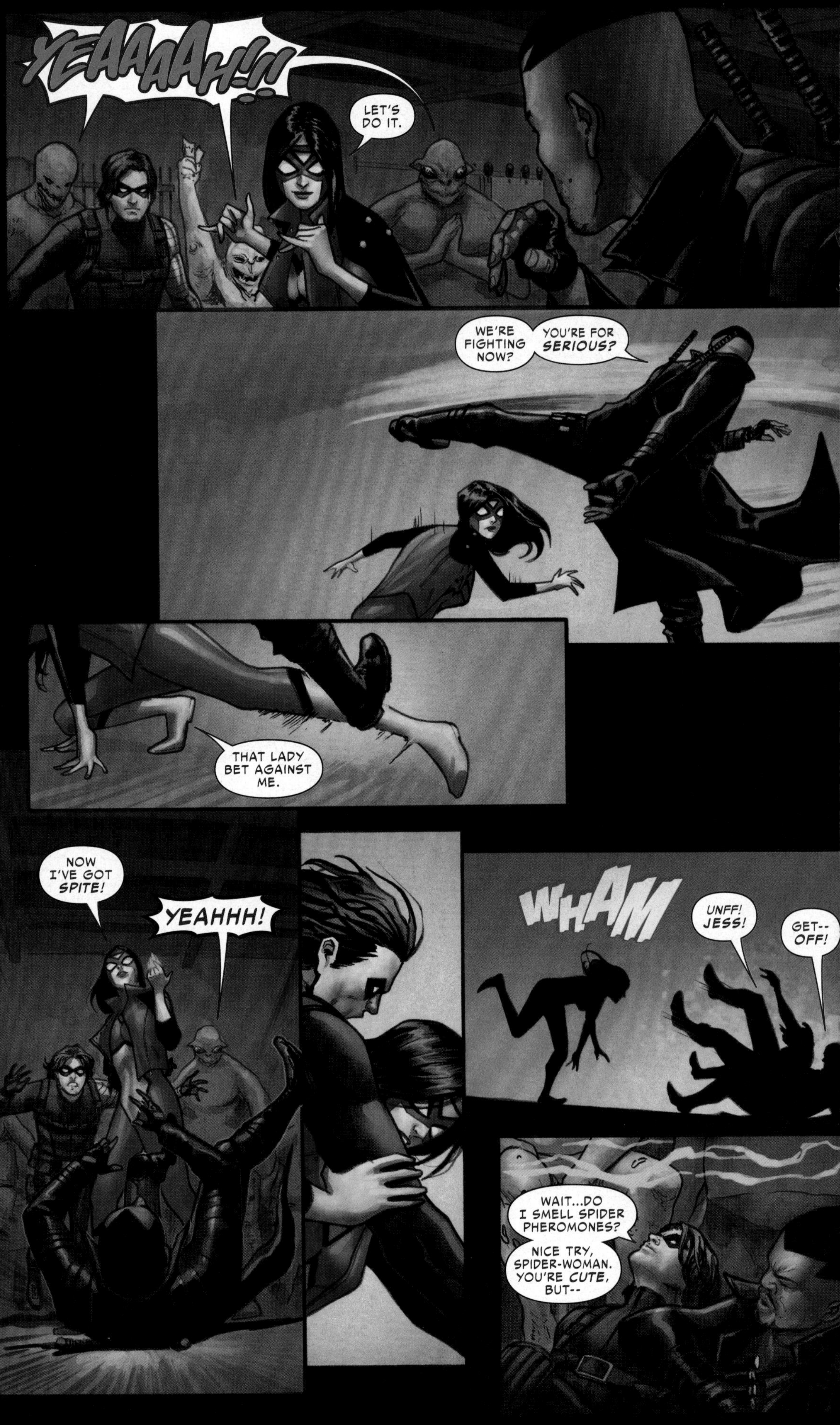
YEAAAAH!!!
LET'S DO IT.
WE'RE FIGHTING NOW?
YOU'RE FOR SERIOUS?
THAT LADY BET AGAINST ME.
NOW I'VE GOT SPITE!
YEAHHH!
WHAM
UNFF! JESS!
GET-- OFF!
WAIT...DO I SMELL SPIDER PHEROMONES?
NICE TRY, SPIDER-WOMAN. YOU'RE CUTE, BUT--

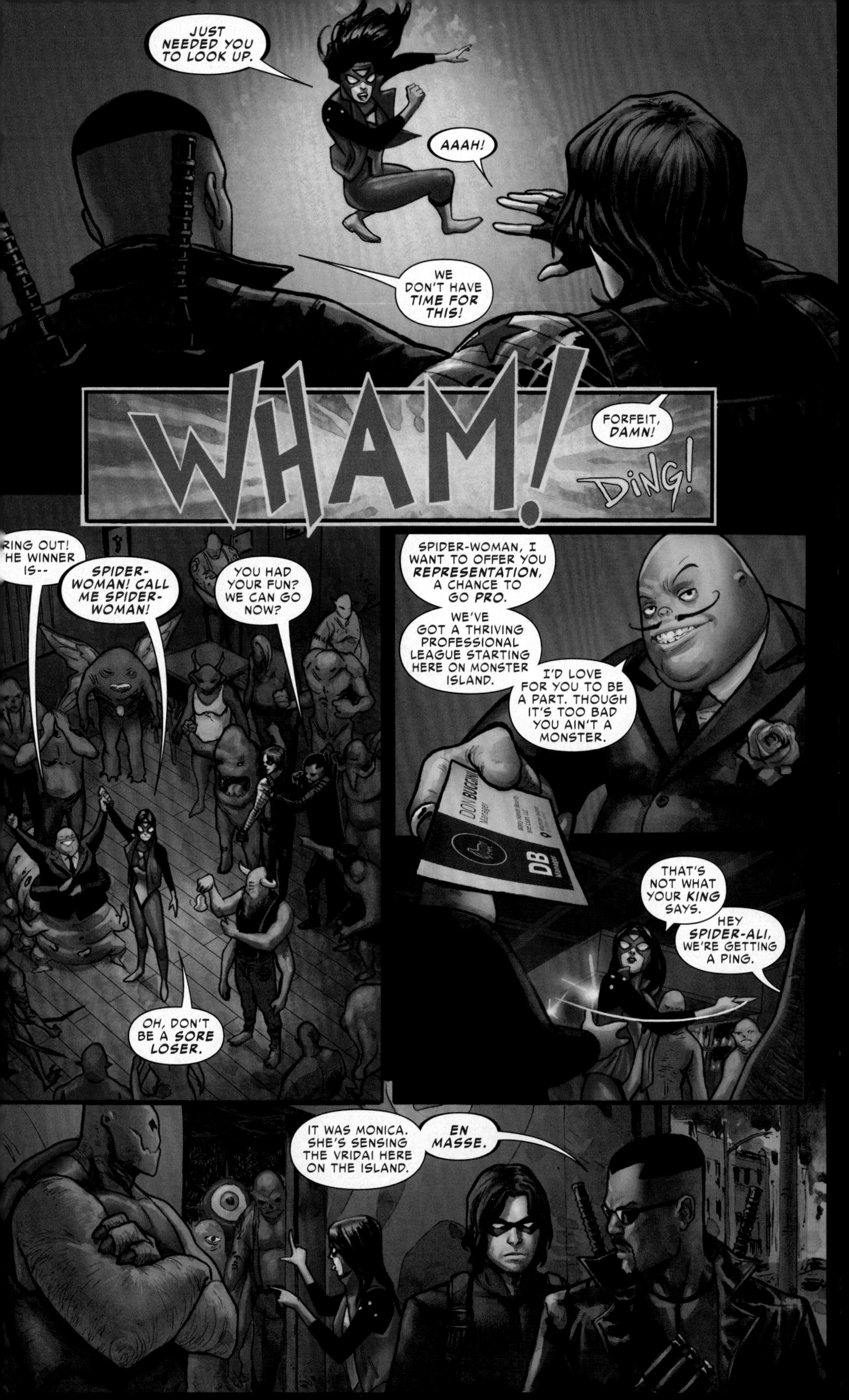
JUST NEEDED YOU TO LOOK UP.
AAAH!
WE DON'T HAVE TIME FOR THIS!
WHAM!
FORFEIT, DAMN!
DING!
RING OUT! THE WINNER IS--
SPIDER-WOMAN! CALL ME SPIDER-WOMAN!
YOU HAD YOUR FUN? WE CAN GO NOW?
OH, DON'T BE A SORE LOSER.
SPIDER-WOMAN, I WANT TO OFFER YOU REPRESENTATION, A CHANCE TO GO PRO.
WE'VE GOT A THRIVING PROFESSIONAL LEAGUE STARTING HERE ON MONSTER ISLAND.
I'D LOVE FOR YOU TO BE A PART. THOUGH IT'S TOO BAD YOU AIN'T A MONSTER.
DON BUCCINI
Manager
DB
THAT'S NOT WHAT YOUR KING SAYS.
HEY SPIDER-ALI, WE'RE GETTING A PING.
IT WAS MONICA. SHE'S SENSING THE VRIDAI HERE ON THE ISLAND.
EN MASSE.

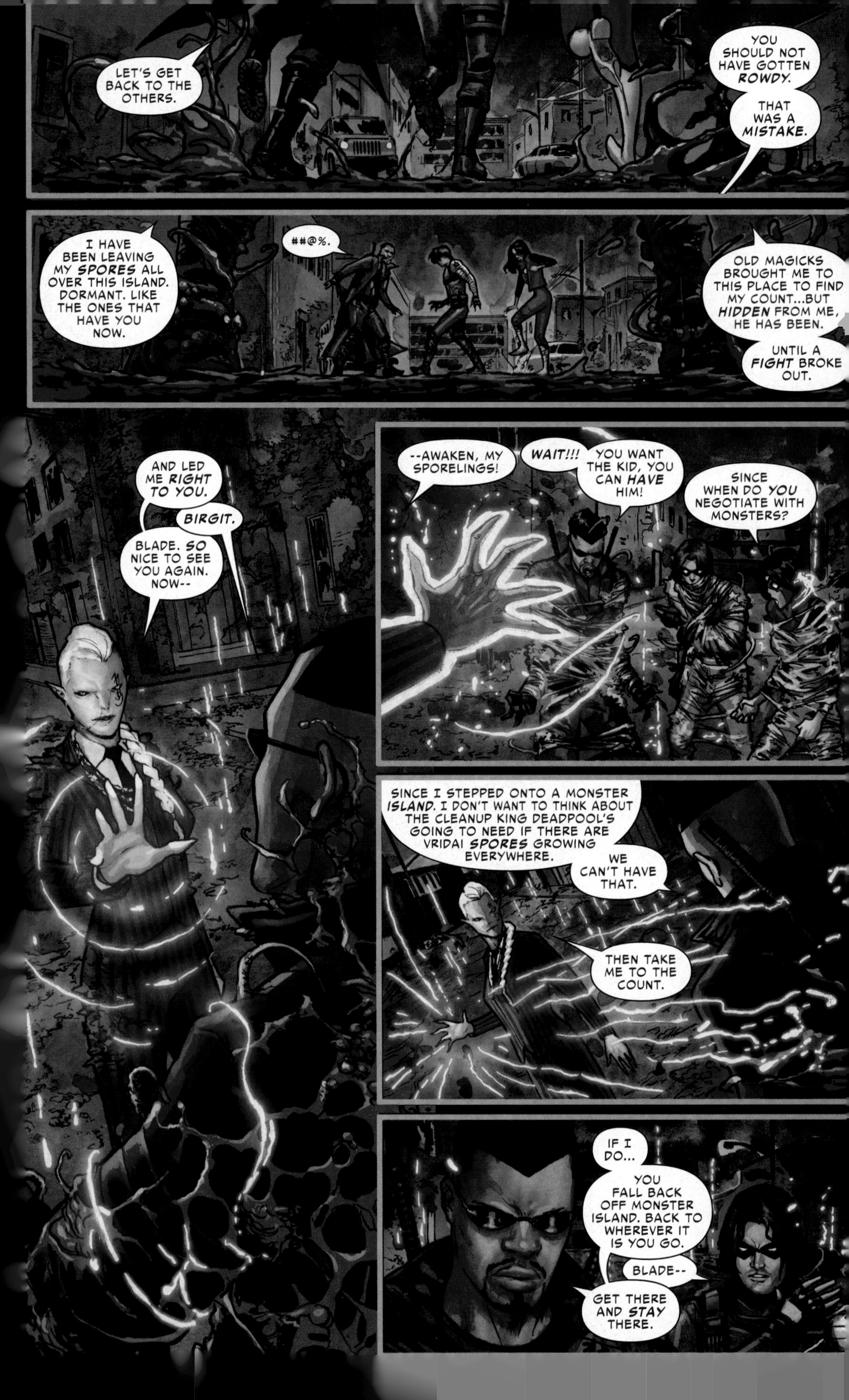
LET'S GET BACK TO THE OTHERS.
YOU SHOULD NOT HAVE GOTTEN ROWDY.
THAT WAS A MISTAKE.
I HAVE BEEN LEAVING MY SPORES ALL OVER THIS ISLAND. DORMANT. LIKE THE ONES THAT HAVE YOU NOW.
##@%.
OLD MAGICKS BROUGHT ME TO THIS PLACE TO FIND MY COUNT...BUT HIDDEN FROM ME, HE HAS BEEN.
UNTIL A FIGHT BROKE OUT.
AND LED ME RIGHT TO YOU.
BIRGIT.
BLADE. SO NICE TO SEE YOU AGAIN. NOW--
--AWAKEN, MY SPORELINGS!
WAIT!!!
YOU WANT THE KID, YOU CAN HAVE HIM!
SINCE WHEN DO YOU NEGOTIATE WITH MONSTERS?
SINCE I STEPPED ONTO A MONSTER ISLAND. I DON'T WANT TO THINK ABOUT THE CLEANUP KING DEADPOOL'S GOING TO NEED IF THERE ARE VRIDAI SPORES GROWING EVERYWHERE.
WE CAN'T HAVE THAT.
THEN TAKE ME TO THE COUNT.
IF I DO...
YOU FALL BACK OFF MONSTER ISLAND. BACK TO WHEREVER IT IS YOU GO.
BLADE--
GET THERE AND STAY THERE.

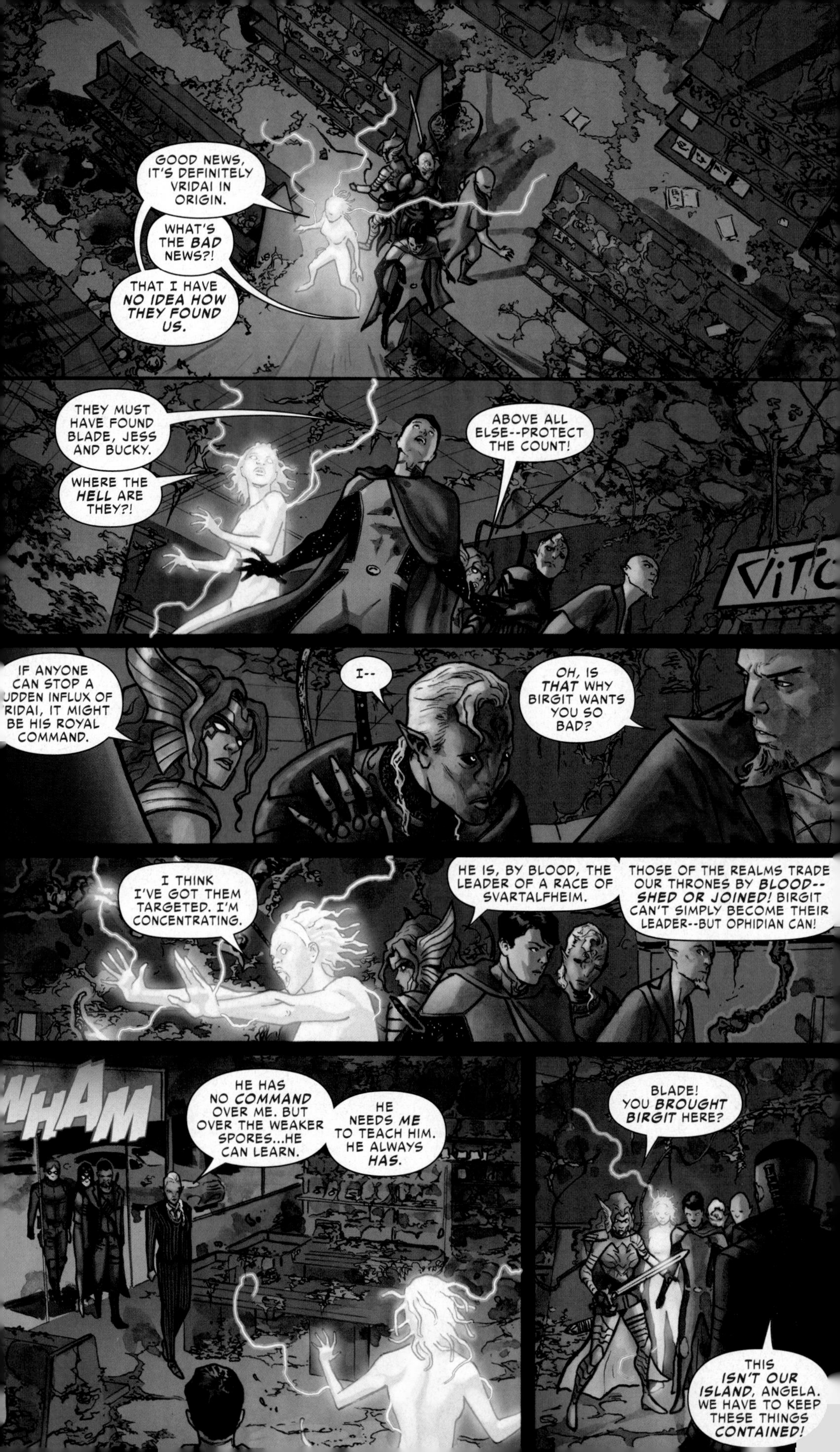
GOOD NEWS, IT'S DEFINITELY VRIDAI IN ORIGIN.
WHAT'S THE *BAD* NEWS?!
THAT I HAVE *NO IDEA HOW THEY FOUND US.*
THEY MUST HAVE FOUND BLADE, JESS AND BUCKY.
WHERE THE *HELL* ARE THEY?!
ABOVE ALL ELSE--PROTECT THE COUNT!
VITC
IF ANYONE CAN STOP A UDDEN INFLUX OF RIDAI, IT MIGHT BE HIS ROYAL COMMAND.
I--
OH, IS THAT WHY BIRGIT WANTS YOU SO BAD?
I THINK I'VE GOT THEM TARGETED. I'M CONCENTRATING.
HE IS, BY BLOOD, THE LEADER OF A RACE OF SVARTALFHEIM.
THOSE OF THE REALMS TRADE OUR THRONES BY *BLOOD--SHED OR JOINED!* BIRGIT CAN'T SIMPLY BECOME THEIR LEADER--BUT OPHIDIAN CAN!
WHAM
HE HAS NO *COMMAND* OVER ME. BUT OVER THE WEAKER SPORES...HE CAN LEARN.
HE NEEDS *ME* TO TEACH HIM. HE ALWAYS *HAS.*
BLADE! YOU *BROUGHT BIRGIT* HERE?
THIS *ISN'T OUR ISLAND,* ANGELA. WE HAVE TO KEEP THESE THINGS *CONTAINED!*

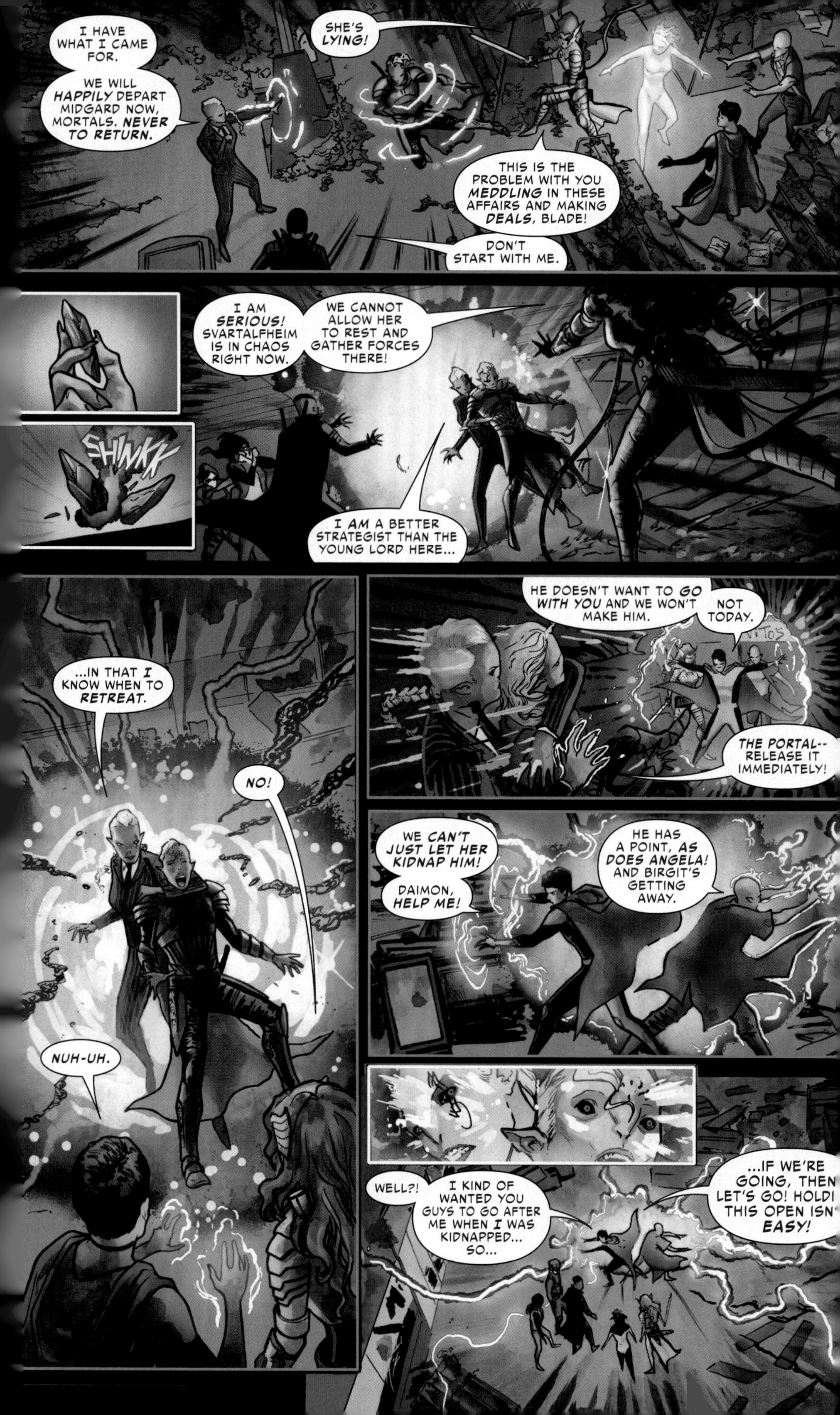

I HAVE WHAT I CAME FOR.
WE WILL HAPPILY DEPART MIDGARD NOW, MORTALS. NEVER TO RETURN.
SHE'S LYING!
THIS IS THE PROBLEM WITH YOU MEDDLING IN THESE AFFAIRS AND MAKING DEALS, BLADE!
DON'T START WITH ME.
SHINKK
I AM SERIOUS! SVARTALFHEIM IS IN CHAOS RIGHT NOW.
WE CANNOT ALLOW HER TO REST AND GATHER FORCES THERE!
I AM A BETTER STRATEGIST THAN THE YOUNG LORD HERE...
...IN THAT I KNOW WHEN TO RETREAT.
NO!
NUH-UH.
HE DOESN'T WANT TO GO WITH YOU AND WE WON'T MAKE HIM.
NOT TODAY.
THE PORTAL-- RELEASE IT IMMEDIATELY!
WE CAN'T JUST LET HER KIDNAP HIM!
DAIMON, HELP ME!
HE HAS A POINT, AS DOES ANGELA! AND BIRGIT'S GETTING AWAY.
WELL?!
I KIND OF WANTED YOU GUYS TO GO AFTER ME WHEN I WAS KIDNAPPED... SO...
...IF WE'RE GOING, THEN LET'S GO! HOLDI THIS OPEN ISN' EASY!

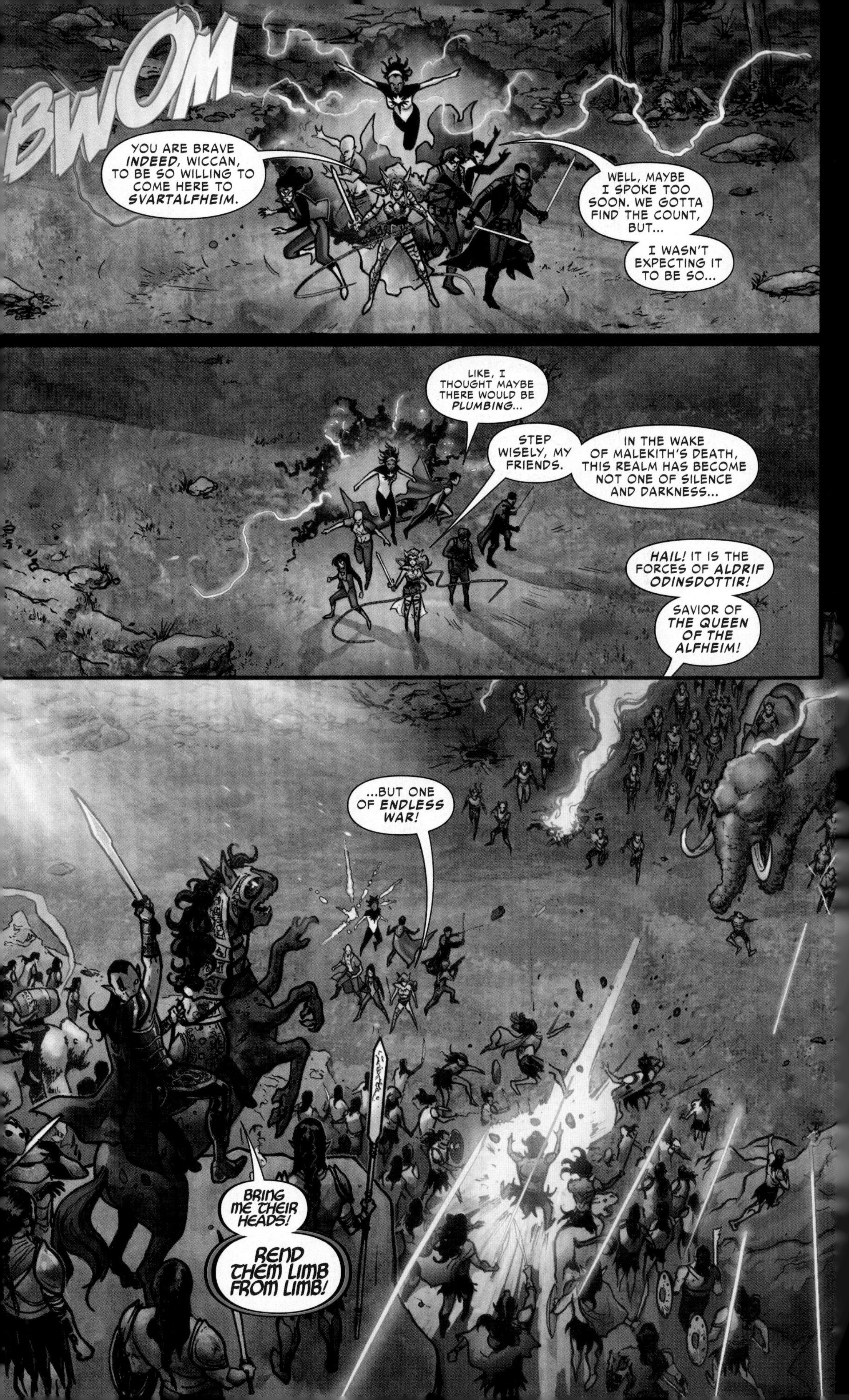
BWOM
YOU ARE BRAVE INDEED, WICCAN, TO BE SO WILLING TO COME HERE TO SVARTALFHEIM.
WELL, MAYBE I SPOKE TOO SOON. WE GOTTA FIND THE COUNT, BUT...
I WASN'T EXPECTING IT TO BE SO...
LIKE, I THOUGHT MAYBE THERE WOULD BE PLUMBING...
STEP WISELY, MY FRIENDS.
IN THE WAKE OF MALEKITH'S DEATH, THIS REALM HAS BECOME NOT ONE OF SILENCE AND DARKNESS...
HAIL! IT IS THE FORCES OF ALDRIF ODINSDOTTIR!
SAVIOR OF THE QUEEN OF THE ALFHEIM!
...BUT ONE OF ENDLESS WAR!
BRING ME THEIR HEADS!
REND THEM LIMB FROM LIMB!

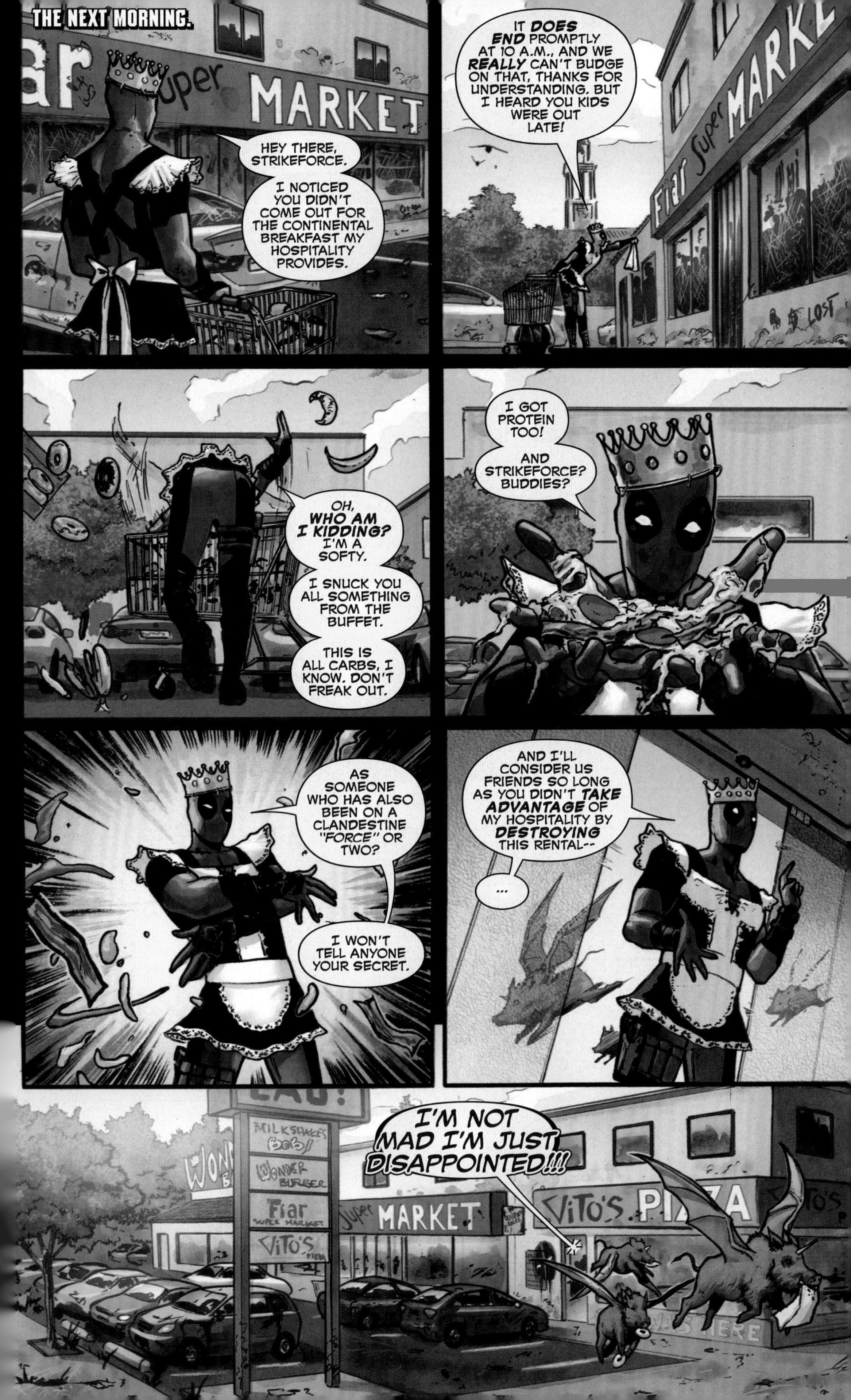
THE NEXT MORNING.
Fiar Super MARKET
HEY THERE, STRIKEFORCE.
I NOTICED YOU DIDN'T COME OUT FOR THE CONTINENTAL BREAKFAST MY HOSPITALITY PROVIDES.
IT DOES END PROMPTLY AT 10 A.M., AND WE REALLY CAN'T BUDGE ON THAT, THANKS FOR UNDERSTANDING. BUT I HEARD YOU KIDS WERE OUT LATE!
OH, WHO AM I KIDDING? I'M A SOFTY.
I SNUCK YOU ALL SOMETHING FROM THE BUFFET.
THIS IS ALL CARBS, I KNOW. DON'T FREAK OUT.
I GOT PROTEIN TOO!
AND STRIKEFORCE? BUDDIES?
AS SOMEONE WHO HAS ALSO BEEN ON A CLANDESTINE "FORCE" OR TWO?
I WON'T TELL ANYONE YOUR SECRET.
AND I'LL CONSIDER US FRIENDS SO LONG AS YOU DIDN'T TAKE ADVANTAGE OF MY HOSPITALITY BY DESTROYING THIS RENTAL--
...
MILKSHAKES
WONDER BURGER
Fiar SUPER MARKET
VITO'S
Super MARKET
VITO'S PIZZA
I'M NOT MAD I'M JUST DISAPPOINTED!!!

8

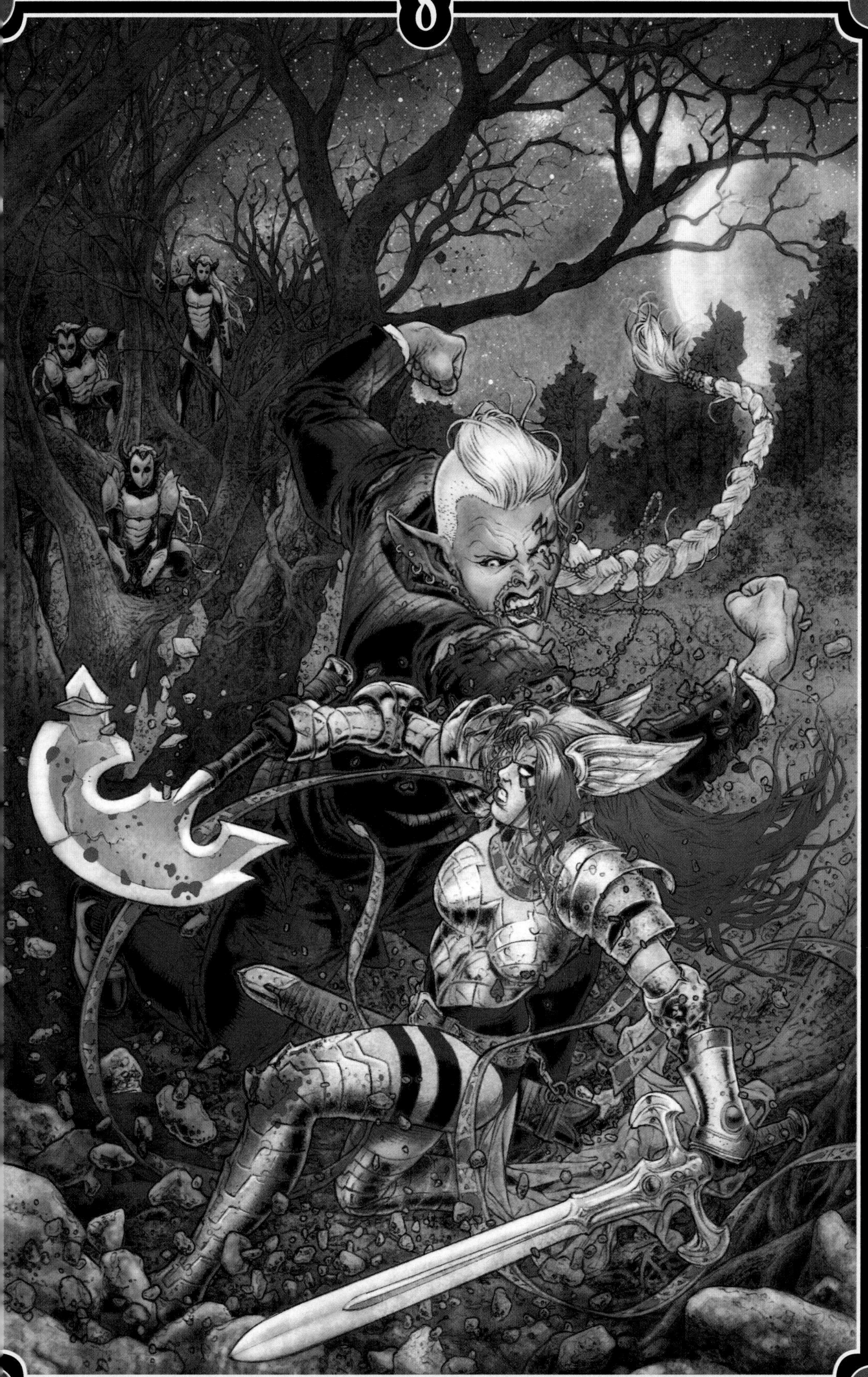

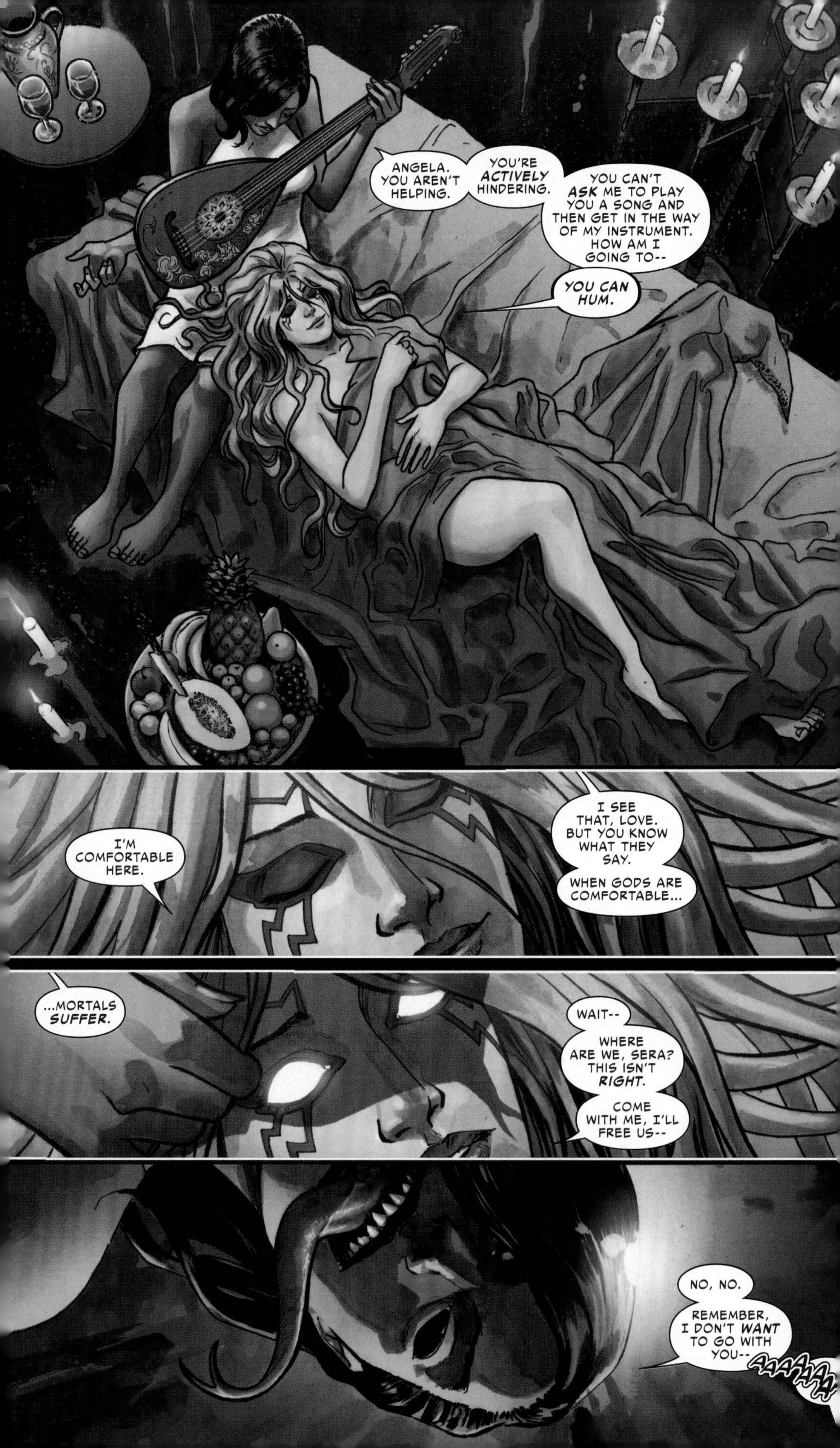
ANGELA. YOU AREN'T HELPING.
YOU'RE ACTIVELY HINDERING.
YOU CAN'T ASK ME TO PLAY YOU A SONG AND THEN GET IN THE WAY OF MY INSTRUMENT. HOW AM I GOING TO--
YOU CAN HUM.
I'M COMFORTABLE HERE.
I SEE THAT, LOVE. BUT YOU KNOW WHAT THEY SAY.
WHEN GODS ARE COMFORTABLE...
...MORTALS SUFFER.
WAIT--
WHERE ARE WE, SERA? THIS ISN'T RIGHT.
COME WITH ME, I'LL FREE US--
NO, NO.
REMEMBER, I DON'T WANT TO GO WITH YOU--
AAAAAAA

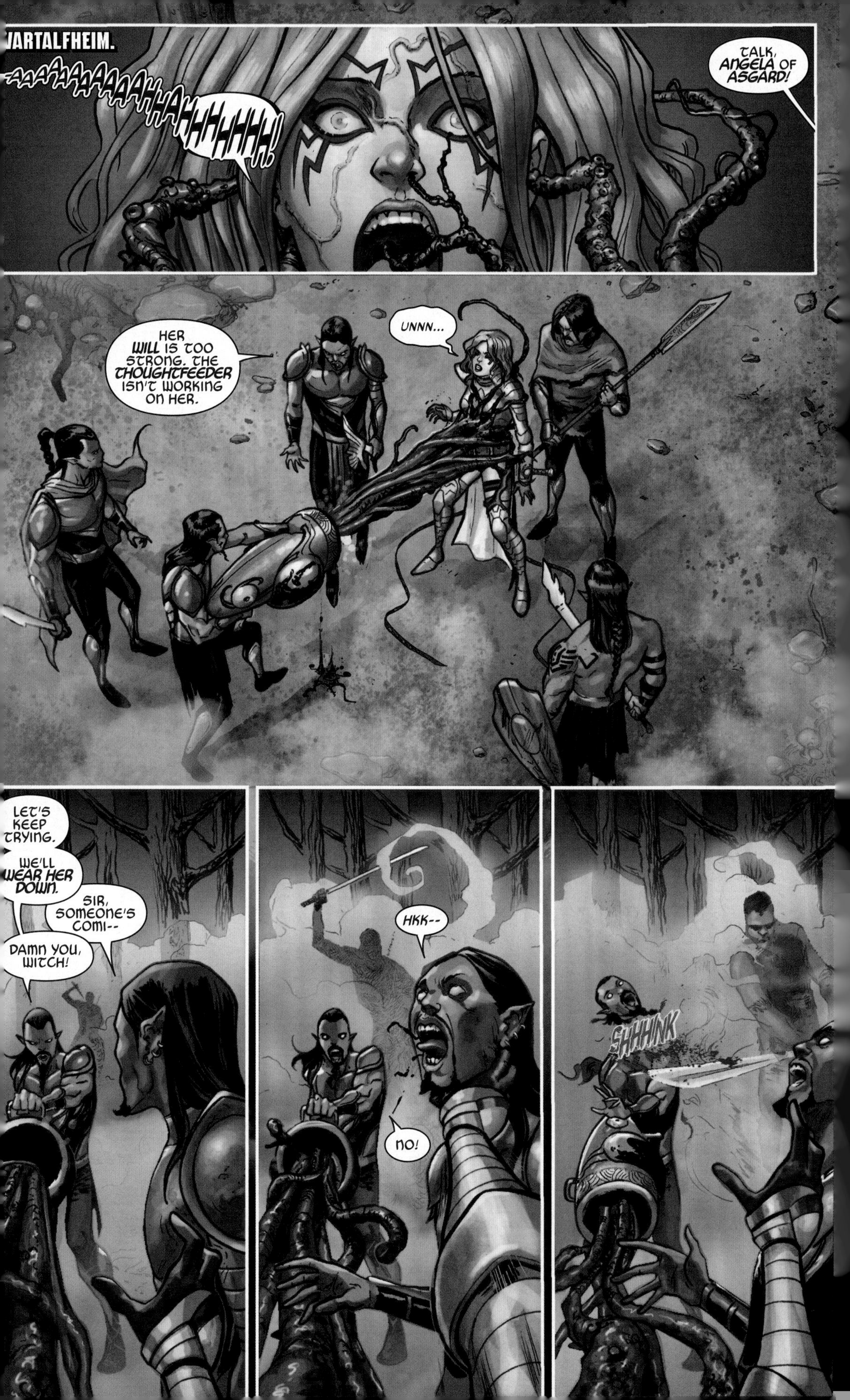

VARTALFHEIM.
AAAAAAAAAAAAHHAHHHHHH!
TALK, ANGELA OF ASGARD!
HER WILL IS TOO STRONG. THE THOUGHTFEEDER ISN'T WORKING ON HER.
UNNN...
LET'S KEEP TRYING.
WE'LL WEAR HER DOWN.
SIR, SOMEONE'S COMI--
DAMN YOU, WITCH!
HKK--
NO!
SHHHINK

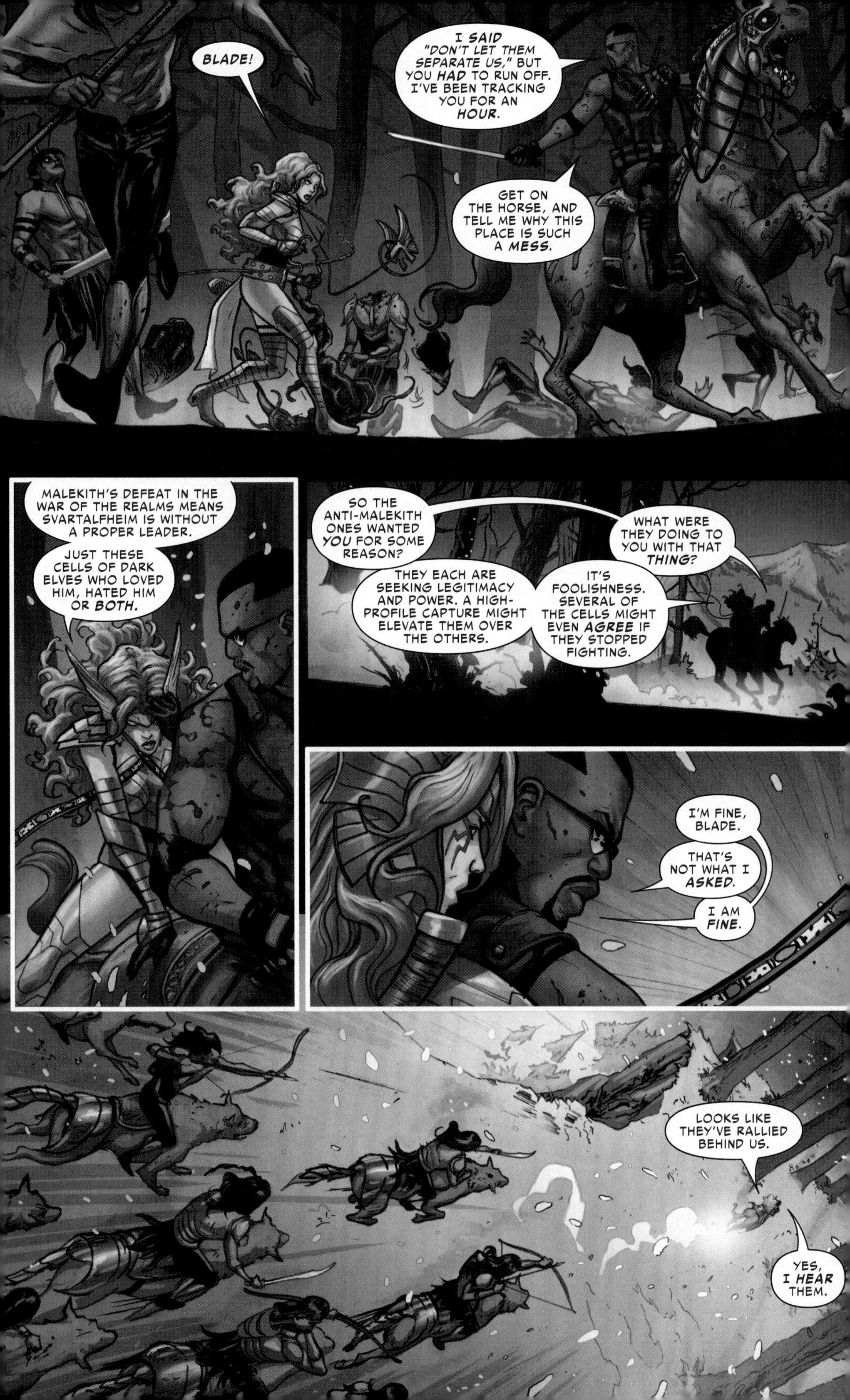
BLADE!
I SAID "DON'T LET THEM SEPARATE US," BUT YOU HAD TO RUN OFF. I'VE BEEN TRACKING YOU FOR AN HOUR.
GET ON THE HORSE, AND TELL ME WHY THIS PLACE IS SUCH A MESS.
MALEKITH'S DEFEAT IN THE WAR OF THE REALMS MEANS SVARTALFHEIM IS WITHOUT A PROPER LEADER.
JUST THESE CELLS OF DARK ELVES WHO LOVED HIM, HATED HIM OR BOTH.
SO THE ANTI-MALEKITH ONES WANTED YOU FOR SOME REASON?
THEY EACH ARE SEEKING LEGITIMACY AND POWER. A HIGH-PROFILE CAPTURE MIGHT ELEVATE THEM OVER THE OTHERS.
WHAT WERE THEY DOING TO YOU WITH THAT THING?
IT'S FOOLISHNESS. SEVERAL OF THE CELLS MIGHT EVEN AGREE IF THEY STOPPED FIGHTING.
I'M FINE, BLADE.
THAT'S NOT WHAT I ASKED.
I AM FINE.
LOOKS LIKE THEY'VE RALLIED BEHIND US.
YES, I HEAR THEM.

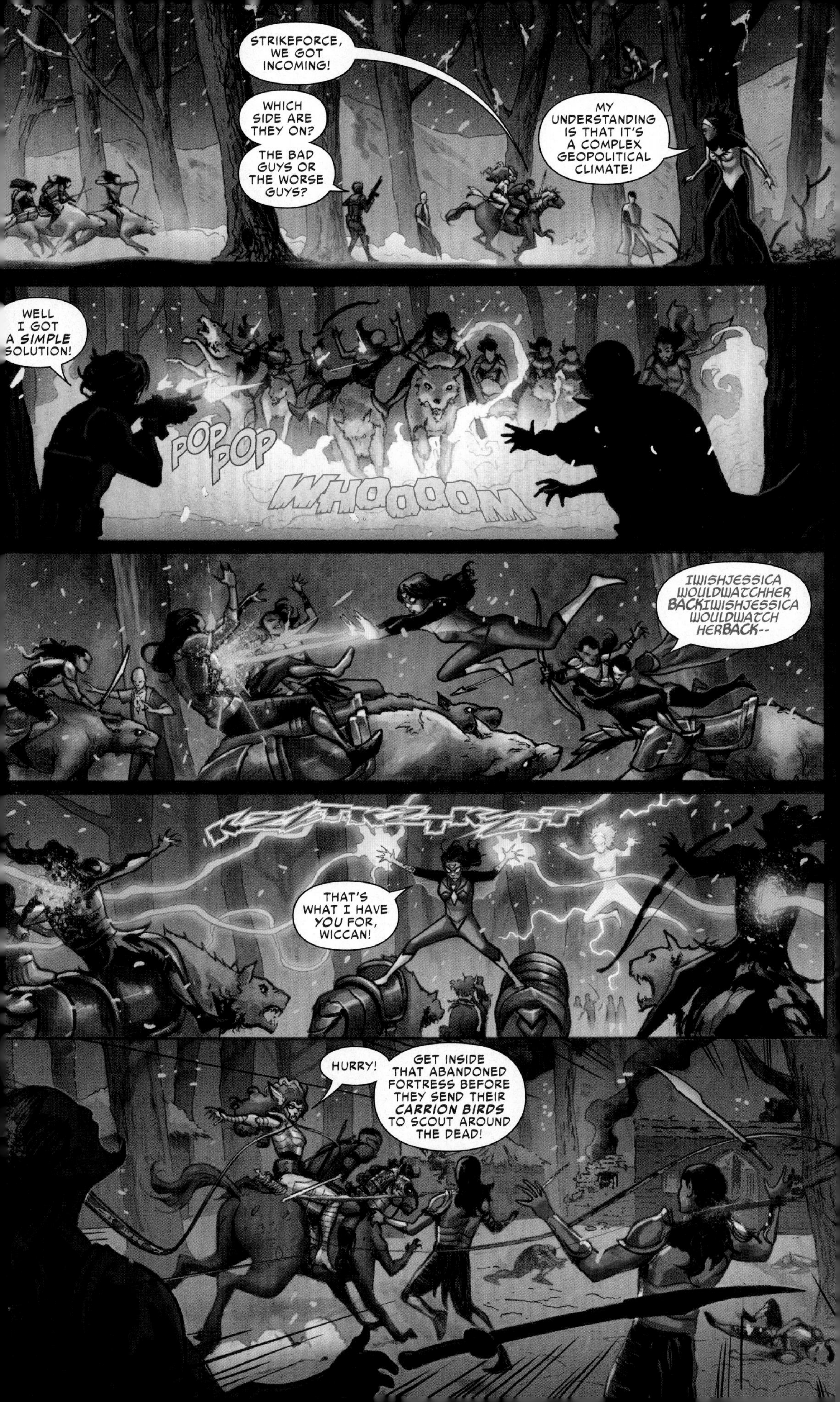

STRIKEFORCE, WE GOT INCOMING!
WHICH SIDE ARE THEY ON?
THE BAD GUYS OR THE WORSE GUYS?
MY UNDERSTANDING IS THAT IT'S A COMPLEX GEOPOLITICAL CLIMATE!
WELL I GOT A SIMPLE SOLUTION!
POP POP
WHOOOOM
IWISHJESSICA WOULDWATCHHER BACKIWISHJESSICA WOULDWATCH HERBACK--
KZZT KZZT KZZT
THAT'S WHAT I HAVE YOU FOR, WICCAN!
HURRY!
GET INSIDE THAT ABANDONED FORTRESS BEFORE THEY SEND THEIR CARRION BIRDS TO SCOUT AROUND THE DEAD!

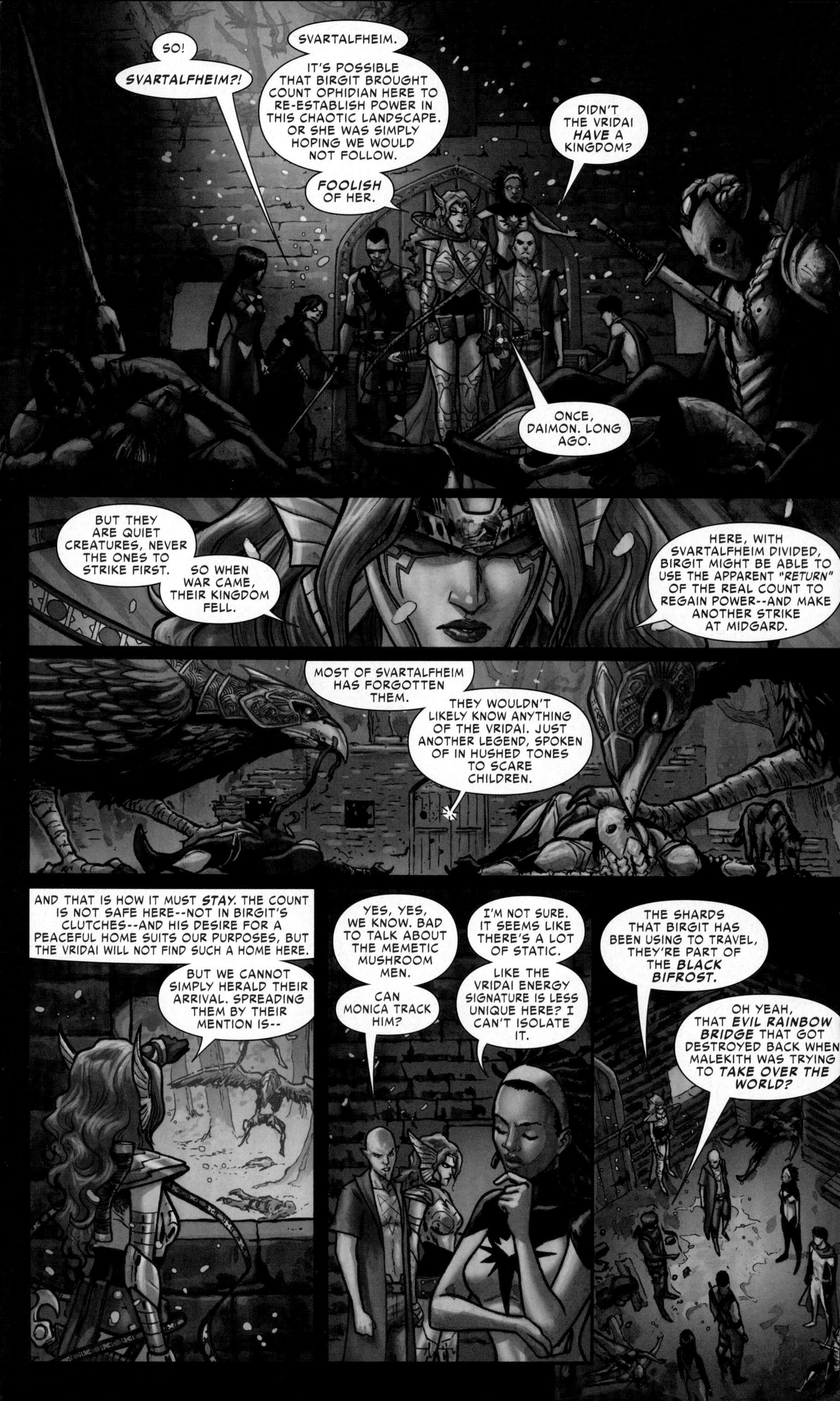
SO!
SVARTALFHEIM?!
SVARTALFHEIM.
IT'S POSSIBLE THAT BIRGIT BROUGHT COUNT OPHIDIAN HERE TO RE-ESTABLISH POWER IN THIS CHAOTIC LANDSCAPE. OR SHE WAS SIMPLY HOPING WE WOULD NOT FOLLOW.
FOOLISH OF HER.
DIDN'T THE VRIDAI HAVE A KINGDOM?
ONCE, DAIMON. LONG AGO.
BUT THEY ARE QUIET CREATURES, NEVER THE ONES TO STRIKE FIRST.
SO WHEN WAR CAME, THEIR KINGDOM FELL.
HERE, WITH SVARTALFHEIM DIVIDED, BIRGIT MIGHT BE ABLE TO USE THE APPARENT "RETURN" OF THE REAL COUNT TO REGAIN POWER--AND MAKE ANOTHER STRIKE AT MIDGARD.
MOST OF SVARTALFHEIM HAS FORGOTTEN THEM.
THEY WOULDN'T LIKELY KNOW ANYTHING OF THE VRIDAI. JUST ANOTHER LEGEND, SPOKEN OF IN HUSHED TONES TO SCARE CHILDREN.
AND THAT IS HOW IT MUST STAY. THE COUNT IS NOT SAFE HERE--NOT IN BIRGIT'S CLUTCHES--AND HIS DESIRE FOR A PEACEFUL HOME SUITS OUR PURPOSES, BUT THE VRIDAI WILL NOT FIND SUCH A HOME HERE.
BUT WE CANNOT SIMPLY HERALD THEIR ARRIVAL. SPREADING THEM BY THEIR MENTION IS--
YES, YES, WE KNOW. BAD TO TALK ABOUT THE MEMETIC MUSHROOM MEN.
CAN MONICA TRACK HIM?
I'M NOT SURE. IT SEEMS LIKE THERE'S A LOT OF STATIC.
LIKE THE VRIDAI ENERGY SIGNATURE IS LESS UNIQUE HERE? I CAN'T ISOLATE IT.
THE SHARDS THAT BIRGIT HAS BEEN USING TO TRAVEL, THEY'RE PART OF THE BLACK BIFROST.
OH YEAH, THAT EVIL RAINBOW BRIDGE THAT GOT DESTROYED BACK WHEN MALEKITH WAS TRYING TO TAKE OVER THE WORLD?

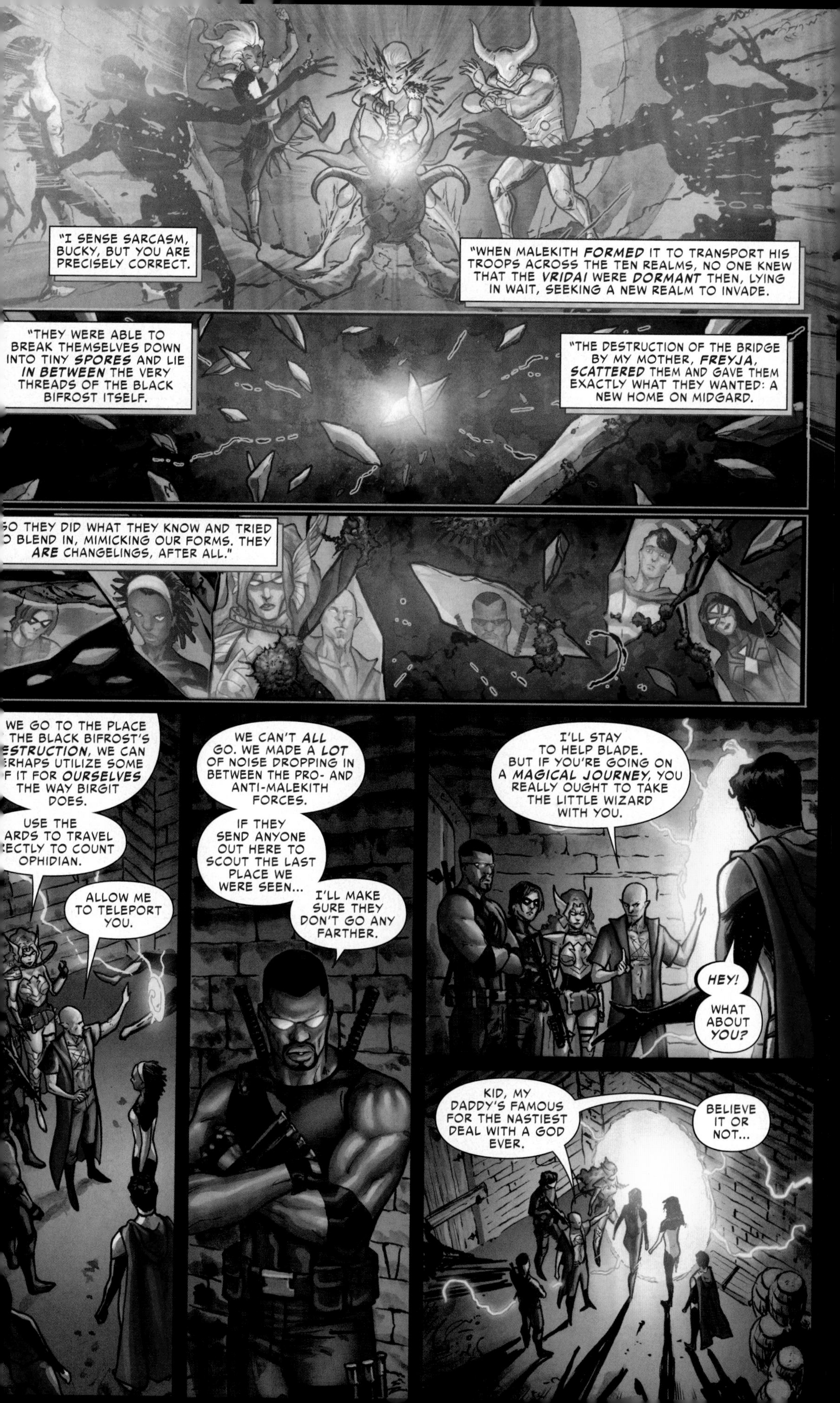

"I SENSE SARCASM, BUCKY, BUT YOU ARE PRECISELY CORRECT.
"WHEN MALEKITH FORMED IT TO TRANSPORT HIS TROOPS ACROSS THE TEN REALMS, NO ONE KNEW THAT THE VRIDAI WERE DORMANT THEN, LYING IN WAIT, SEEKING A NEW REALM TO INVADE.
"THEY WERE ABLE TO BREAK THEMSELVES DOWN INTO TINY SPORES AND LIE IN BETWEEN THE VERY THREADS OF THE BLACK BIFROST ITSELF.
"THE DESTRUCTION OF THE BRIDGE BY MY MOTHER, FREYJA, SCATTERED THEM AND GAVE THEM EXACTLY WHAT THEY WANTED: A NEW HOME ON MIDGARD.
O THEY DID WHAT THEY KNOW AND TRIED O BLEND IN, MIMICKING OUR FORMS. THEY ARE CHANGELINGS, AFTER ALL."
WE GO TO THE PLACE THE BLACK BIFROST'S ESTRUCTION, WE CAN ERHAPS UTILIZE SOME F IT FOR OURSELVES THE WAY BIRGIT DOES.
USE THE ARDS TO TRAVEL ECTLY TO COUNT OPHIDIAN.
ALLOW ME TO TELEPORT YOU.
WE CAN'T ALL GO. WE MADE A LOT OF NOISE DROPPING IN BETWEEN THE PRO- AND ANTI-MALEKITH FORCES.
IF THEY SEND ANYONE OUT HERE TO SCOUT THE LAST PLACE WE WERE SEEN...
I'LL MAKE SURE THEY DON'T GO ANY FARTHER.
I'LL STAY TO HELP BLADE. BUT IF YOU'RE GOING ON A MAGICAL JOURNEY, YOU REALLY OUGHT TO TAKE THE LITTLE WIZARD WITH YOU.
HEY!
WHAT ABOUT YOU?
KID, MY DADDY'S FAMOUS FOR THE NASTIEST DEAL WITH A GOD EVER.
BELIEVE IT OR NOT...

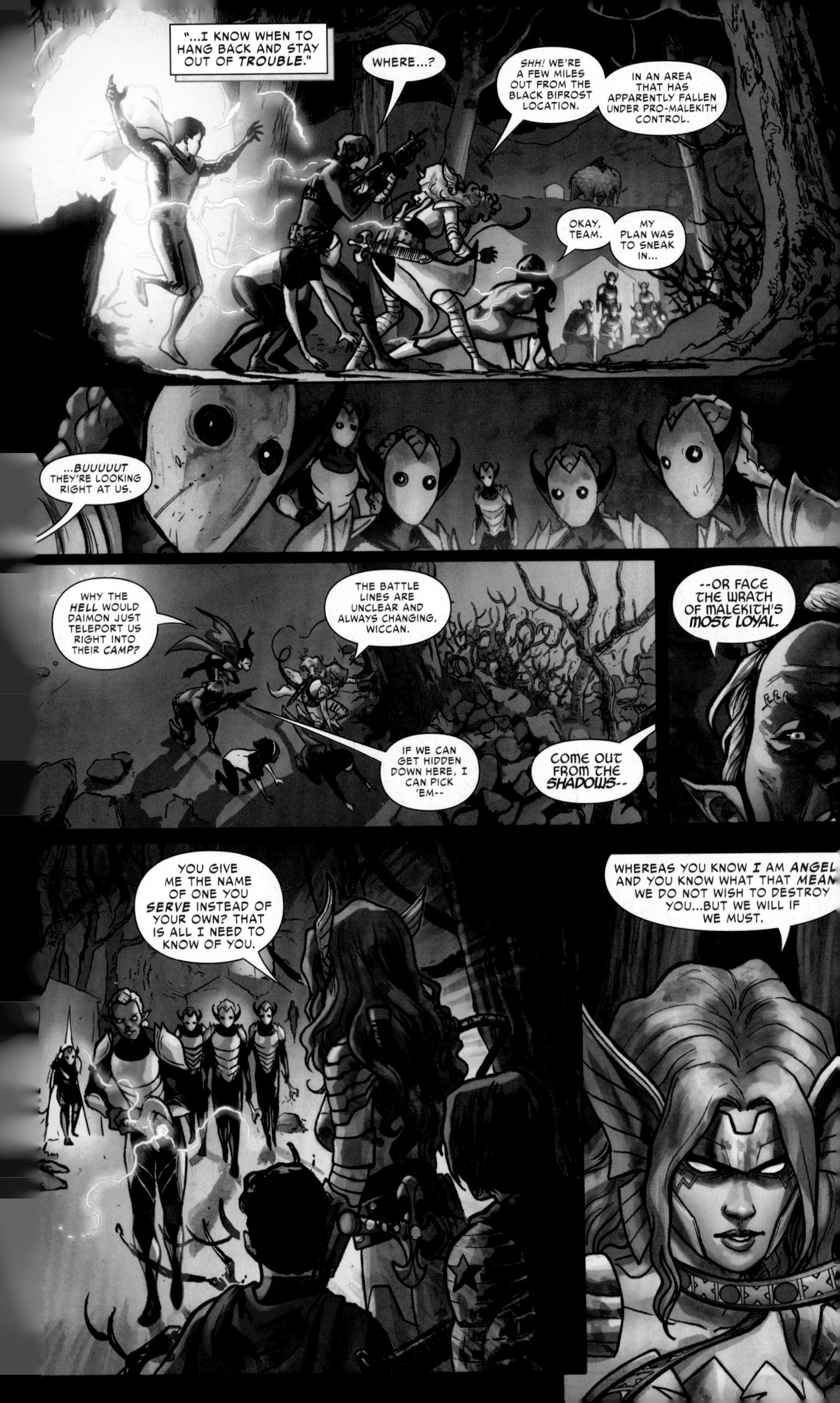

"...I KNOW WHEN TO HANG BACK AND STAY OUT OF TROUBLE."
WHERE...?
SHH! WE'RE A FEW MILES OUT FROM THE BLACK BIFROST LOCATION.
IN AN AREA THAT HAS APPARENTLY FALLEN UNDER PRO-MALEKITH CONTROL.
OKAY, TEAM.
MY PLAN WAS TO SNEAK IN...
...BUUUUUT THEY'RE LOOKING RIGHT AT US.
WHY THE HELL WOULD DAIMON JUST TELEPORT US RIGHT INTO THEIR CAMP?
THE BATTLE LINES ARE UNCLEAR AND ALWAYS CHANGING, WICCAN.
IF WE CAN GET HIDDEN DOWN HERE, I CAN PICK 'EM--
COME OUT FROM THE SHADOWS--
--OR FACE THE WRATH OF MALEKITH'S MOST LOYAL.
YOU GIVE ME THE NAME OF ONE YOU SERVE INSTEAD OF YOUR OWN? THAT IS ALL I NEED TO KNOW OF YOU.
WHEREAS YOU KNOW I AM ANGEL AND YOU KNOW WHAT THAT MEAN WE DO NOT WISH TO DESTROY YOU...BUT WE WILL IF WE MUST.

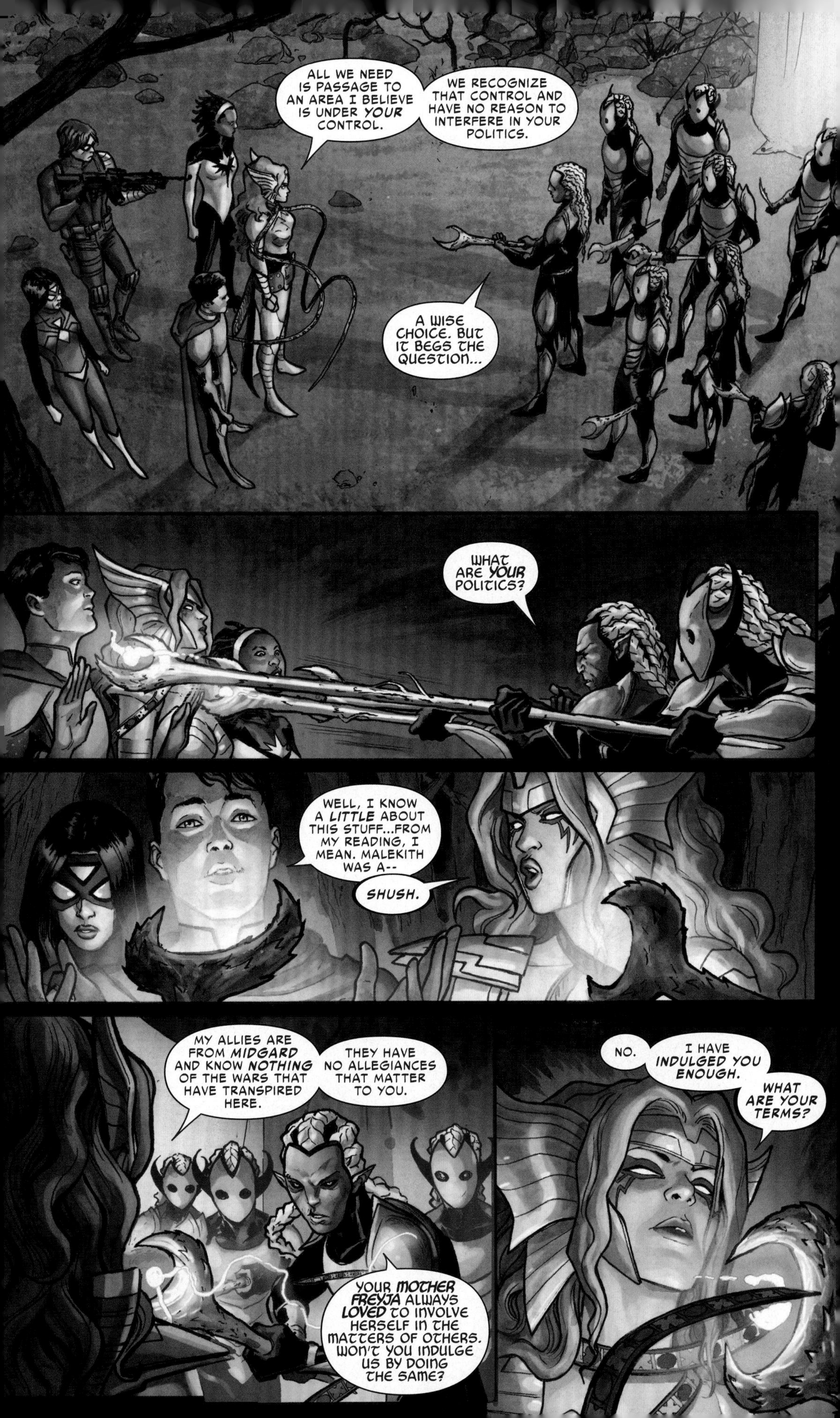
ALL WE NEED IS PASSAGE TO AN AREA I BELIEVE IS UNDER YOUR CONTROL.
WE RECOGNIZE THAT CONTROL AND HAVE NO REASON TO INTERFERE IN YOUR POLITICS.
A WISE CHOICE. BUT IT BEGS THE QUESTION...
WHAT ARE YOUR POLITICS?
WELL, I KNOW A LITTLE ABOUT THIS STUFF...FROM MY READING, I MEAN. MALEKITH WAS A--
SHUSH.
MY ALLIES ARE FROM MIDGARD AND KNOW NOTHING OF THE WARS THAT HAVE TRANSPIRED HERE.
THEY HAVE NO ALLEGIANCES THAT MATTER TO YOU.
YOUR MOTHER FREYJA ALWAYS LOVED TO INVOLVE HERSELF IN THE MATTERS OF OTHERS. WON'T YOU INDULGE US BY DOING THE SAME?
NO.
I HAVE INDULGED YOU ENOUGH.
WHAT ARE YOUR TERMS?

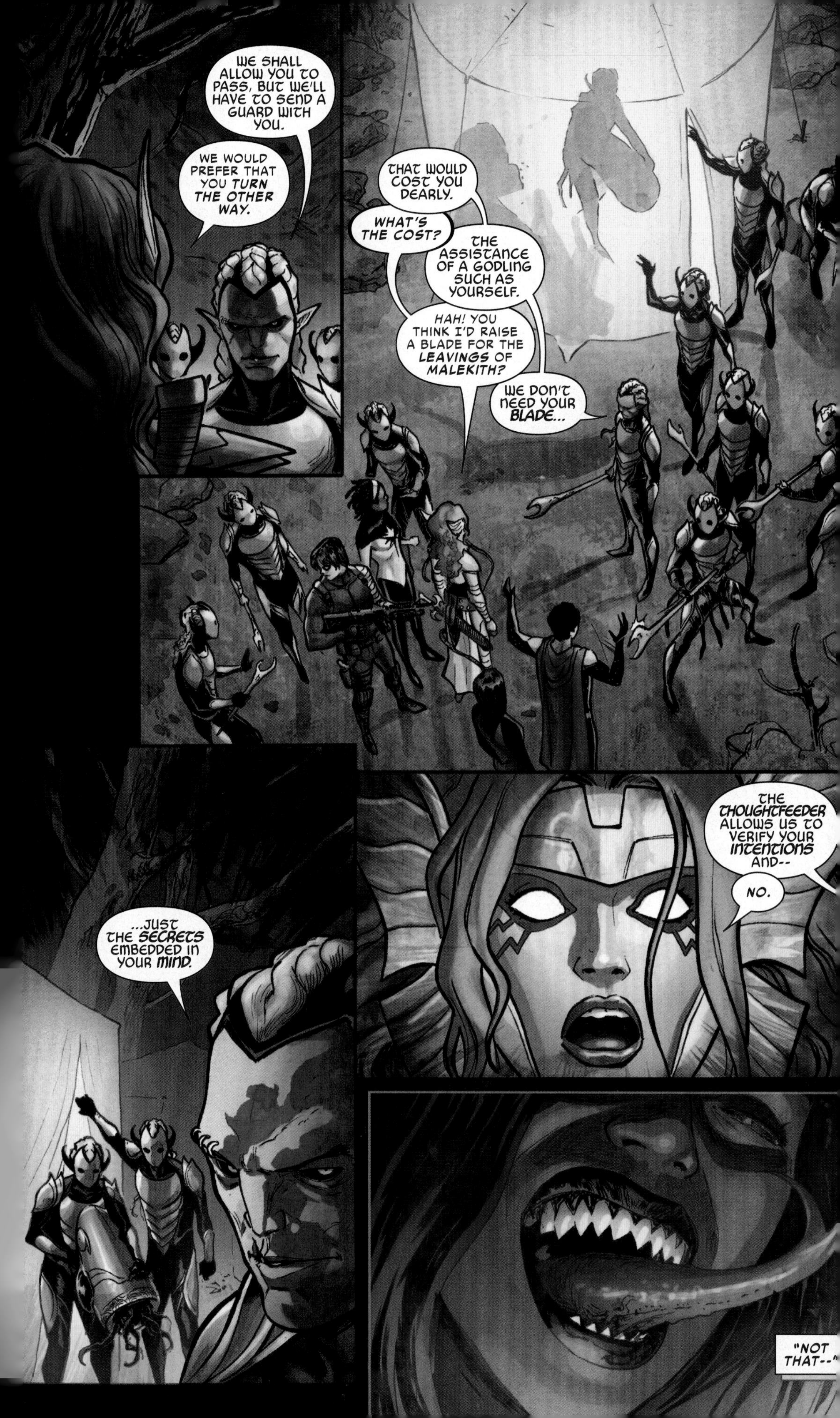
WE SHALL ALLOW YOU TO PASS, BUT WE'LL HAVE TO SEND A GUARD WITH YOU.
WE WOULD PREFER THAT YOU TURN THE OTHER WAY.
THAT WOULD COST YOU DEARLY.
WHAT'S THE COST?
THE ASSISTANCE OF A GODLING SUCH AS YOURSELF.
HAH! YOU THINK I'D RAISE A BLADE FOR THE LEAVINGS OF MALEKITH?
WE DON'T NEED YOUR BLADE...
...JUST THE SECRETS EMBEDDED IN YOUR MIND.
THE THOUGHTFEEDER ALLOWS US TO VERIFY YOUR INTENTIONS AND--
NO.
"NOT THAT--"

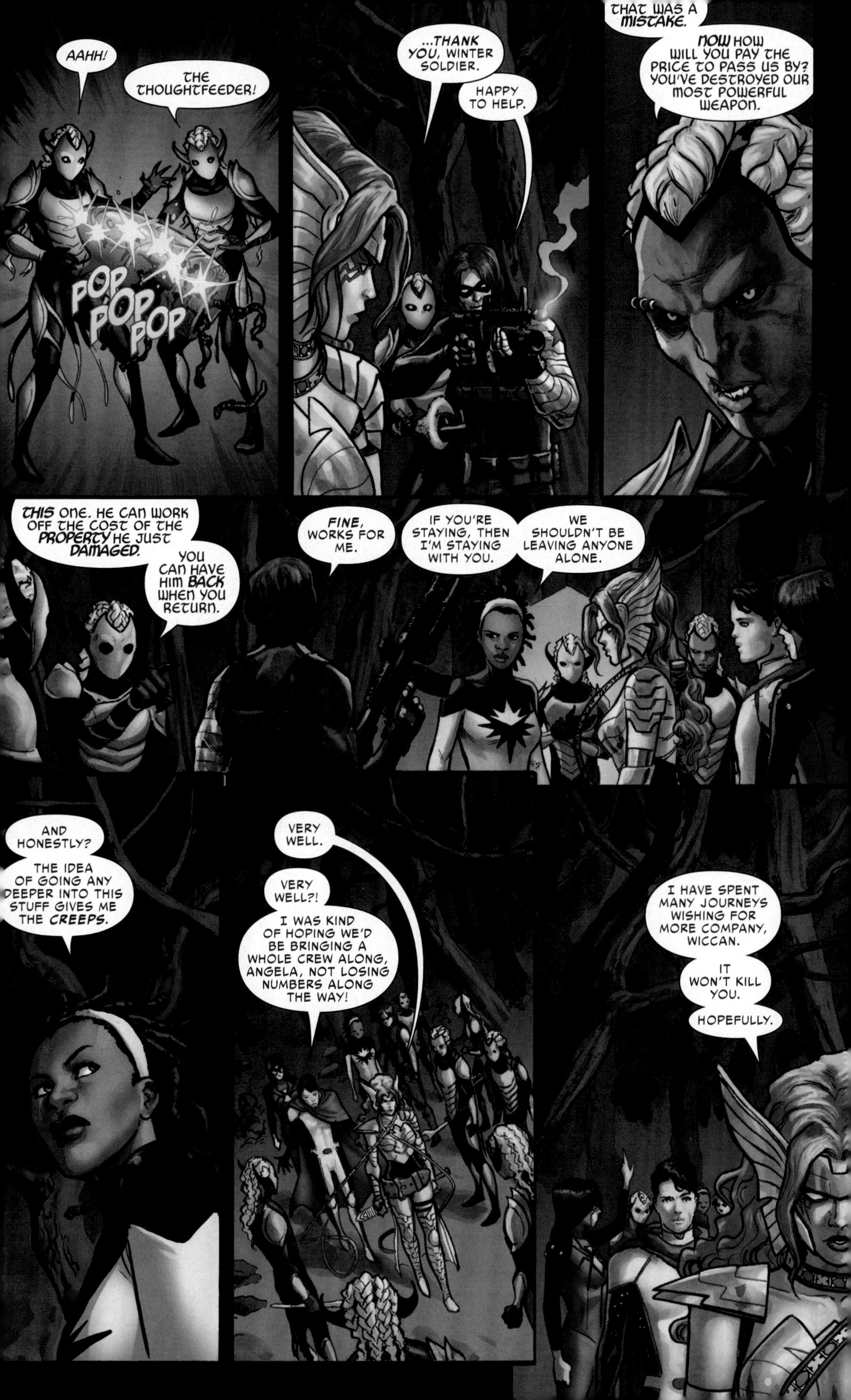
AAHH!
THE THOUGHTFEEDER!
POP POP POP
...THANK YOU, WINTER SOLDIER.
HAPPY TO HELP.
THAT WAS A MISTAKE.
NOW HOW WILL YOU PAY THE PRICE TO PASS US BY? YOU'VE DESTROYED OUR MOST POWERFUL WEAPON.
THIS ONE. HE CAN WORK OFF THE COST OF THE PROPERTY HE JUST DAMAGED.
YOU CAN HAVE HIM BACK WHEN YOU RETURN.
FINE, WORKS FOR ME.
IF YOU'RE STAYING, THEN I'M STAYING WITH YOU.
WE SHOULDN'T BE LEAVING ANYONE ALONE.
AND HONESTLY?
THE IDEA OF GOING ANY DEEPER INTO THIS STUFF GIVES ME THE CREEPS.
VERY WELL.
VERY WELL?!
I WAS KIND OF HOPING WE'D BE BRINGING A WHOLE CREW ALONG, ANGELA, NOT LOSING NUMBERS ALONG THE WAY!
I HAVE SPENT MANY JOURNEYS WISHING FOR MORE COMPANY, WICCAN.
IT WON'T KILL YOU.
HOPEFULLY.

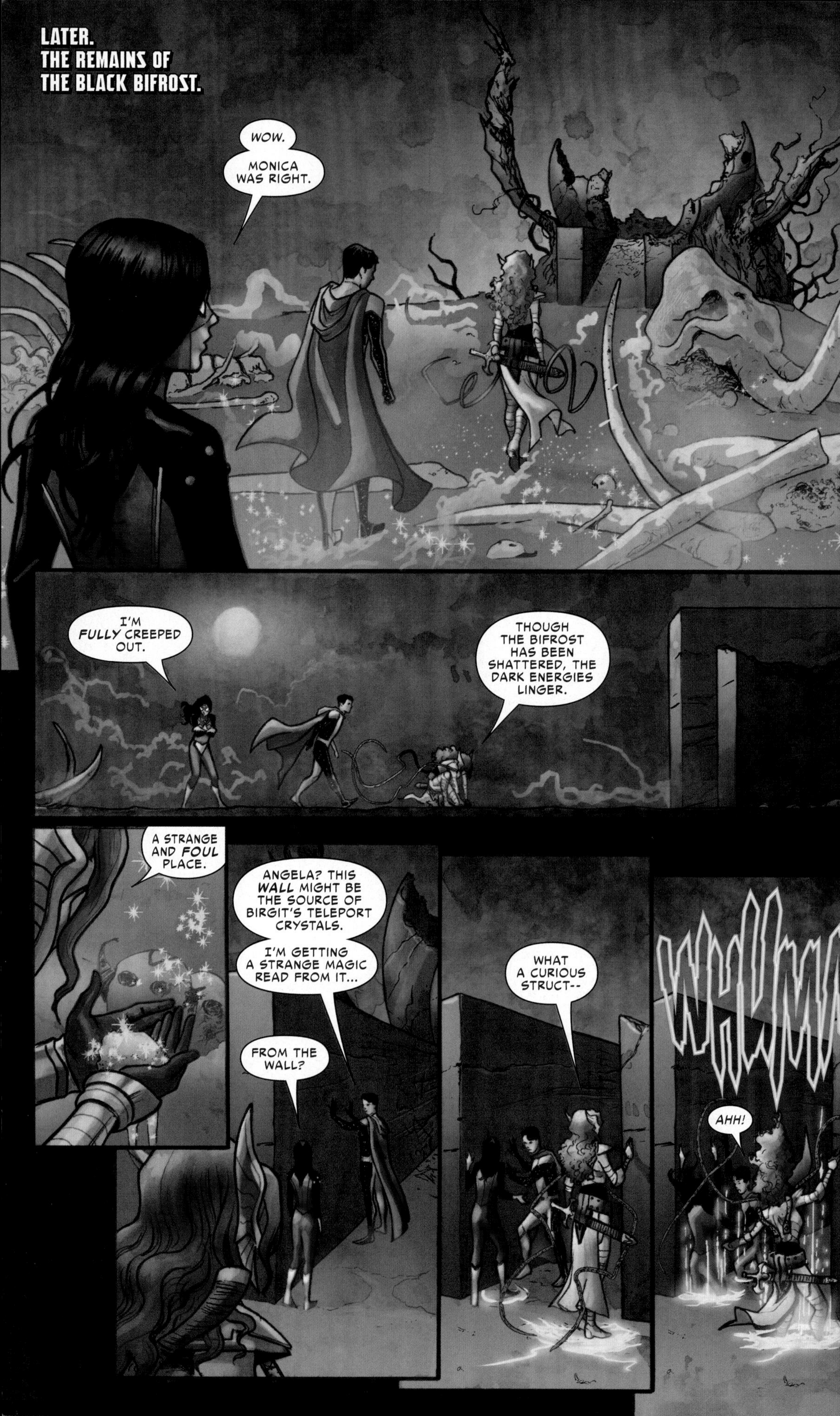
LATER.
THE REMAINS OF THE BLACK BIFROST.
WOW.
MONICA WAS RIGHT.
I'M FULLY CREEPED OUT.
THOUGH THE BIFROST HAS BEEN SHATTERED, THE DARK ENERGIES LINGER.
A STRANGE AND FOUL PLACE.
ANGELA? THIS WALL MIGHT BE THE SOURCE OF BIRGIT'S TELEPORT CRYSTALS.
I'M GETTING A STRANGE MAGIC READ FROM IT...
FROM THE WALL?
WHAT A CURIOUS STRUCT--
AHH!

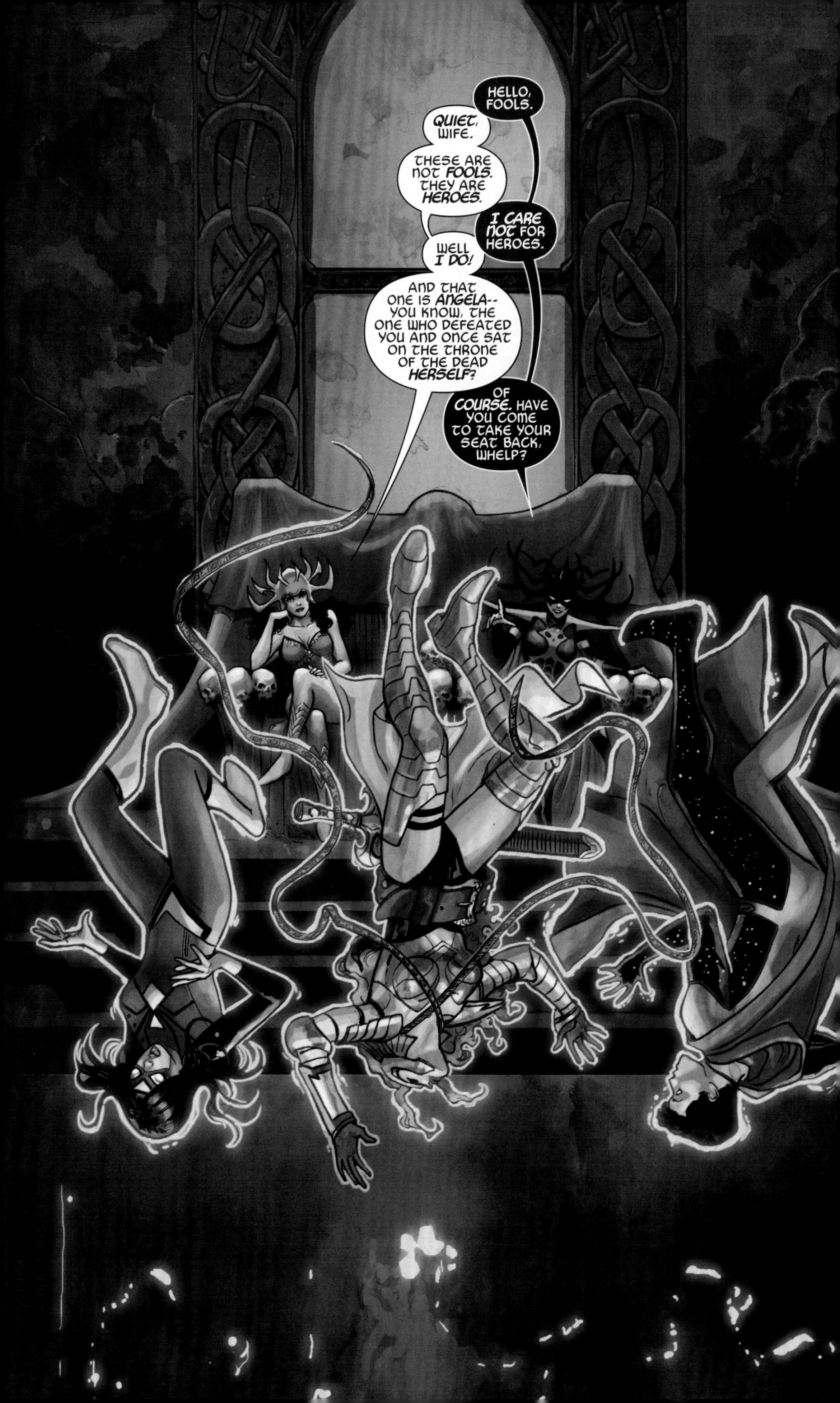
HELLO, FOOLS.
QUIET, WIFE.
THESE ARE NOT FOOLS. THEY ARE HEROES.
I CARE NOT FOR HEROES.
WELL I DO!
AND THAT ONE IS ANGELA--YOU KNOW, THE ONE WHO DEFEATED YOU AND ONCE SAT ON THE THRONE OF THE DEAD HERSELF?
OF COURSE. HAVE YOU COME TO TAKE YOUR SEAT BACK, WHELP?

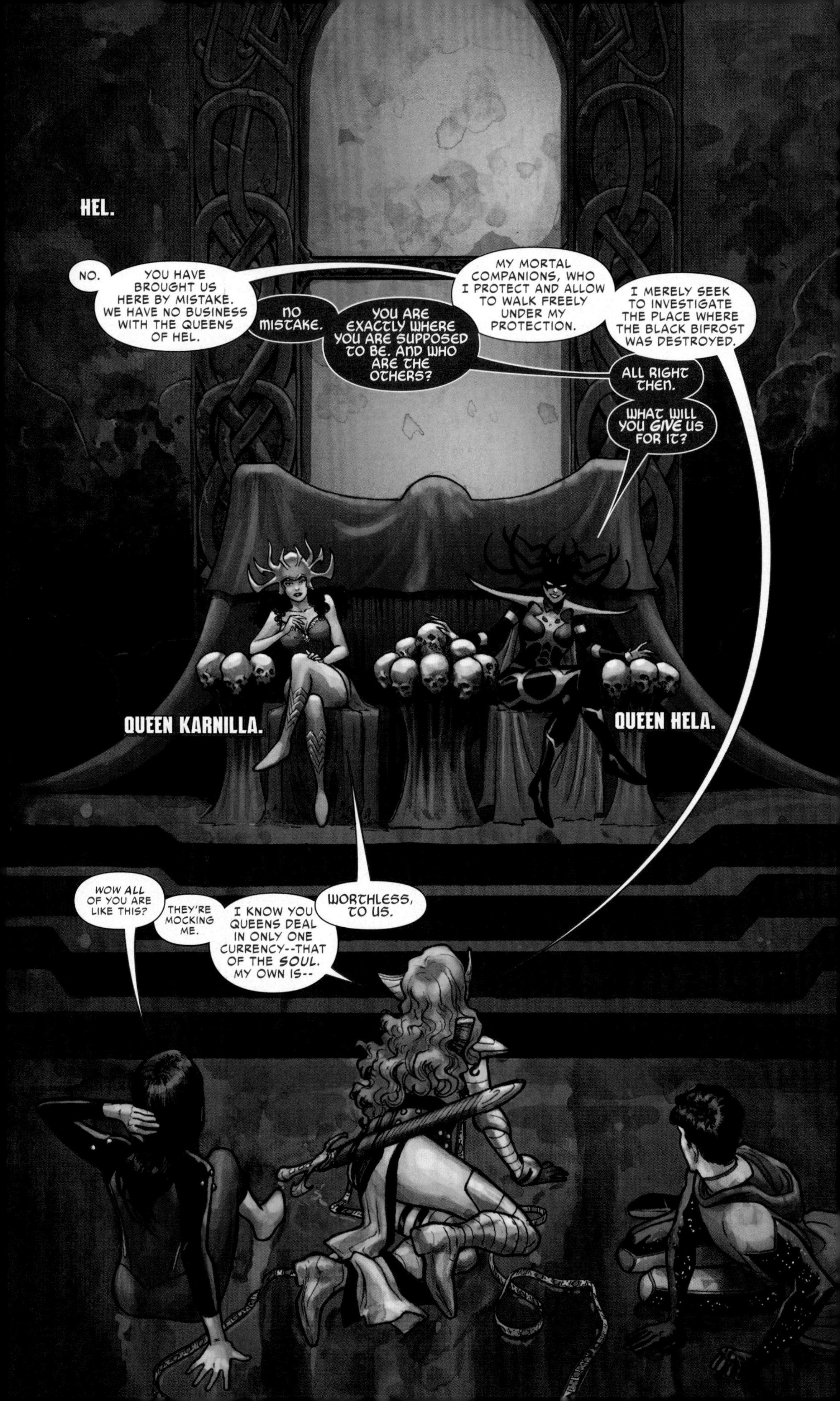

HEL.
NO.
YOU HAVE BROUGHT US HERE BY MISTAKE. WE HAVE NO BUSINESS WITH THE QUEENS OF HEL.
NO MISTAKE.
YOU ARE EXACTLY WHERE YOU ARE SUPPOSED TO BE. AND WHO ARE THE OTHERS?
MY MORTAL COMPANIONS, WHO I PROTECT AND ALLOW TO WALK FREELY UNDER MY PROTECTION.
I MERELY SEEK TO INVESTIGATE THE PLACE WHERE THE BLACK BIFROST WAS DESTROYED.
ALL RIGHT THEN.
WHAT WILL YOU GIVE US FOR IT?
QUEEN KARNILLA.
QUEEN HELA.
I KNOW YOU QUEENS DEAL IN ONLY ONE CURRENCY--THAT OF THE SOUL. MY OWN IS--
WORTHLESS, TO US.
THEY'RE MOCKING ME.
WOW ALL OF YOU ARE LIKE THIS?

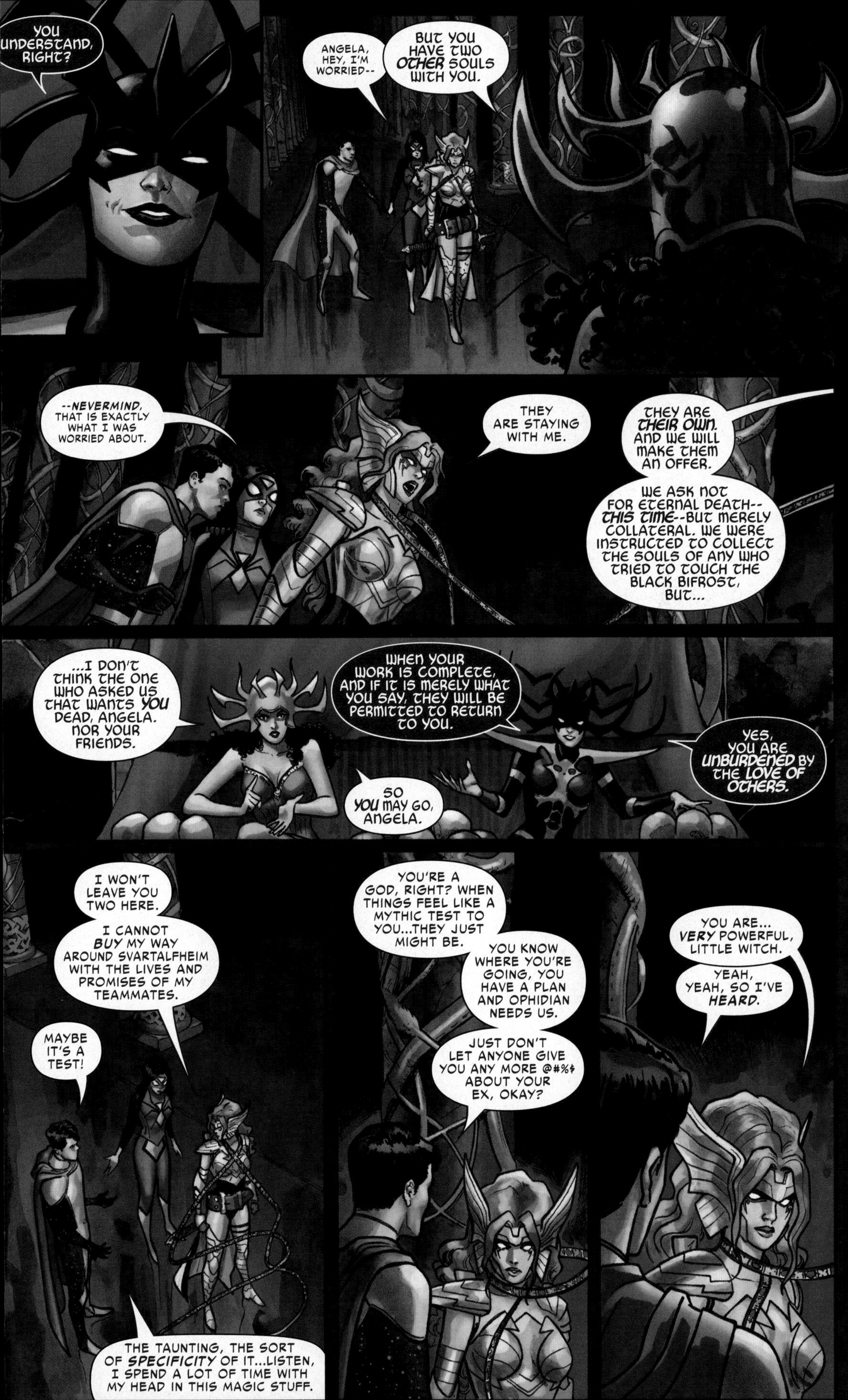
YOU UNDERSTAND, RIGHT?
ANGELA, HEY, I'M WORRIED--
BUT YOU HAVE TWO OTHER SOULS WITH YOU.
--NEVERMIND, THAT IS EXACTLY WHAT I WAS WORRIED ABOUT.
THEY ARE STAYING WITH ME.
THEY ARE THEIR OWN. AND WE WILL MAKE THEM AN OFFER.
WE ASK NOT FOR ETERNAL DEATH-- THIS TIME--BUT MERELY COLLATERAL. WE WERE INSTRUCTED TO COLLECT THE SOULS OF ANY WHO TRIED TO TOUCH THE BLACK BIFROST, BUT...
...I DON'T THINK THE ONE WHO ASKED US THAT WANTS YOU DEAD, ANGELA. NOR YOUR FRIENDS.
WHEN YOUR WORK IS COMPLETE, AND IF IT IS MERELY WHAT YOU SAY, THEY WILL BE PERMITTED TO RETURN TO YOU.
SO YOU MAY GO, ANGELA.
YES, YOU ARE UNBURDENED BY THE LOVE OF OTHERS.
I WON'T LEAVE YOU TWO HERE.
I CANNOT BUY MY WAY AROUND SVARTALFHEIM WITH THE LIVES AND PROMISES OF MY TEAMMATES.
MAYBE IT'S A TEST!
THE TAUNTING, THE SORT OF SPECIFICITY OF IT...LISTEN, I SPEND A LOT OF TIME WITH MY HEAD IN THIS MAGIC STUFF.
YOU'RE A GOD, RIGHT? WHEN THINGS FEEL LIKE A MYTHIC TEST TO YOU...THEY JUST MIGHT BE.
YOU KNOW WHERE YOU'RE GOING, YOU HAVE A PLAN AND OPHIDIAN NEEDS US.
JUST DON'T LET ANYONE GIVE YOU ANY MORE @#%$ ABOUT YOUR EX, OKAY?
YOU ARE... VERY POWERFUL, LITTLE WITCH.
YEAH, YEAH, SO I'VE HEARD.

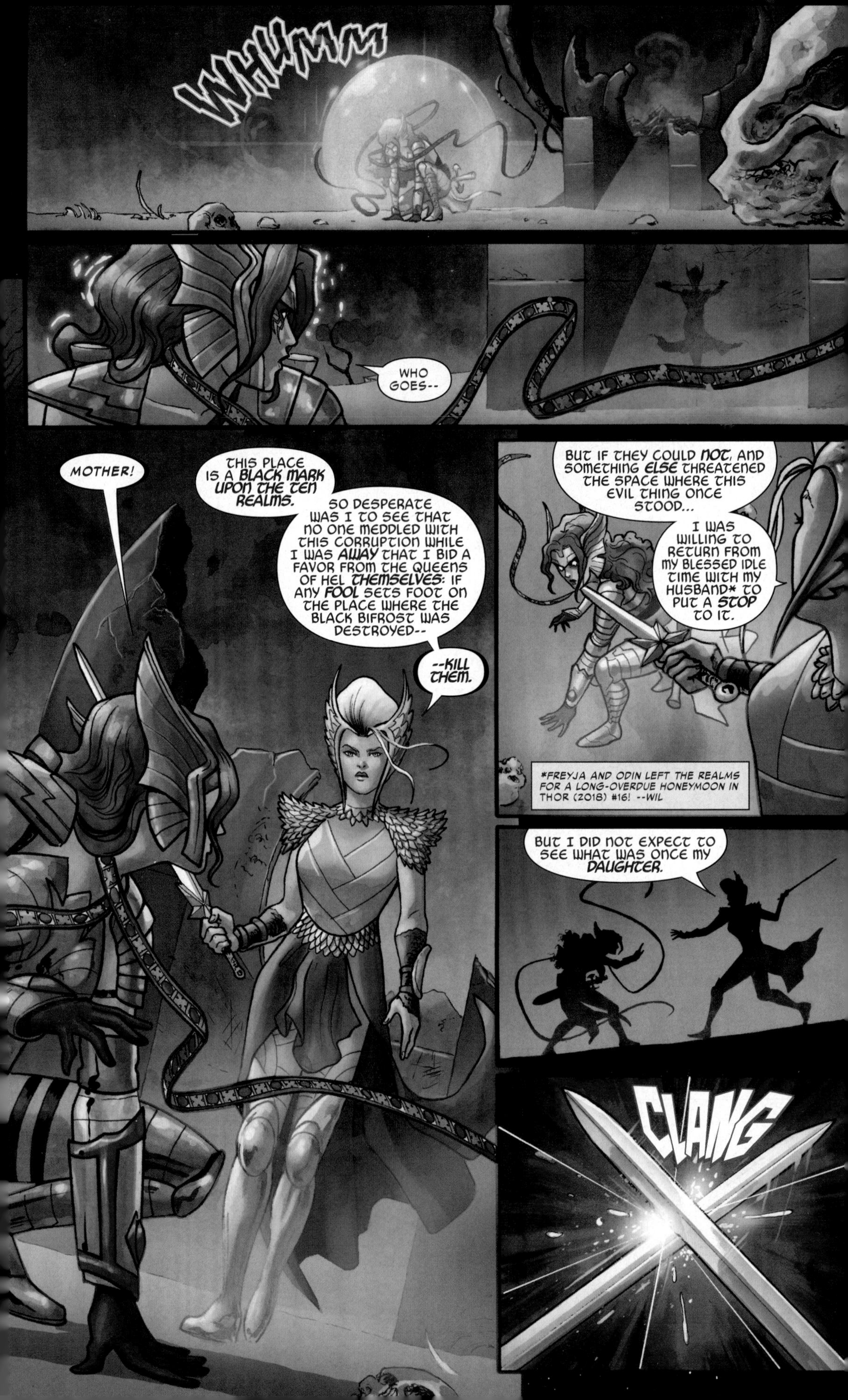
WHUMMM
WHO GOES--
MOTHER!
THIS PLACE IS A BLACK MARK UPON THE TEN REALMS.
SO DESPERATE WAS I TO SEE THAT NO ONE MEDDLED WITH THIS CORRUPTION WHILE I WAS AWAY THAT I BID A FAVOR FROM THE QUEENS OF HEL THEMSELVES: IF ANY FOOL SETS FOOT ON THE PLACE WHERE THE BLACK BIFROST WAS DESTROYED--
--KILL THEM.
BUT IF THEY COULD NOT, AND SOMETHING ELSE THREATENED THE SPACE WHERE THIS EVIL THING ONCE STOOD...
I WAS WILLING TO RETURN FROM MY BLESSED IDLE TIME WITH MY HUSBAND* TO PUT A STOP TO IT.
*FREYJA AND ODIN LEFT THE REALMS FOR A LONG-OVERDUE HONEYMOON IN THOR (2018) #16! --WIL
BUT I DID NOT EXPECT TO SEE WHAT WAS ONCE MY DAUGHTER.
CLANG

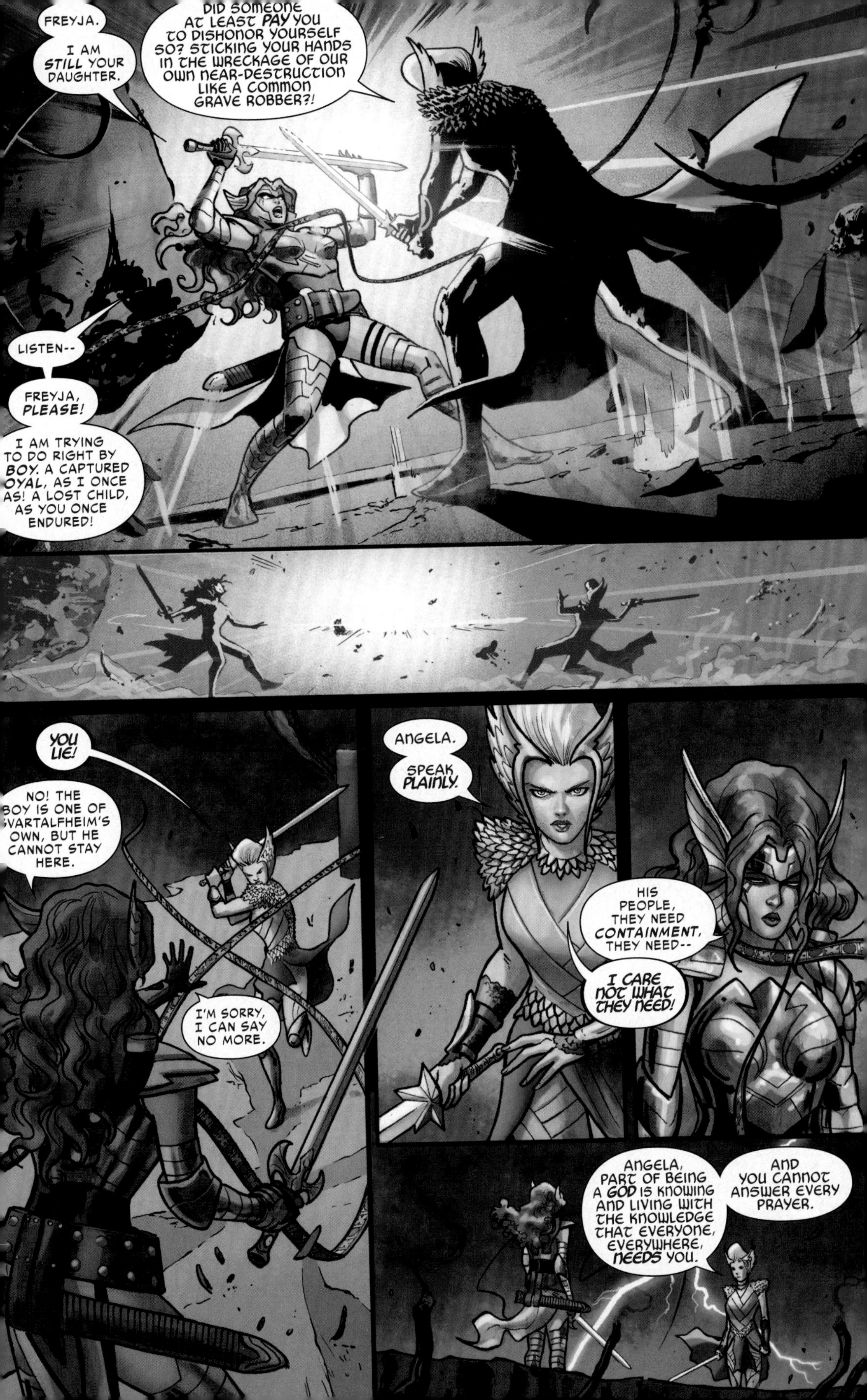
FREYJA.
I AM STILL YOUR DAUGHTER.
DID SOMEONE AT LEAST PAY YOU TO DISHONOR YOURSELF SO? STICKING YOUR HANDS IN THE WRECKAGE OF OUR OWN NEAR-DESTRUCTION LIKE A COMMON GRAVE ROBBER?!
LISTEN--
FREYJA, PLEASE!
I AM TRYING TO DO RIGHT BY BOY. A CAPTURED OYAL, AS I ONCE AS! A LOST CHILD, AS YOU ONCE ENDURED!
YOU LIE!
NO! THE BOY IS ONE OF VARTALFHEIM'S OWN, BUT HE CANNOT STAY HERE.
I'M SORRY, I CAN SAY NO MORE.
ANGELA.
SPEAK PLAINLY.
HIS PEOPLE, THEY NEED CONTAINMENT, THEY NEED--
I CARE NOT WHAT THEY NEED!
ANGELA, PART OF BEING A GOD IS KNOWING AND LIVING WITH THE KNOWLEDGE THAT EVERYONE, EVERYWHERE, NEEDS YOU.
AND YOU CANNOT ANSWER EVERY PRAYER.

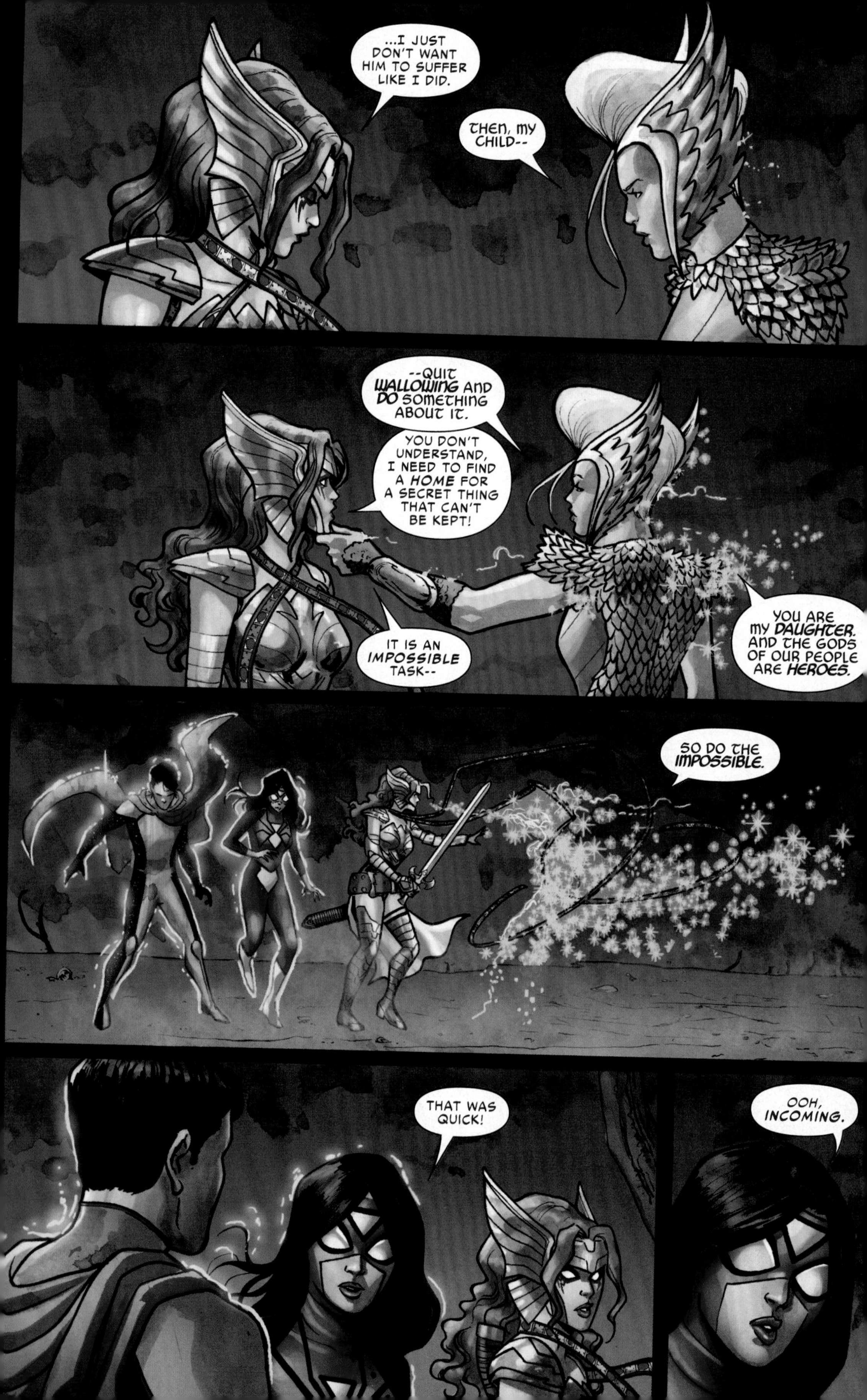
...I JUST DON'T WANT HIM TO SUFFER LIKE I DID.
THEN, MY CHILD--
--QUIT WALLOWING AND DO SOMETHING ABOUT IT.
YOU DON'T UNDERSTAND, I NEED TO FIND A HOME FOR A SECRET THING THAT CAN'T BE KEPT!
IT IS AN IMPOSSIBLE TASK--
YOU ARE MY DAUGHTER. AND THE GODS OF OUR PEOPLE ARE HEROES.
SO DO THE IMPOSSIBLE.
THAT WAS QUICK!
OOH, INCOMING.

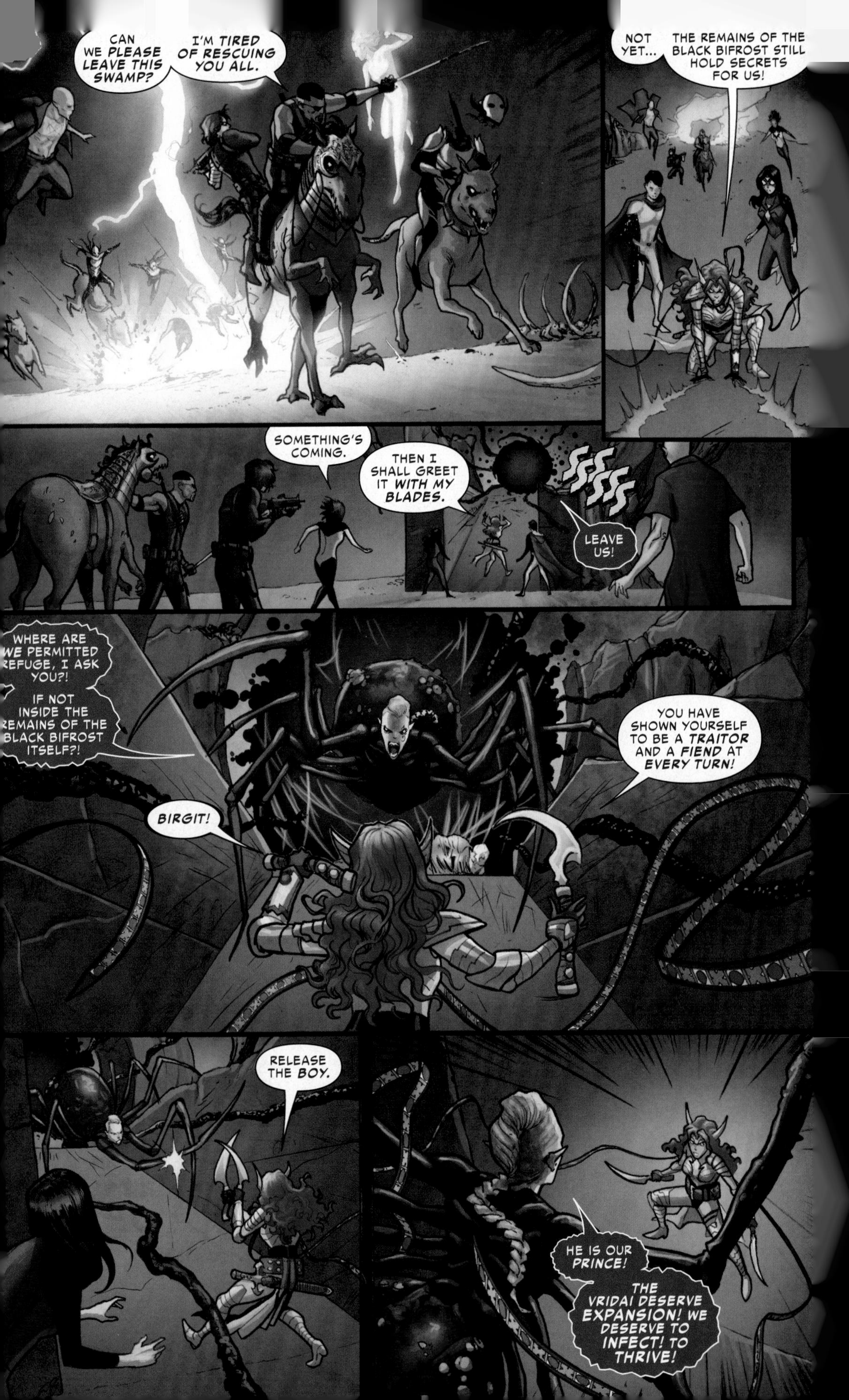
CAN WE PLEASE LEAVE THIS SWAMP?
I'M TIRED OF RESCUING YOU ALL.
NOT YET...
THE REMAINS OF THE BLACK BIFROST STILL HOLD SECRETS FOR US!
SOMETHING'S COMING.
THEN I SHALL GREET IT WITH MY BLADES.
SSSSS
LEAVE US!
WHERE ARE WE PERMITTED REFUGE, I ASK YOU?!
IF NOT INSIDE THE REMAINS OF THE BLACK BIFROST ITSELF?!
YOU HAVE SHOWN YOURSELF TO BE A TRAITOR AND A FIEND AT EVERY TURN!
BIRGIT!
RELEASE THE BOY.
HE IS OUR PRINCE!
THE VRIDAI DESERVE EXPANSION! WE DESERVE TO INFECT! TO THRIVE!

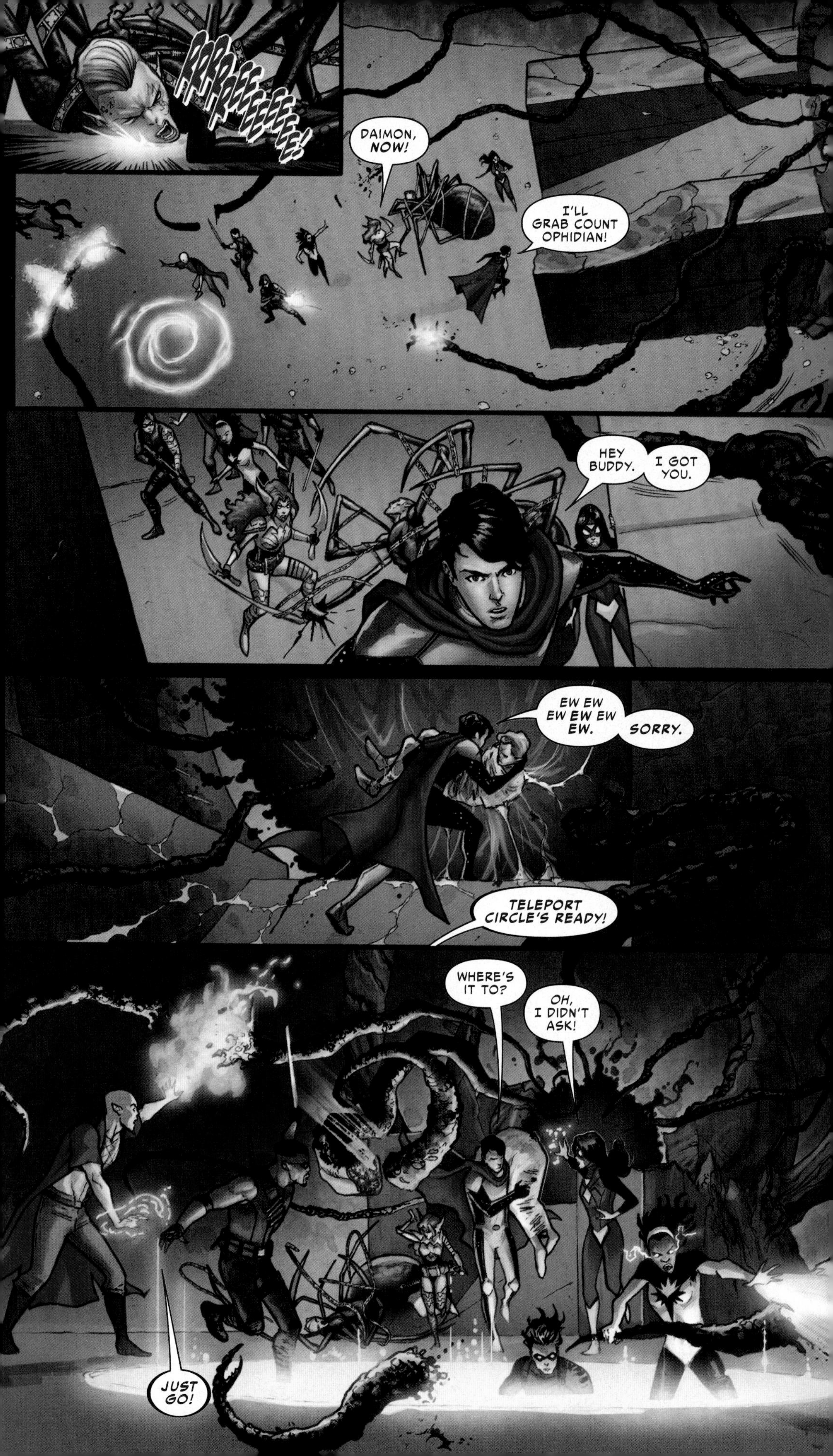
RRRREEEEEEEE!
DAIMON, NOW!
I'LL GRAB COUNT OPHIDIAN!
HEY BUDDY.
I GOT YOU.
EW EW EW EW EW EW.
SORRY.
TELEPORT CIRCLE'S READY!
WHERE'S IT TO?
OH, I DIDN'T ASK!
JUST GO!

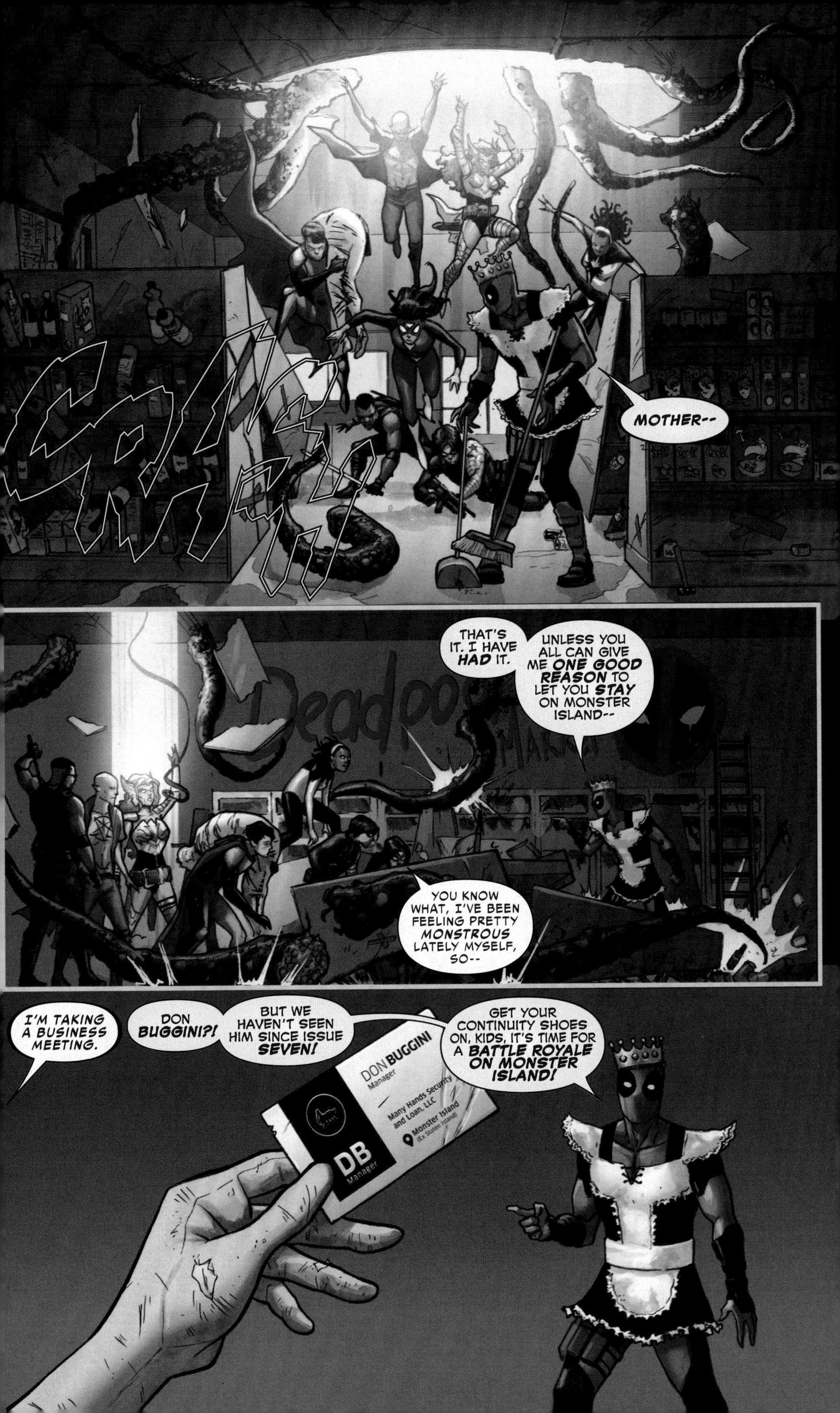
MOTHER--
THAT'S IT. I HAVE HAD IT.
UNLESS YOU ALL CAN GIVE ME ONE GOOD REASON TO LET YOU STAY ON MONSTER ISLAND--
YOU KNOW WHAT, I'VE BEEN FEELING PRETTY MONSTROUS LATELY MYSELF, SO--
I'M TAKING A BUSINESS MEETING.
DON BUGGINI?!
BUT WE HAVEN'T SEEN HIM SINCE ISSUE SEVEN!
GET YOUR CONTINUITY SHOES ON, KIDS, IT'S TIME FOR A BATTLE ROYALE ON MONSTER ISLAND!
DON BUGGINI
Manager
Many Hands Security and Loan, LLC
Monster Island
(Ex Staten Island)
DB
Manager

9

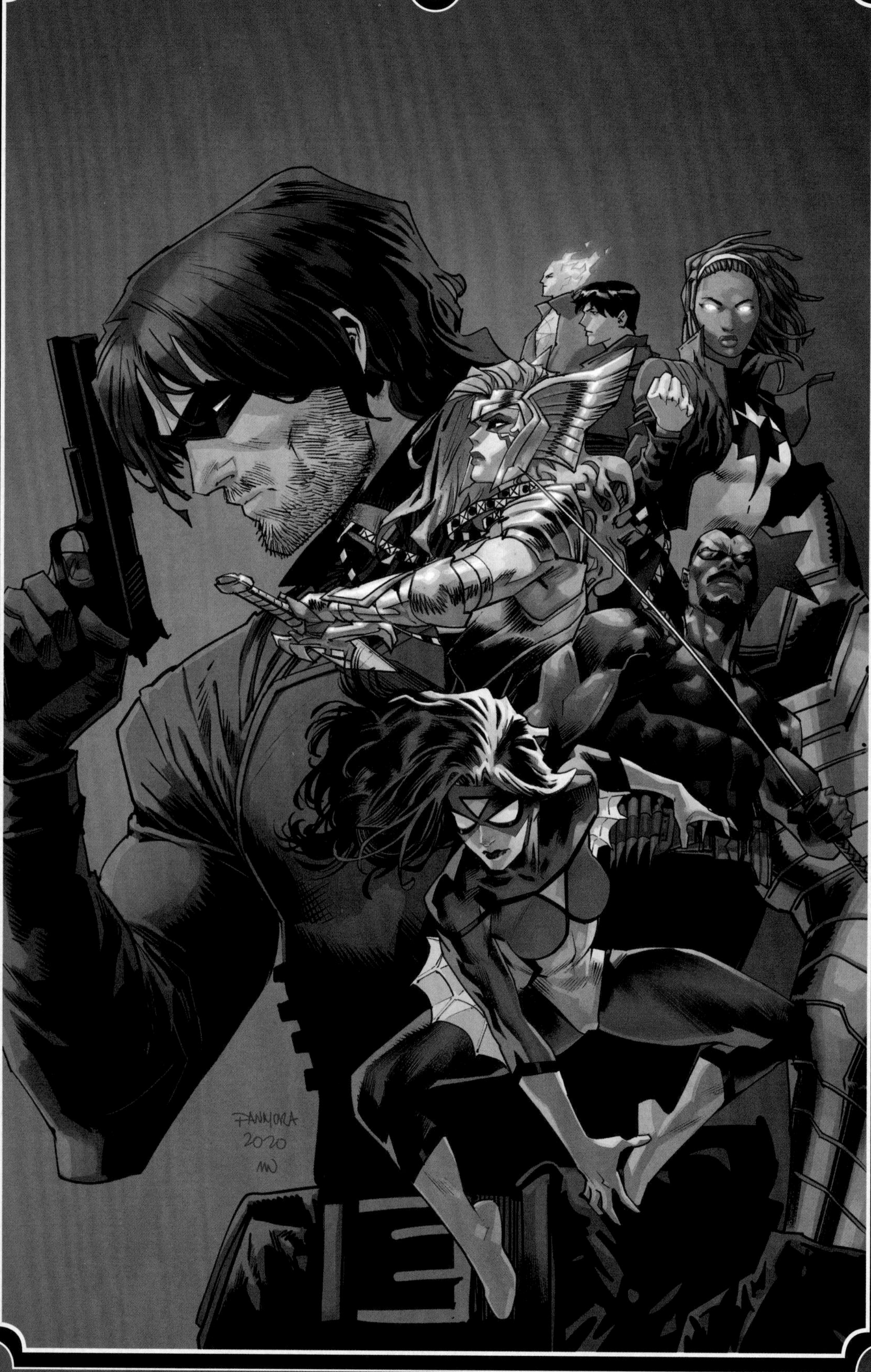
DANMORA
2020
MW

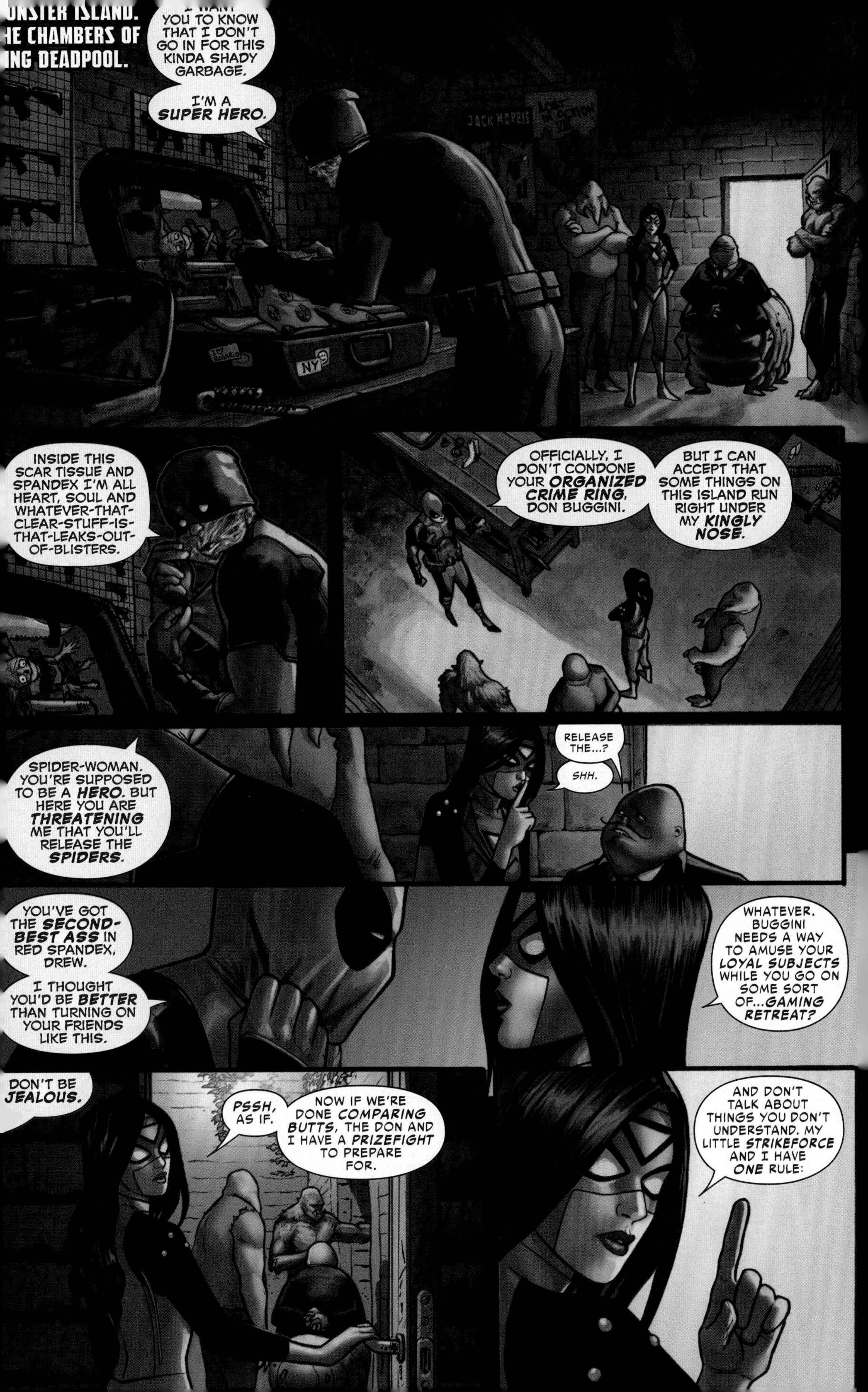

NSTER ISLAND.
HE CHAMBERS OF
NG DEADPOOL.
YOU TO KNOW THAT I DON'T GO IN FOR THIS KINDA SHADY GARBAGE.
I'M A SUPER HERO.
INSIDE THIS SCAR TISSUE AND SPANDEX I'M ALL HEART, SOUL AND WHATEVER-THAT-CLEAR-STUFF-IS-THAT-LEAKS-OUT-OF-BLISTERS.
OFFICIALLY, I DON'T CONDONE YOUR ORGANIZED CRIME RING, DON BUGGINI.
BUT I CAN ACCEPT THAT SOME THINGS ON THIS ISLAND RUN RIGHT UNDER MY KINGLY NOSE.
SPIDER-WOMAN. YOU'RE SUPPOSED TO BE A HERO. BUT HERE YOU ARE THREATENING ME THAT YOU'LL RELEASE THE SPIDERS.
RELEASE THE...?
SHH.
YOU'VE GOT THE SECOND-BEST ASS IN RED SPANDEX, DREW.
I THOUGHT YOU'D BE BETTER THAN TURNING ON YOUR FRIENDS LIKE THIS.
WHATEVER. BUGGINI NEEDS A WAY TO AMUSE YOUR LOYAL SUBJECTS WHILE YOU GO ON SOME SORT OF...GAMING RETREAT?
DON'T BE JEALOUS.
PSSH, AS IF.
NOW IF WE'RE DONE COMPARING BUTTS, THE DON AND I HAVE A PRIZEFIGHT TO PREPARE FOR.
AND DON'T TALK ABOUT THINGS YOU DON'T UNDERSTAND. MY LITTLE STRIKEFORCE AND I HAVE ONE RULE:

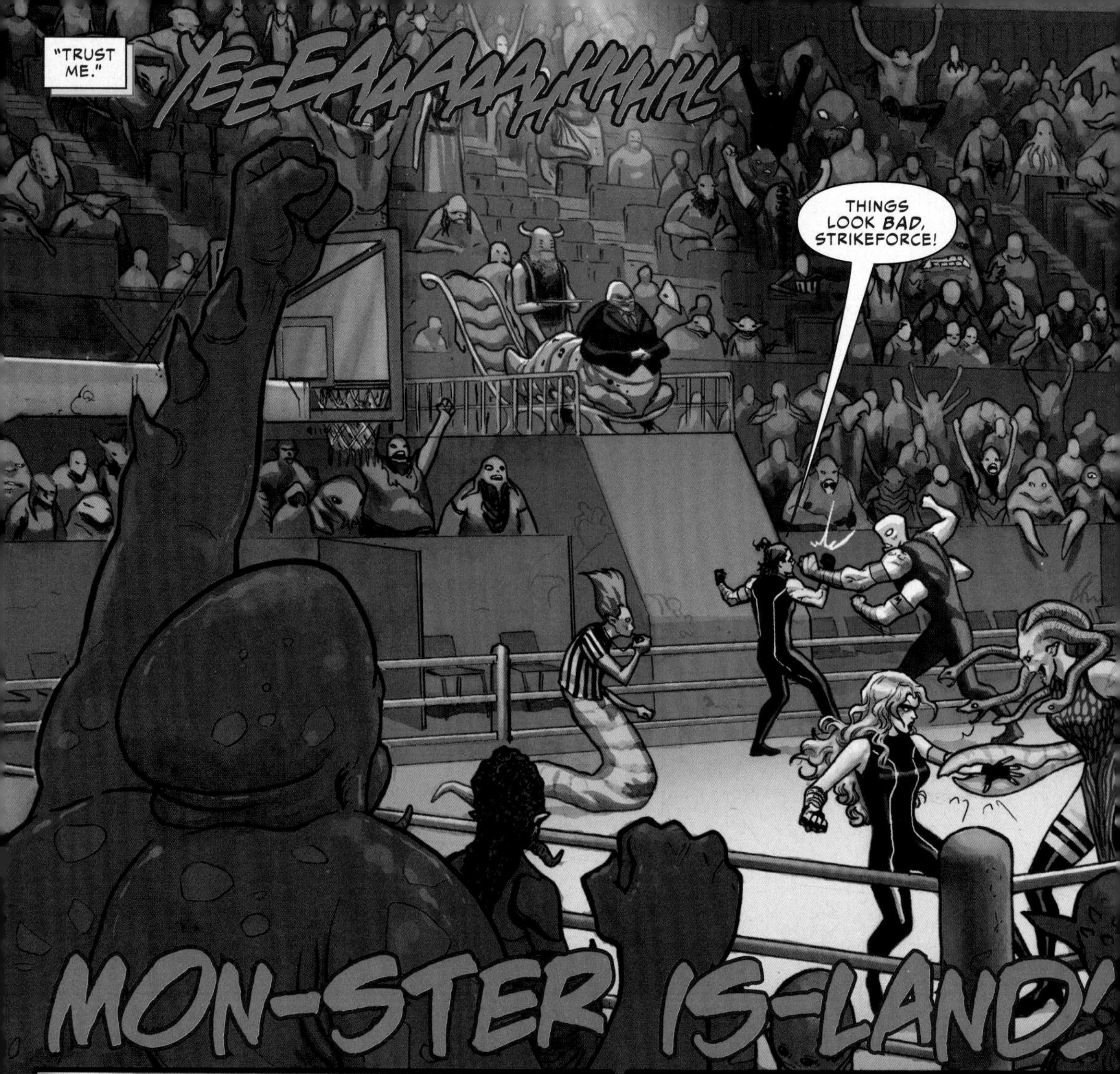
"TRUST ME."
YEEEAAAAAHHHH!
THINGS LOOK BAD, STRIKEFORCE!
MON-STER IS-LAND!

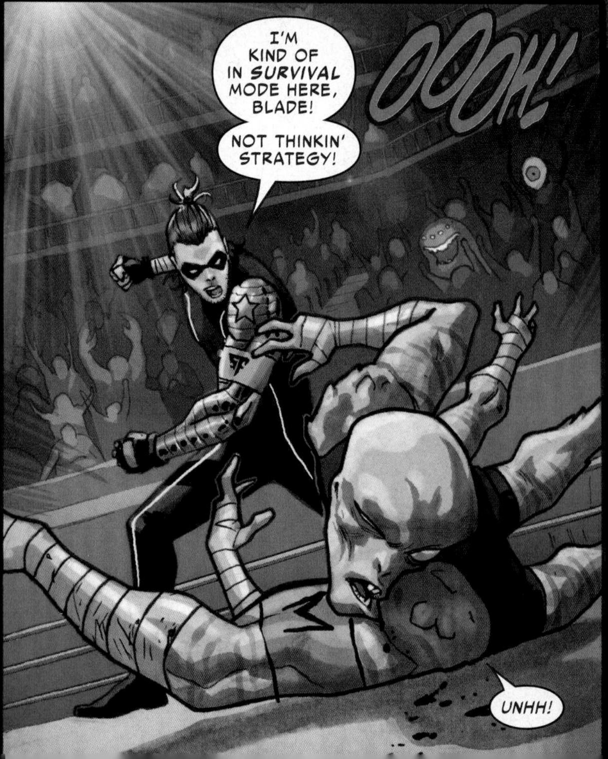
I'M KIND OF IN SURVIVAL MODE HERE, BLADE!
NOT THINKIN' STRATEGY!
OOOH!
UNHH!

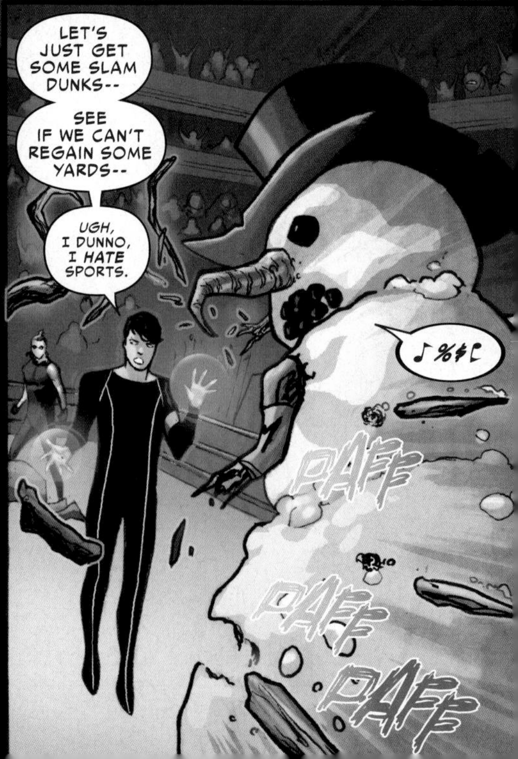
LET'S JUST GET SOME SLAM DUNKS--
SEE IF WE CAN'T REGAIN SOME YARDS--
UGH, I DUNNO, I HATE SPORTS.
♪%$⊏
PAFF
PAFF
PAFF

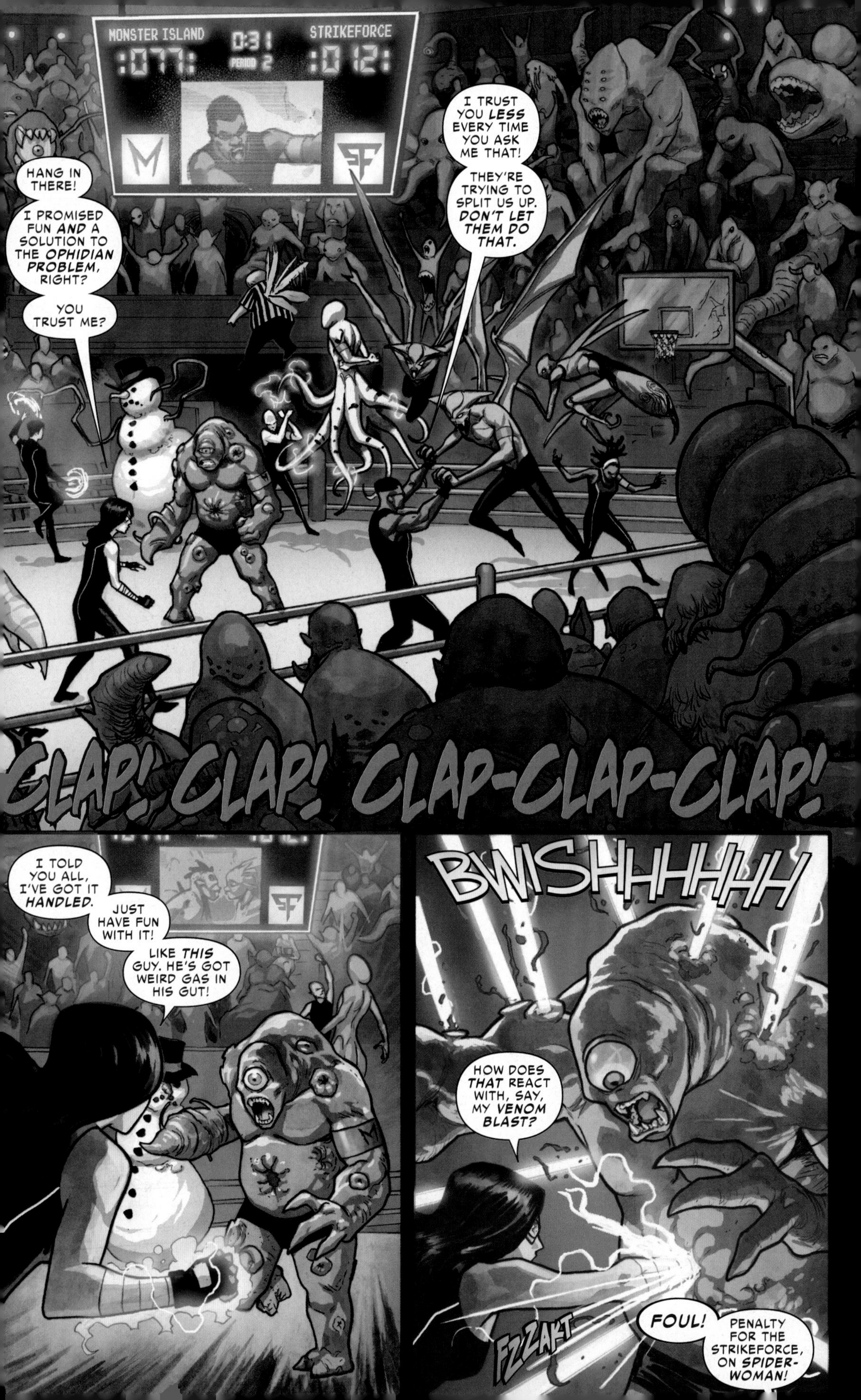

MONSTER ISLAND
0:31
PERIOD 2
STRIKEFORCE
:077:
:012:
HANG IN THERE!
I PROMISED FUN AND A SOLUTION TO THE OPHIDIAN PROBLEM, RIGHT?
YOU TRUST ME?
I TRUST YOU LESS EVERY TIME YOU ASK ME THAT!
THEY'RE TRYING TO SPLIT US UP. DON'T LET THEM DO THAT.
CLAP! CLAP! CLAP-CLAP-CLAP!
I TOLD YOU ALL, I'VE GOT IT HANDLED.
JUST HAVE FUN WITH IT!
LIKE THIS GUY. HE'S GOT WEIRD GAS IN HIS GUT!
BWISHHHHHH
HOW DOES THAT REACT WITH, SAY, MY VENOM BLAST?
FZZAKT
FOUL!
PENALTY FOR THE STRIKEFORCE, ON SPIDER-WOMAN!

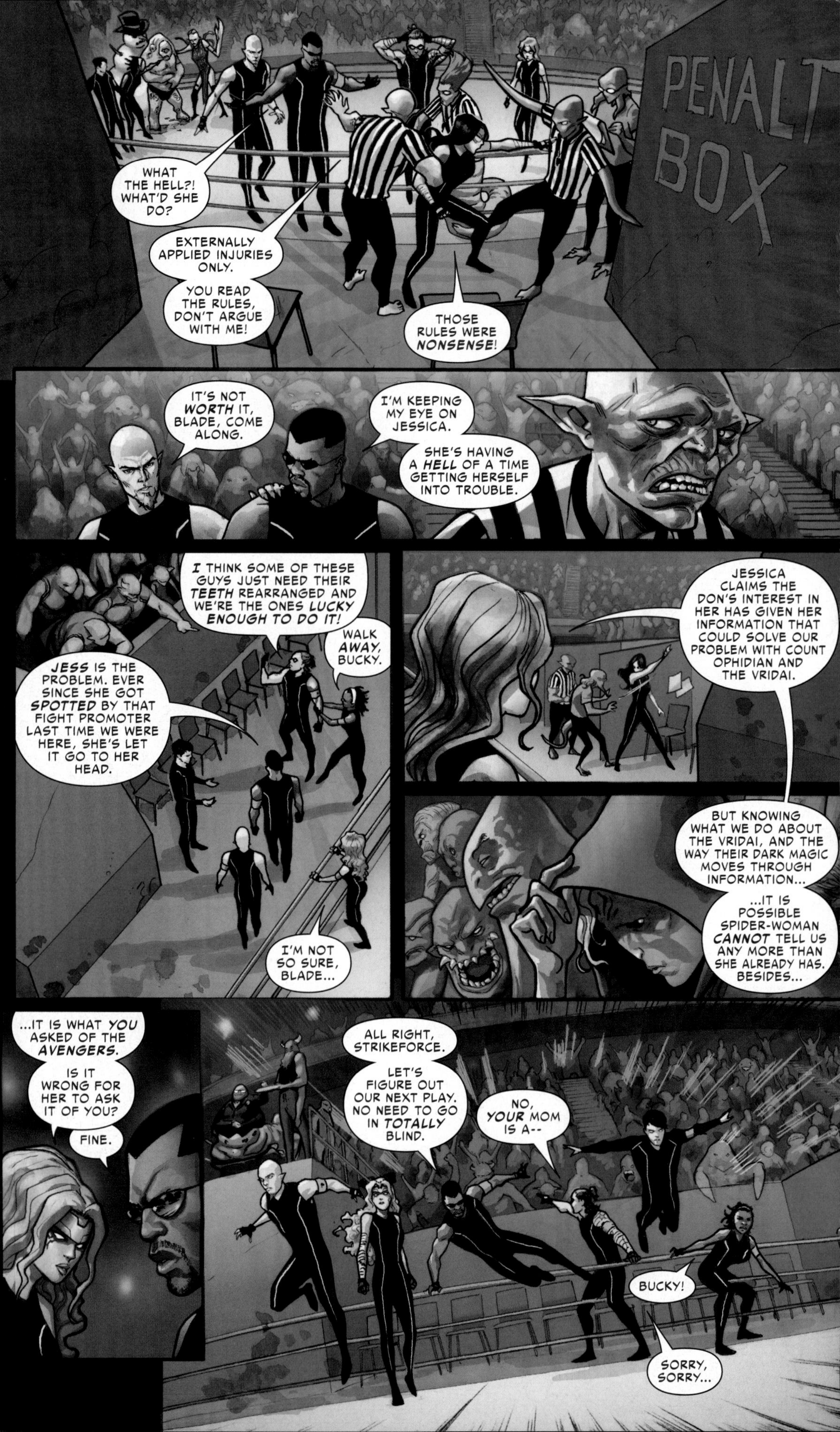
PENALTY BOX
WHAT THE HELL?! WHAT'D SHE DO?
EXTERNALLY APPLIED INJURIES ONLY.
YOU READ THE RULES, DON'T ARGUE WITH ME!
THOSE RULES WERE NONSENSE!
IT'S NOT WORTH IT, BLADE, COME ALONG.
I'M KEEPING MY EYE ON JESSICA.
SHE'S HAVING A HELL OF A TIME GETTING HERSELF INTO TROUBLE.
I THINK SOME OF THESE GUYS JUST NEED THEIR TEETH REARRANGED AND WE'RE THE ONES LUCKY ENOUGH TO DO IT!
WALK AWAY, BUCKY.
JESS IS THE PROBLEM. EVER SINCE SHE GOT SPOTTED BY THAT FIGHT PROMOTER LAST TIME WE WERE HERE, SHE'S LET IT GO TO HER HEAD.
I'M NOT SO SURE, BLADE...
JESSICA CLAIMS THE DON'S INTEREST IN HER HAS GIVEN HER INFORMATION THAT COULD SOLVE OUR PROBLEM WITH COUNT OPHIDIAN AND THE VRIDAI.
BUT KNOWING WHAT WE DO ABOUT THE VRIDAI, AND THE WAY THEIR DARK MAGIC MOVES THROUGH INFORMATION...
...IT IS POSSIBLE SPIDER-WOMAN CANNOT TELL US ANY MORE THAN SHE ALREADY HAS. BESIDES...
...IT IS WHAT YOU ASKED OF THE AVENGERS.
IS IT WRONG FOR HER TO ASK IT OF YOU?
FINE.
ALL RIGHT, STRIKEFORCE.
LET'S FIGURE OUT OUR NEXT PLAY. NO NEED TO GO IN TOTALLY BLIND.
NO, YOUR MOM IS A--
BUCKY!
SORRY, SORRY...

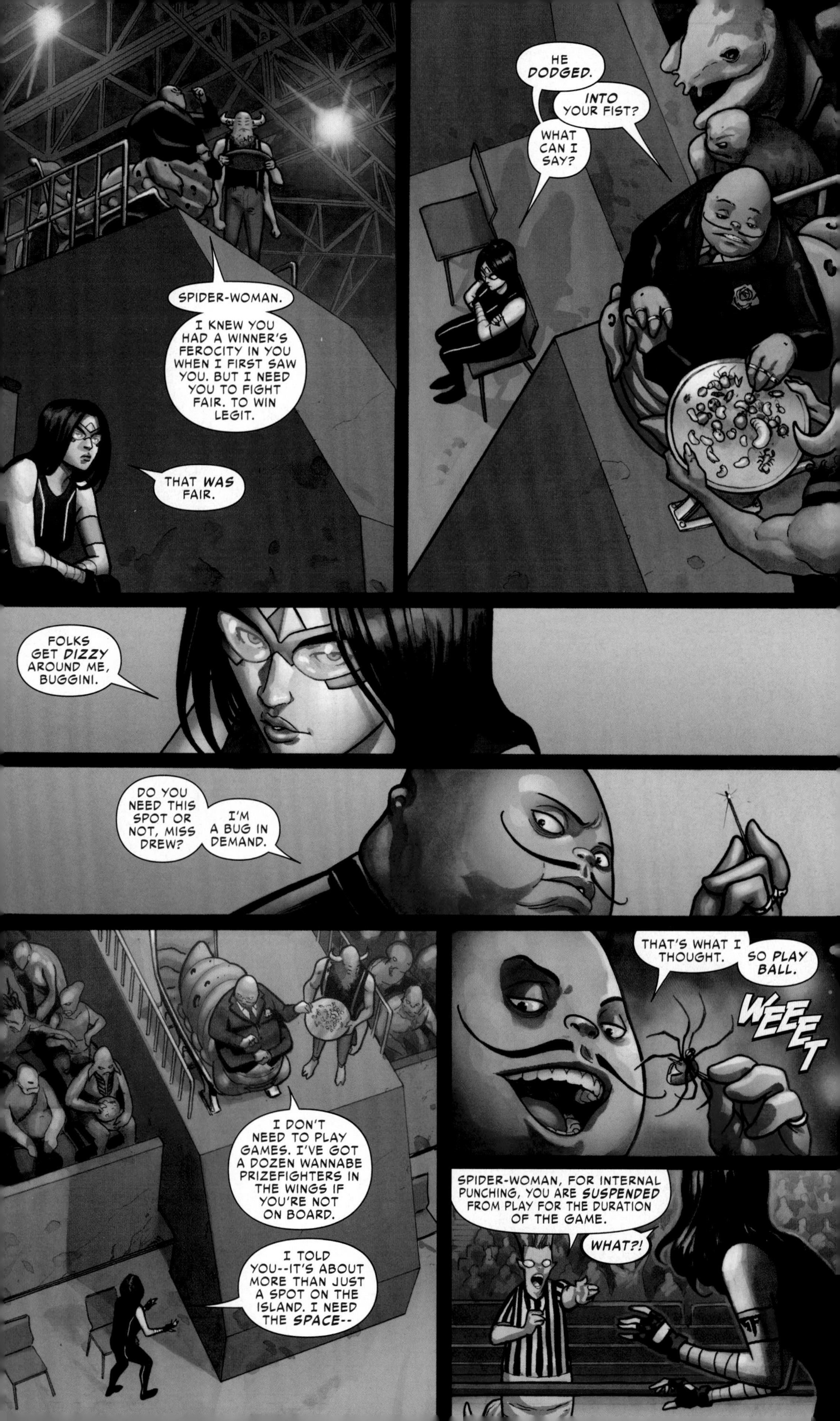
SPIDER-WOMAN.
I KNEW YOU HAD A WINNER'S FEROCITY IN YOU WHEN I FIRST SAW YOU. BUT I NEED YOU TO FIGHT FAIR. TO WIN LEGIT.
THAT *WAS* FAIR.
HE *DODGED*.
INTO YOUR FIST?
WHAT CAN I SAY?
FOLKS GET *DIZZY* AROUND ME, BUGGINI.
DO YOU NEED THIS SPOT OR NOT, MISS DREW?
I'M A BUG IN DEMAND.
I DON'T NEED TO PLAY GAMES. I'VE GOT A DOZEN WANNABE PRIZEFIGHTERS IN THE WINGS IF YOU'RE NOT ON BOARD.
I TOLD YOU--IT'S ABOUT MORE THAN JUST A SPOT ON THE ISLAND. I NEED THE *SPACE*--
THAT'S WHAT I THOUGHT.
SO *PLAY* BALL.
WEEET
SPIDER-WOMAN, FOR INTERNAL PUNCHING, YOU ARE *SUSPENDED* FROM PLAY FOR THE DURATION OF THE GAME.
WHAT?!

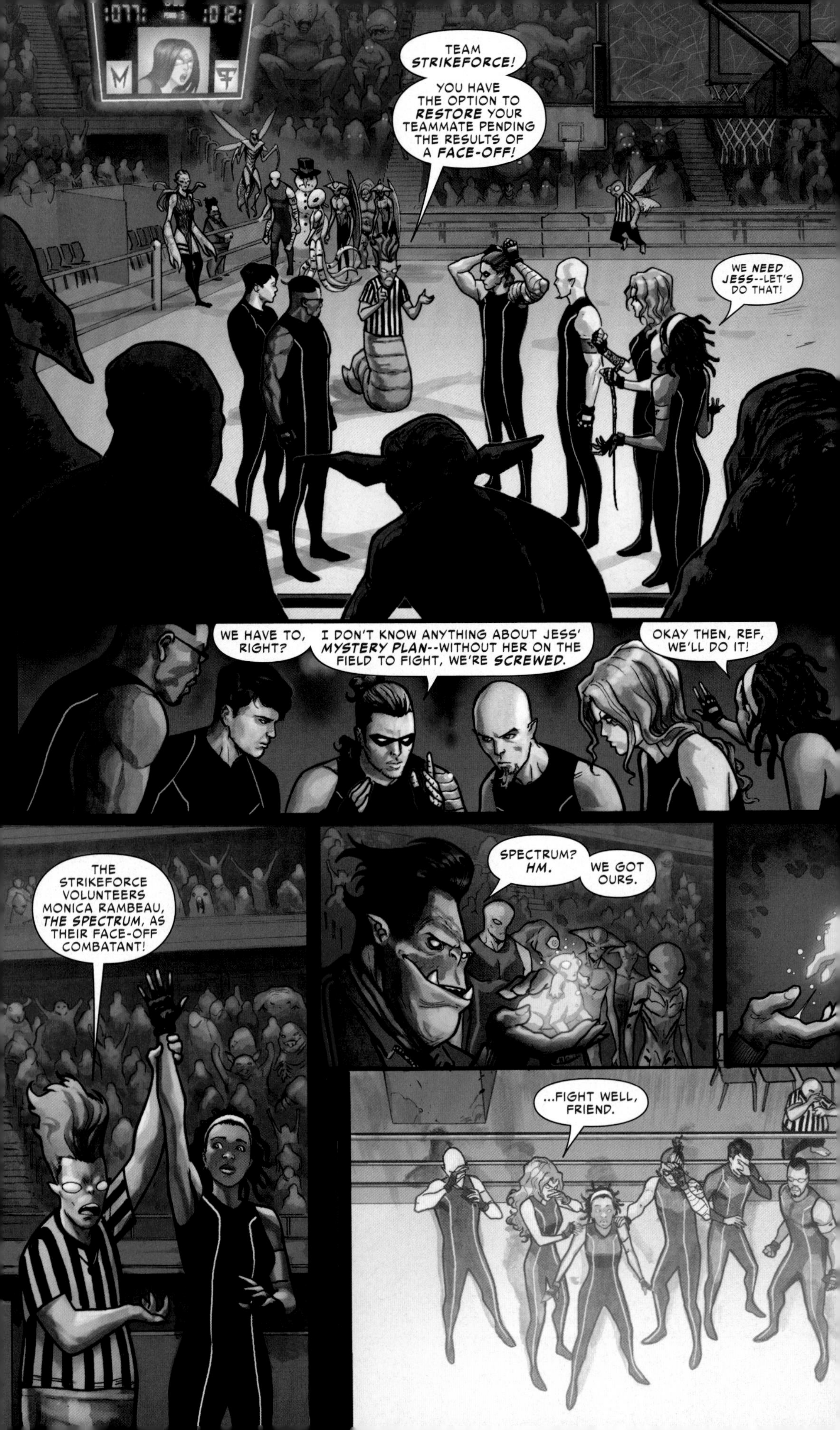
TEAM STRIKEFORCE!
YOU HAVE THE OPTION TO RESTORE YOUR TEAMMATE PENDING THE RESULTS OF A FACE-OFF!
WE NEED JESS--LET'S DO THAT!
WE HAVE TO, RIGHT?
I DON'T KNOW ANYTHING ABOUT JESS' MYSTERY PLAN--WITHOUT HER ON THE FIELD TO FIGHT, WE'RE SCREWED.
OKAY THEN, REF, WE'LL DO IT!
THE STRIKEFORCE VOLUNTEERS MONICA RAMBEAU, THE SPECTRUM, AS THEIR FACE-OFF COMBATANT!
SPECTRUM? HM.
WE GOT OURS.
...FIGHT WELL, FRIEND.

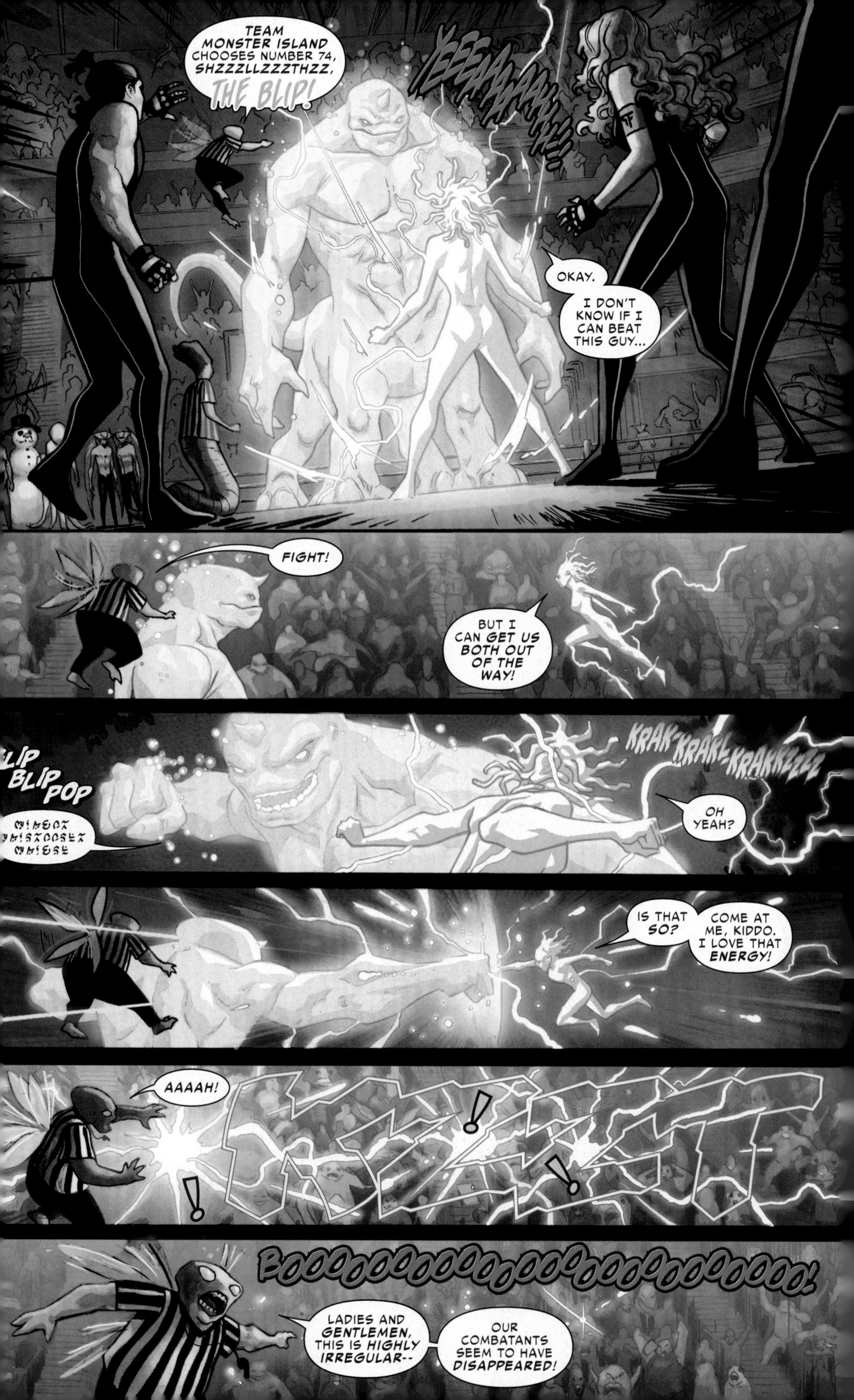
TEAM MONSTER ISLAND CHOOSES NUMBER 74, SHZZZLLZZZTHZZ, THE BLIP!
YEEEAAAAAAHHH!!
OKAY.
I DON'T KNOW IF I CAN BEAT THIS GUY...
FIGHT!
BUT I CAN GET US BOTH OUT OF THE WAY!
BLIP BLIP POP
KRAK-KRAKL-KRAKKZZZ
OH YEAH?
IS THAT SO?
COME AT ME, KIDDO. I LOVE THAT ENERGY!
AAAAH!
BOOOOOOOOOOOOOOOOOOOOOOOOOOOOOOOO!
LADIES AND GENTLEMEN, THIS IS HIGHLY IRREGULAR--
OUR COMBATANTS SEEM TO HAVE DISAPPEARED!

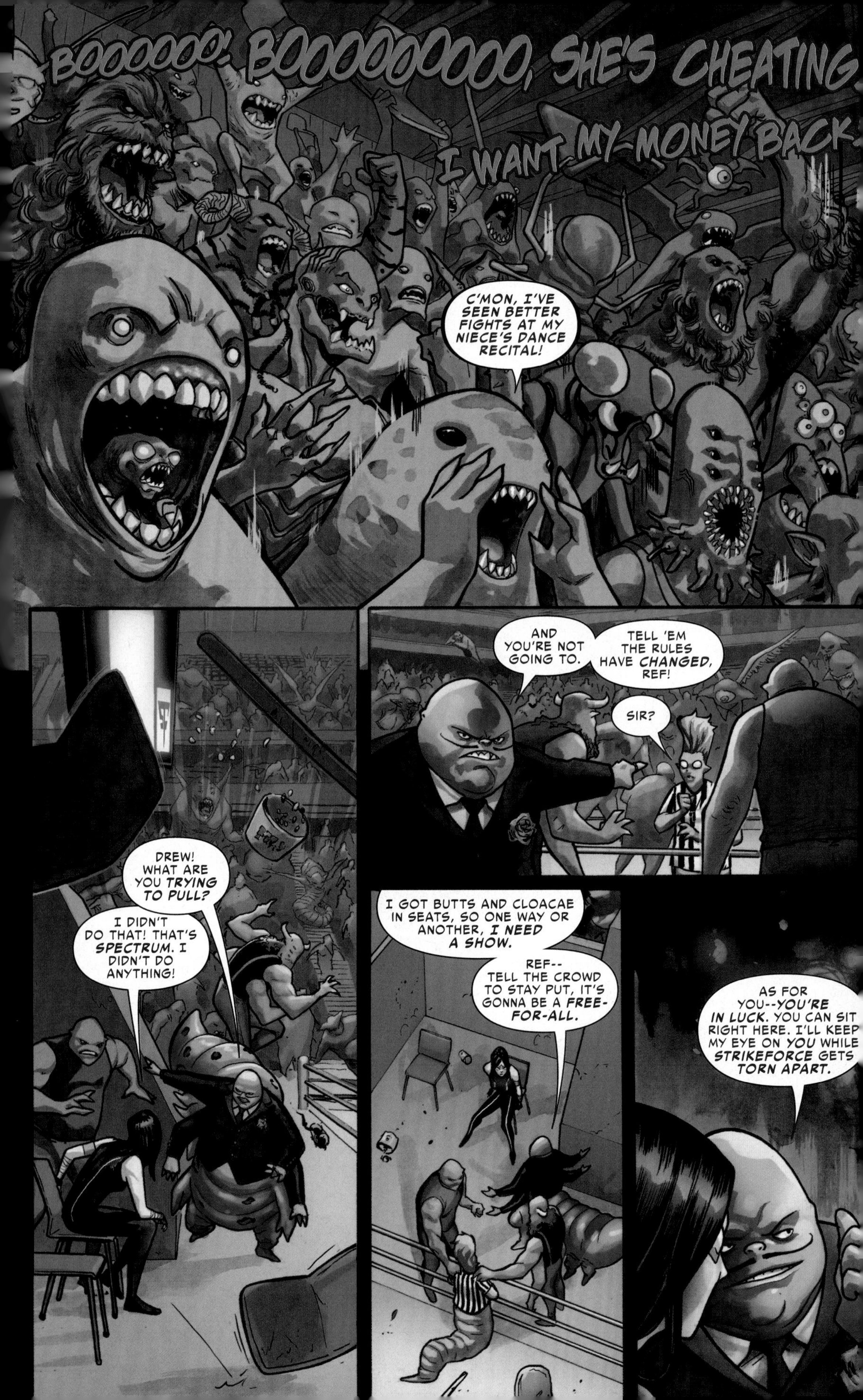
BOOOOOO! BOOOOOOOOO, SHE'S CHEATING!
I WANT MY MONEY BACK!
C'MON, I'VE SEEN BETTER FIGHTS AT MY NIECE'S DANCE RECITAL!
DREW! WHAT ARE YOU TRYING TO PULL?
I DIDN'T DO THAT! THAT'S SPECTRUM. I DIDN'T DO ANYTHING!
AND YOU'RE NOT GOING TO.
TELL 'EM THE RULES HAVE CHANGED, REF!
SIR?
I GOT BUTTS AND CLOACAE IN SEATS, SO ONE WAY OR ANOTHER, I NEED A SHOW.
REF-- TELL THE CROWD TO STAY PUT, IT'S GONNA BE A FREE-FOR-ALL.
AS FOR YOU--YOU'RE IN LUCK. YOU CAN SIT RIGHT HERE. I'LL KEEP MY EYE ON YOU WHILE STRIKEFORCE GETS TORN APART.

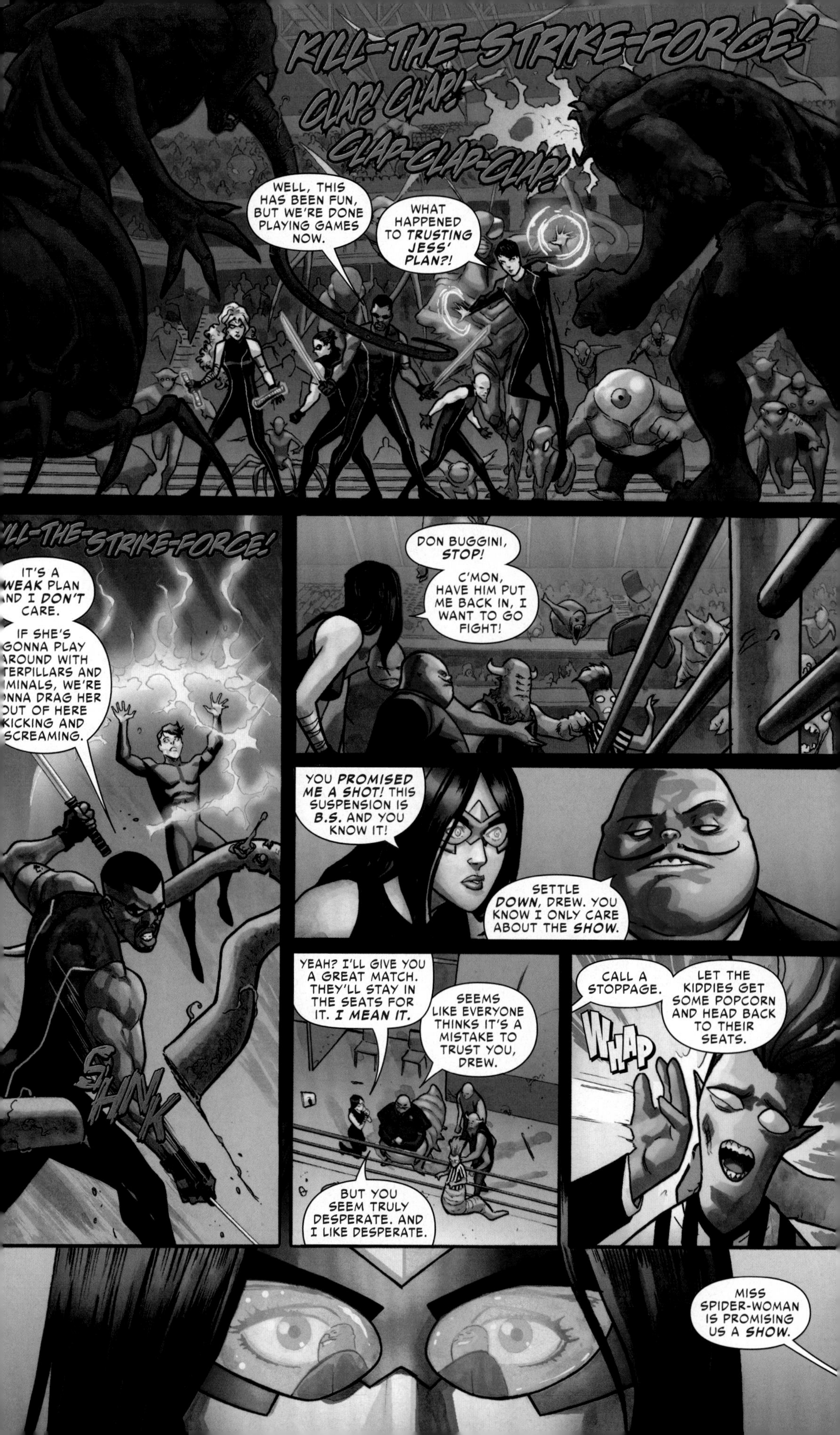
KILL-THE-STRIKE-FORCE!
CLAP! CLAP!
CLAP-CLAP-CLAP!
WELL, THIS HAS BEEN FUN, BUT WE'RE DONE PLAYING GAMES NOW.
WHAT HAPPENED TO TRUSTING JESS' PLAN?!
ILL-THE-STRIKE-FORCE!
IT'S A WEAK PLAN ND I DON'T CARE.
IF SHE'S GONNA PLAY AROUND WITH TERPILLARS AND IMINALS, WE'RE ONNA DRAG HER OUT OF HERE KICKING AND SCREAMING.
SHNK
DON BUGGINI, STOP!
C'MON, HAVE HIM PUT ME BACK IN, I WANT TO GO FIGHT!
YOU PROMISED ME A SHOT! THIS SUSPENSION IS B.S. AND YOU KNOW IT!
SETTLE DOWN, DREW. YOU KNOW I ONLY CARE ABOUT THE SHOW.
YEAH? I'LL GIVE YOU A GREAT MATCH. THEY'LL STAY IN THE SEATS FOR IT. I MEAN IT.
SEEMS LIKE EVERYONE THINKS IT'S A MISTAKE TO TRUST YOU, DREW.
BUT YOU SEEM TRULY DESPERATE. AND I LIKE DESPERATE.
CALL A STOPPAGE.
LET THE KIDDIES GET SOME POPCORN AND HEAD BACK TO THEIR SEATS.
WHAP
MISS SPIDER-WOMAN IS PROMISING US A SHOW.

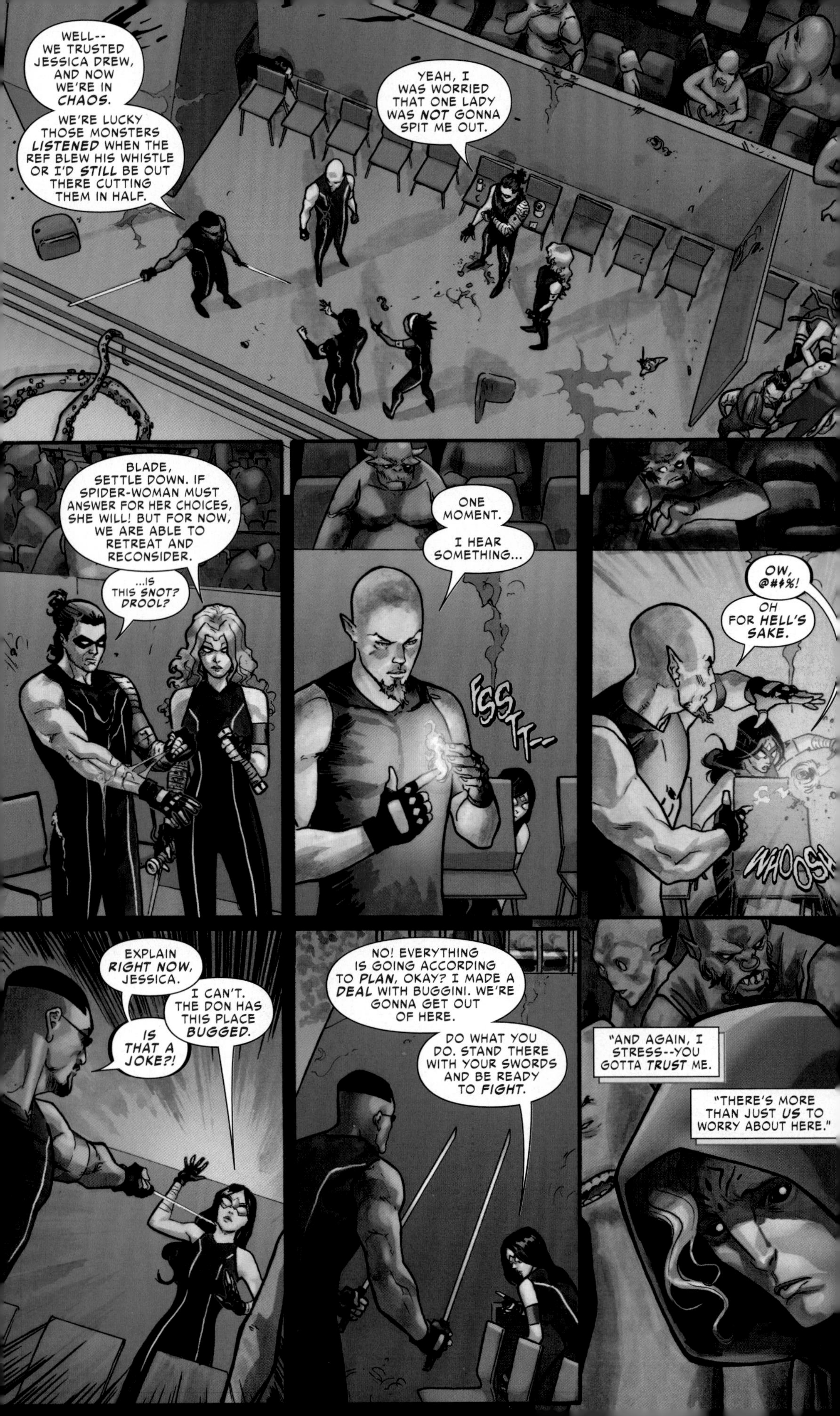
WELL-- WE TRUSTED JESSICA DREW, AND NOW WE'RE IN CHAOS.
WE'RE LUCKY THOSE MONSTERS LISTENED WHEN THE REF BLEW HIS WHISTLE OR I'D STILL BE OUT THERE CUTTING THEM IN HALF.
YEAH, I WAS WORRIED THAT ONE LADY WAS NOT GONNA SPIT ME OUT.
BLADE, SETTLE DOWN. IF SPIDER-WOMAN MUST ANSWER FOR HER CHOICES, SHE WILL! BUT FOR NOW, WE ARE ABLE TO RETREAT AND RECONSIDER.
...IS THIS SNOT? DROOL?
ONE MOMENT.
I HEAR SOMETHING...
FSSTT--
OW, @#$%!
OH FOR HELL'S SAKE.
WHOOSH
EXPLAIN RIGHT NOW, JESSICA.
I CAN'T. THE DON HAS THIS PLACE BUGGED.
IS THAT A JOKE?!
NO! EVERYTHING IS GOING ACCORDING TO PLAN, OKAY? I MADE A DEAL WITH BUGGINI. WE'RE GONNA GET OUT OF HERE.
DO WHAT YOU DO. STAND THERE WITH YOUR SWORDS AND BE READY TO FIGHT.
"AND AGAIN, I STRESS--YOU GOTTA TRUST ME.
"THERE'S MORE THAN JUST US TO WORRY ABOUT HERE."

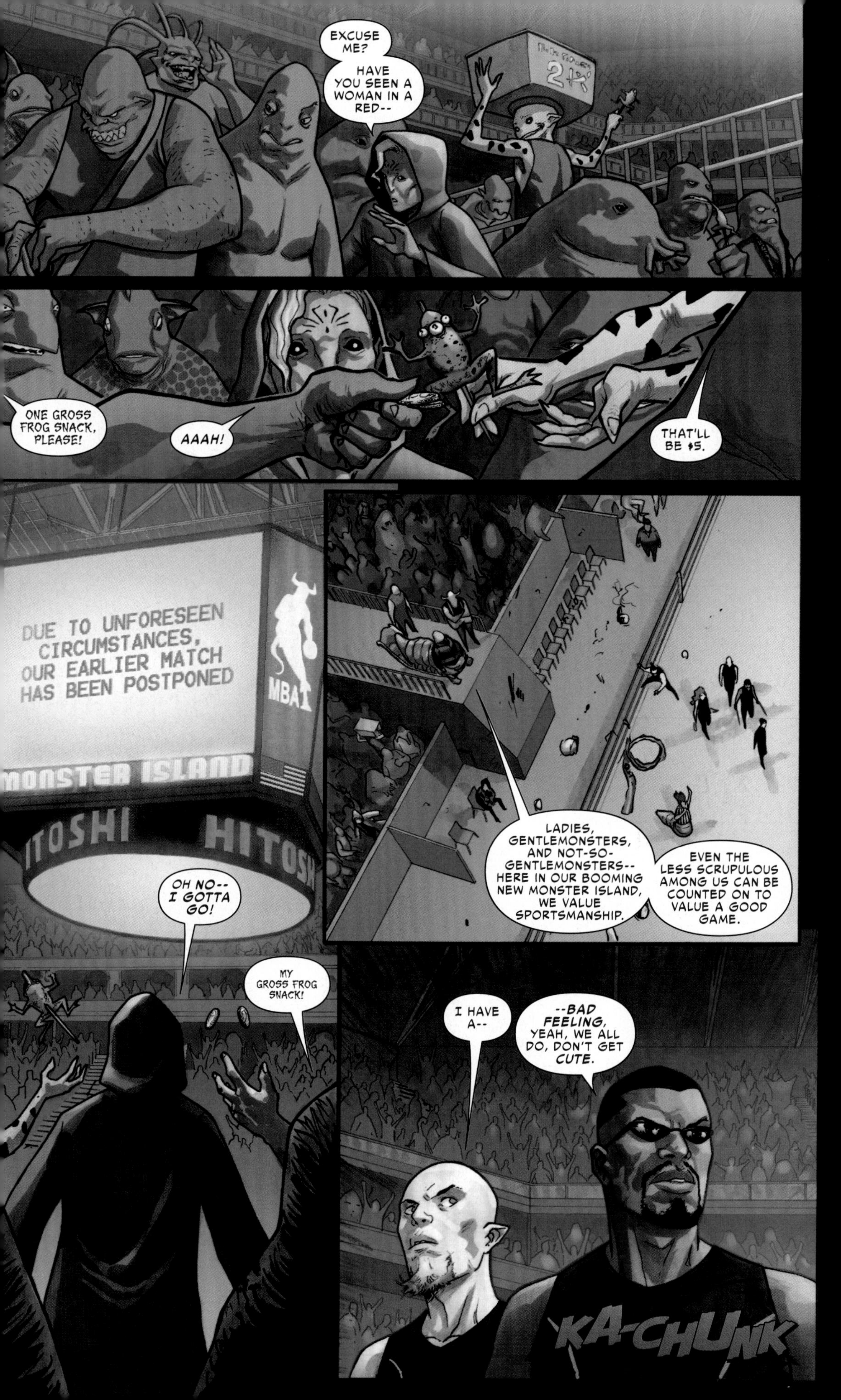

EXCUSE ME?
HAVE YOU SEEN A WOMAN IN A RED--
ONE GROSS FROG SNACK, PLEASE!
AAAH!
THAT'LL BE $5.
DUE TO UNFORESEEN CIRCUMSTANCES, OUR EARLIER MATCH HAS BEEN POSTPONED
MBA
MONSTER ISLAND
HITOSHI
HITOSHI
LADIES, GENTLEMONSTERS, AND NOT-SO-GENTLEMONSTERS-- HERE IN OUR BOOMING NEW MONSTER ISLAND, WE VALUE SPORTSMANSHIP.
EVEN THE LESS SCRUPULOUS AMONG US CAN BE COUNTED ON TO VALUE A GOOD GAME.
OH NO-- I GOTTA GO!
MY GROSS FROG SNACK!
I HAVE A--
--BAD FEELING, YEAH, WE ALL DO, DON'T GET CUTE.
KA-CHUNK

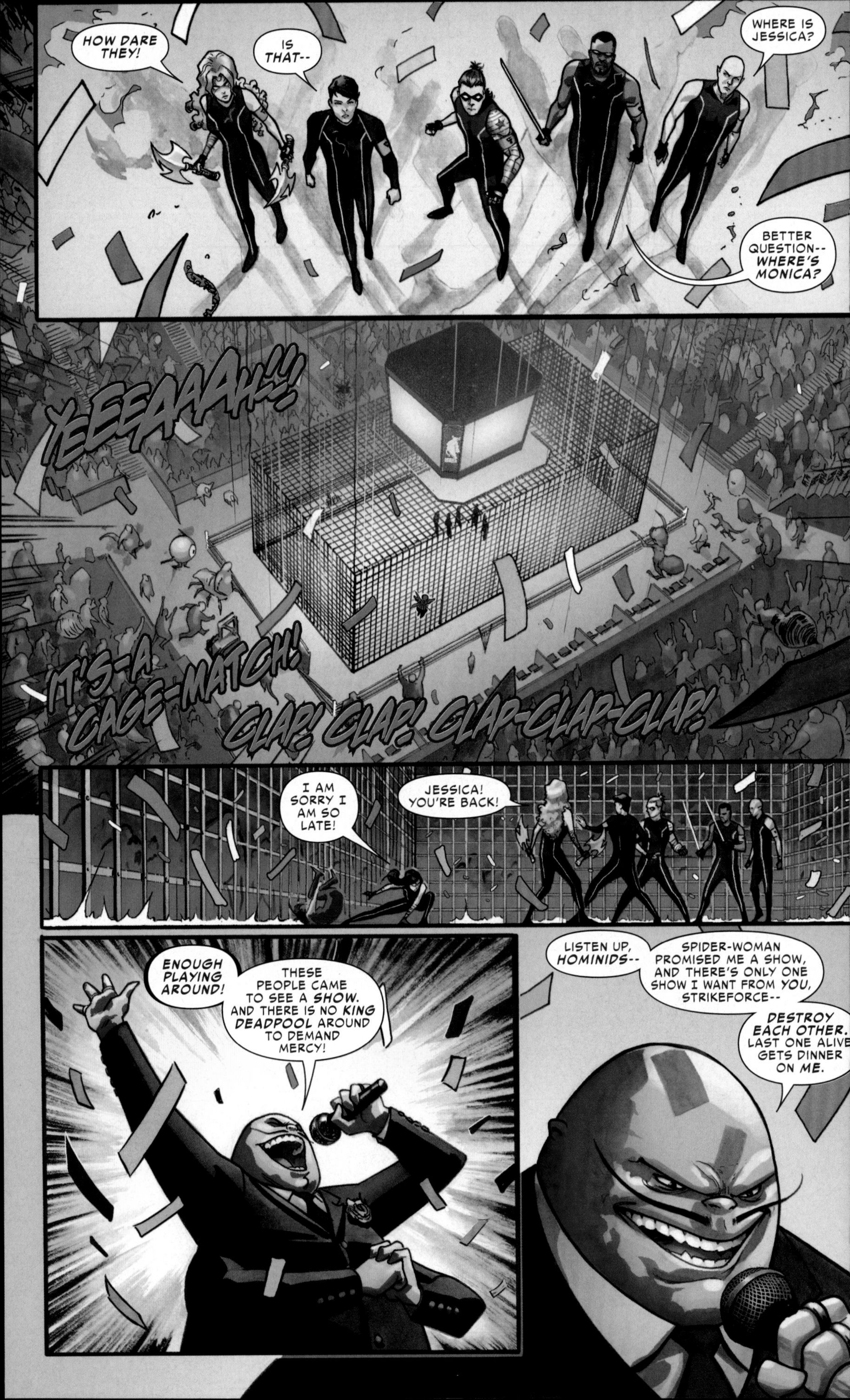

HOW DARE THEY!
IS THAT--
WHERE IS JESSICA?
BETTER QUESTION-- WHERE'S MONICA?
YEEEAAAH!!!
IT'S-A CAGE-MATCH!
CLAP! CLAP! CLAP-CLAP-CLAP!
I AM SORRY I AM SO LATE!
JESSICA! YOU'RE BACK!
ENOUGH PLAYING AROUND!
THESE PEOPLE CAME TO SEE A SHOW. AND THERE IS NO KING DEADPOOL AROUND TO DEMAND MERCY!
LISTEN UP, HOMINIDS--
SPIDER-WOMAN PROMISED ME A SHOW, AND THERE'S ONLY ONE SHOW I WANT FROM YOU, STRIKEFORCE--
DESTROY EACH OTHER. LAST ONE ALIVE GETS DINNER ON ME.

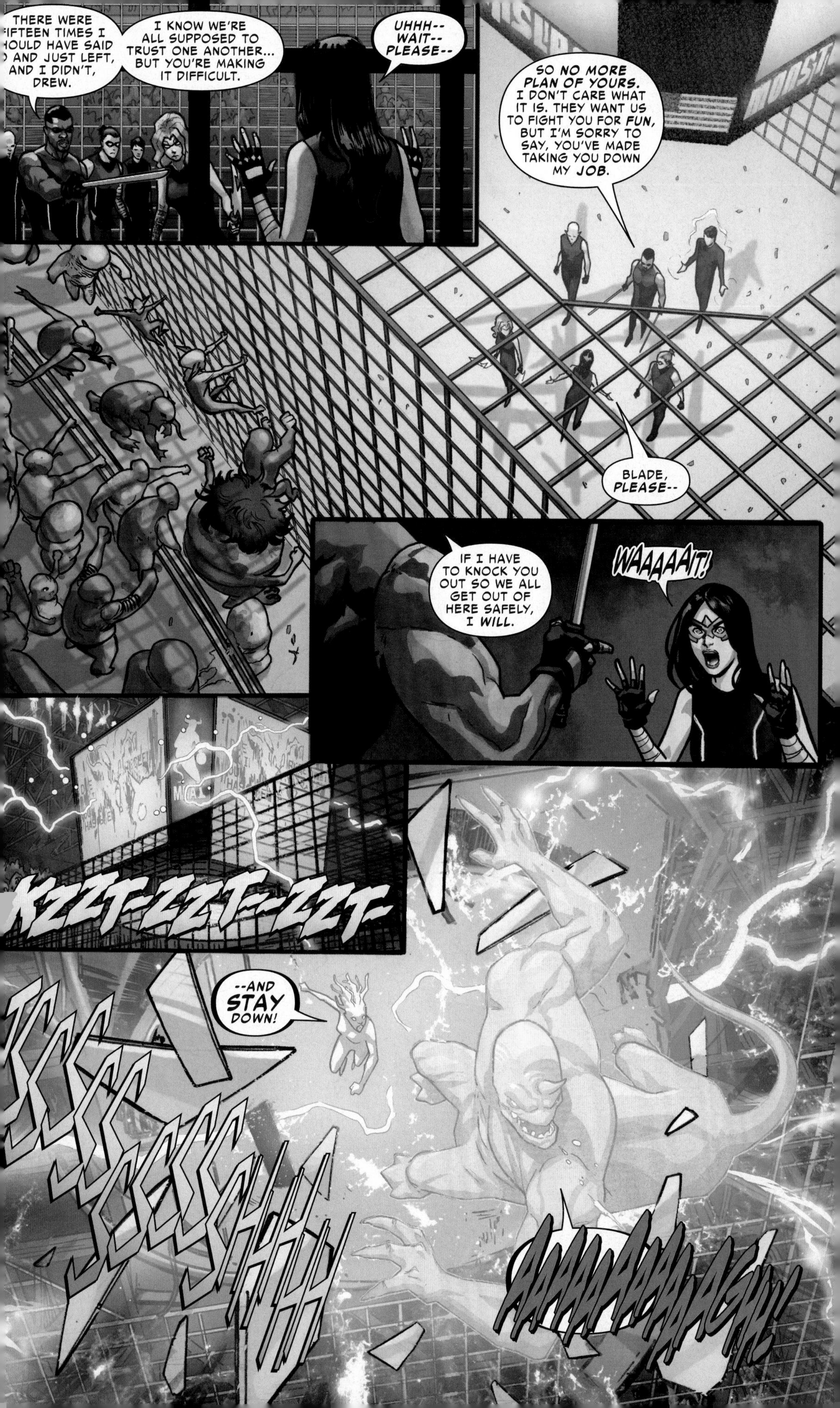

THERE WERE FIFTEEN TIMES I SHOULD HAVE SAID NO AND JUST LEFT, AND I DIDN'T, DREW.
I KNOW WE'RE ALL SUPPOSED TO TRUST ONE ANOTHER... BUT YOU'RE MAKING IT DIFFICULT.
UHHH-- WAIT-- PLEASE--
SO NO MORE PLAN OF YOURS. I DON'T CARE WHAT IT IS. THEY WANT US TO FIGHT YOU FOR FUN, BUT I'M SORRY TO SAY, YOU'VE MADE TAKING YOU DOWN MY JOB.
BLADE, PLEASE--
IF I HAVE TO KNOCK YOU OUT SO WE ALL GET OUT OF HERE SAFELY, I WILL.
WAAAAAIT!
KZZT-ZZT--ZZT-
--AND STAY DOWN!
JSSSSSHHH
AAAAAAAAAAAGH!

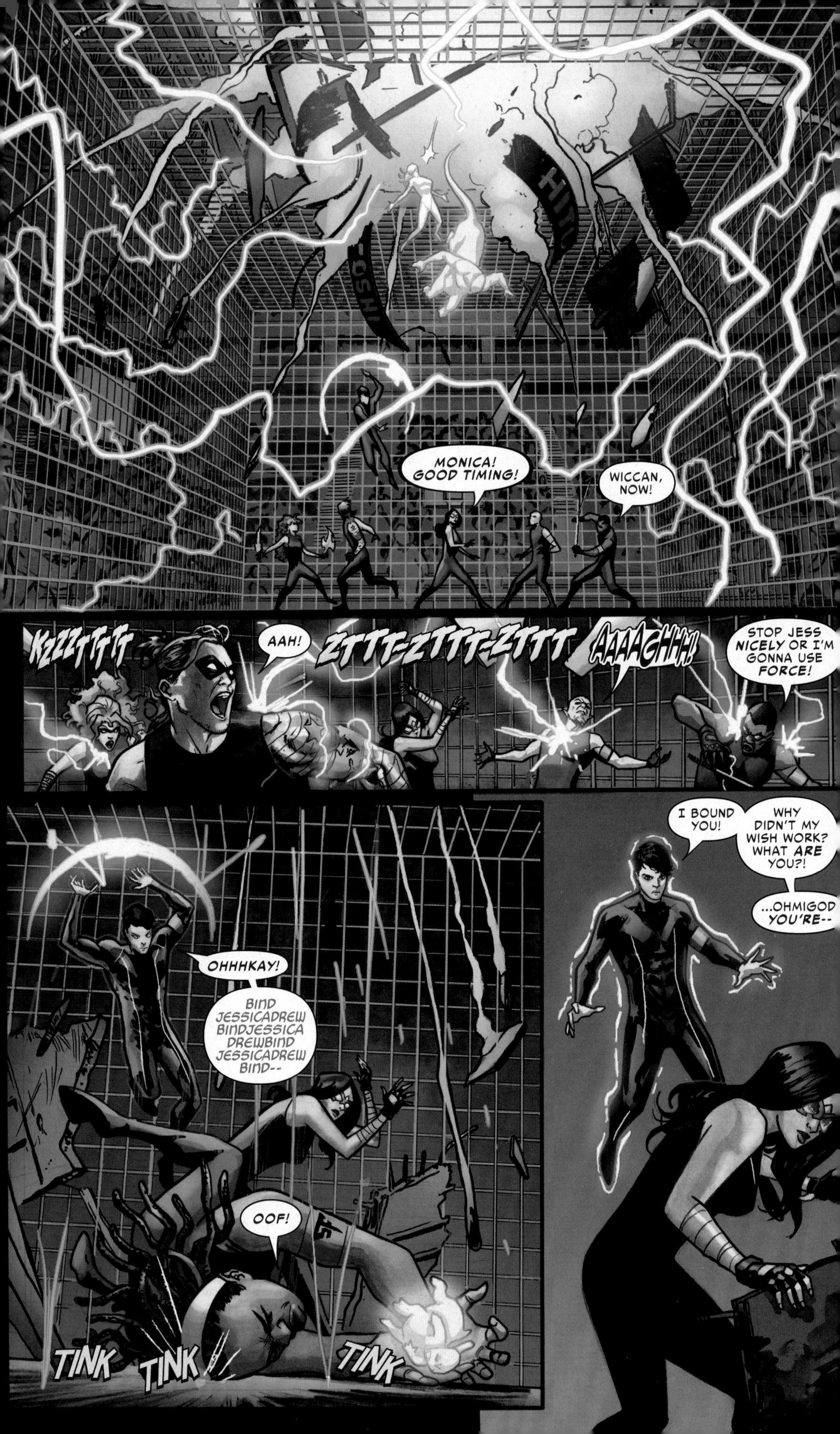
MONICA! GOOD TIMING!
WICCAN, NOW!
KZZZTTTT
AAH!
ZTTT-ZTTT-ZTTT
AAAAGHHH!
STOP JESS NICELY OR I'M GONNA USE FORCE!
OHHHKAY!
BIND JESSICADREW BINDJESSICA DREWBIND JESSICADREW BIND--
OOF!
TINK
TINK
TINK
I BOUND YOU!
WHY DIDN'T MY WISH WORK? WHAT ARE YOU?!
...OHMIGOD YOU'RE--

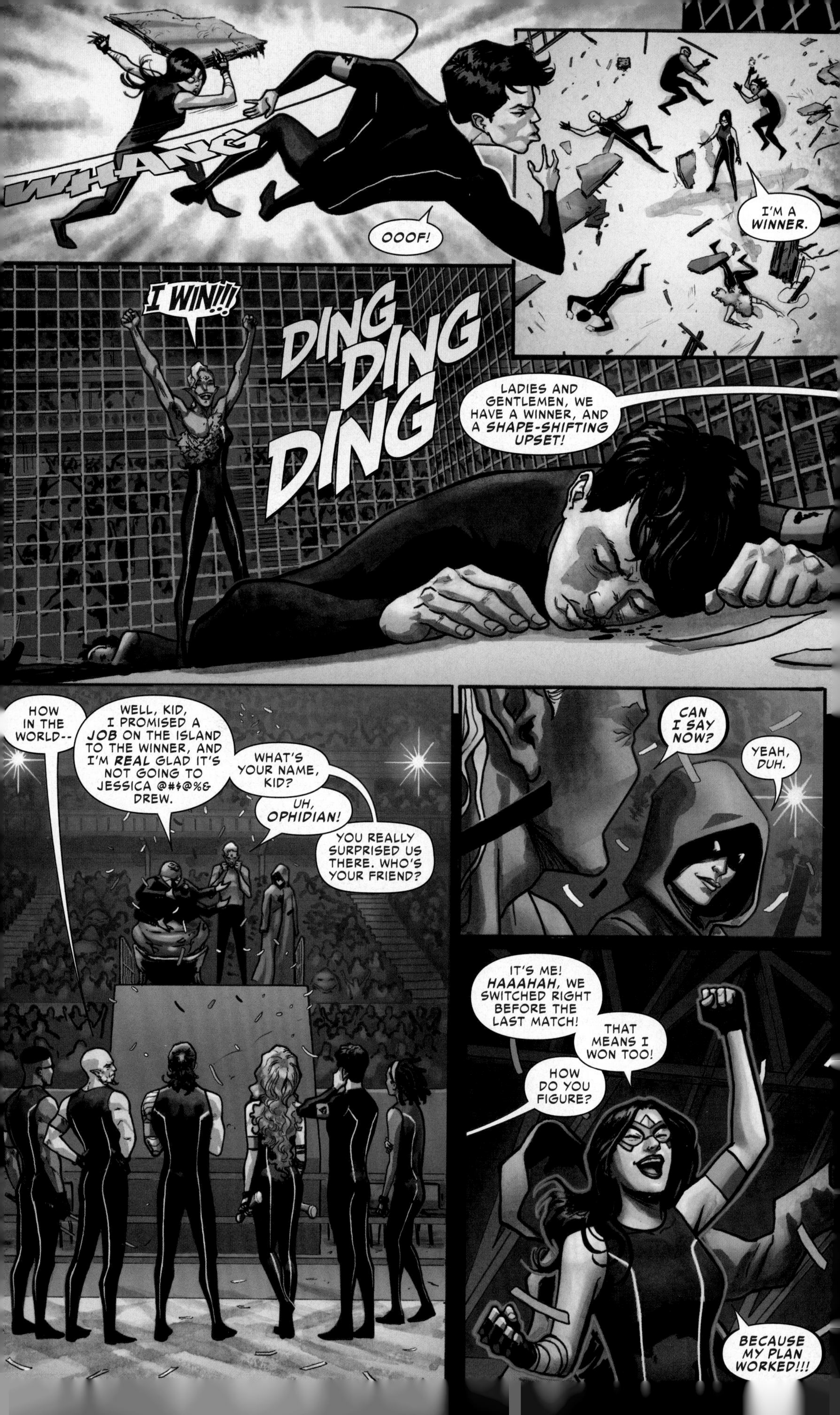
WHANG
OOOF!
I'M A WINNER.
I WIN!!!
DING DING DING
LADIES AND GENTLEMEN, WE HAVE A WINNER, AND A SHAPE-SHIFTING UPSET!
HOW IN THE WORLD--
WELL, KID, I PROMISED A JOB ON THE ISLAND TO THE WINNER, AND I'M REAL GLAD IT'S NOT GOING TO JESSICA @#$@%& DREW.
WHAT'S YOUR NAME, KID?
UH, OPHIDIAN!
YOU REALLY SURPRISED US THERE. WHO'S YOUR FRIEND?
CAN I SAY NOW?
YEAH, DUH.
IT'S ME! HAAAAHAH, WE SWITCHED RIGHT BEFORE THE LAST MATCH!
THAT MEANS I WON TOO!
HOW DO YOU FIGURE?
BECAUSE MY PLAN WORKED!!!

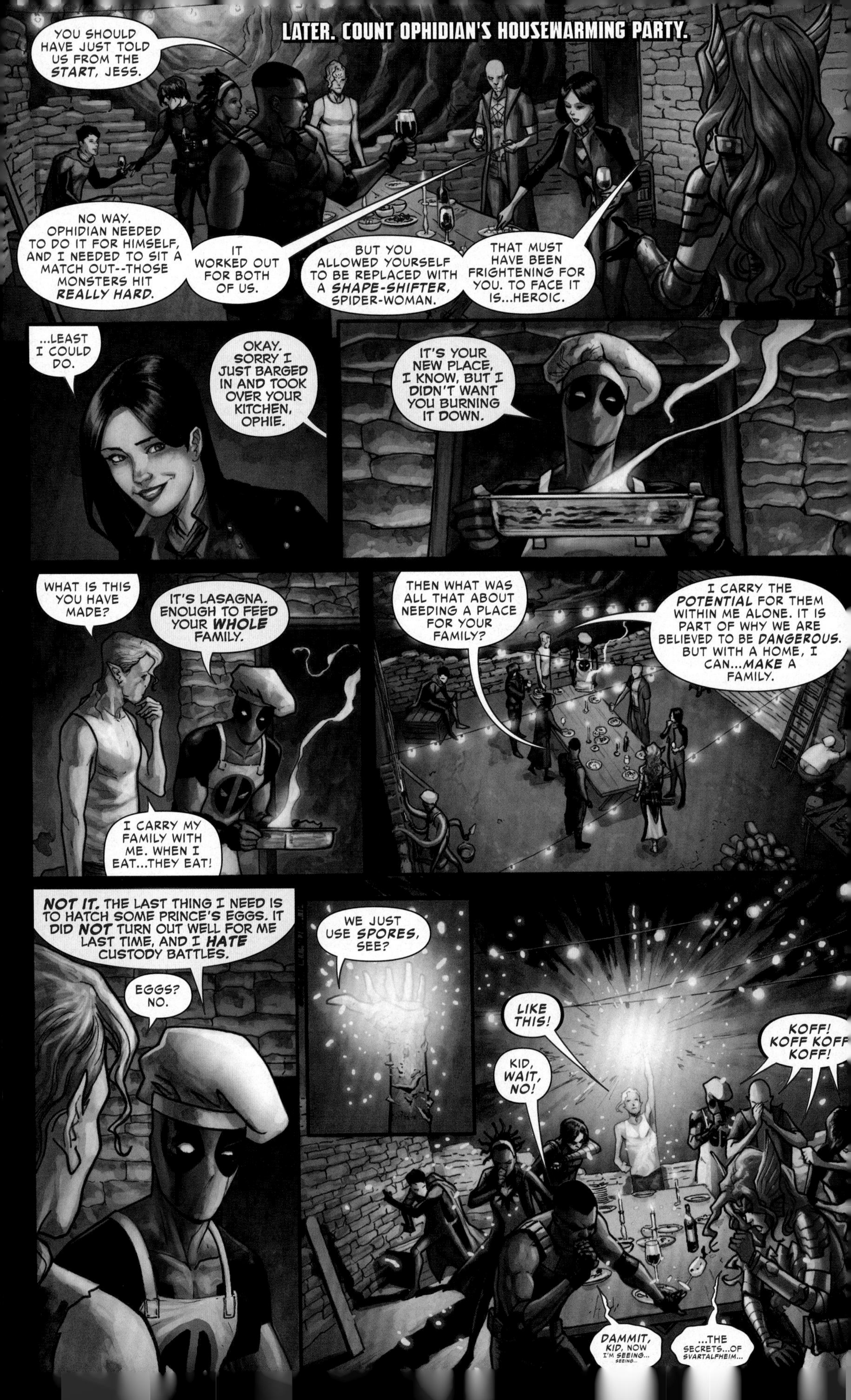
LATER. COUNT OPHIDIAN'S HOUSEWARMING PARTY.
YOU SHOULD HAVE JUST TOLD US FROM THE START, JESS.
NO WAY. OPHIDIAN NEEDED TO DO IT FOR HIMSELF, AND I NEEDED TO SIT A MATCH OUT--THOSE MONSTERS HIT REALLY HARD.
IT WORKED OUT FOR BOTH OF US.
BUT YOU ALLOWED YOURSELF TO BE REPLACED WITH A SHAPE-SHIFTER, SPIDER-WOMAN.
THAT MUST HAVE BEEN FRIGHTENING FOR YOU. TO FACE IT IS...HEROIC.
...LEAST I COULD DO.
OKAY. SORRY I JUST BARGED IN AND TOOK OVER YOUR KITCHEN, OPHIE.
IT'S YOUR NEW PLACE, I KNOW, BUT I DIDN'T WANT YOU BURNING IT DOWN.
WHAT IS THIS YOU HAVE MADE?
IT'S LASAGNA. ENOUGH TO FEED YOUR WHOLE FAMILY.
I CARRY MY FAMILY WITH ME. WHEN I EAT...THEY EAT!
THEN WHAT WAS ALL THAT ABOUT NEEDING A PLACE FOR YOUR FAMILY?
I CARRY THE POTENTIAL FOR THEM WITHIN ME ALONE. IT IS PART OF WHY WE ARE BELIEVED TO BE DANGEROUS. BUT WITH A HOME, I CAN...MAKE A FAMILY.
NOT IT. THE LAST THING I NEED IS TO HATCH SOME PRINCE'S EGGS. IT DID NOT TURN OUT WELL FOR ME LAST TIME, AND I HATE CUSTODY BATTLES.
EGGS? NO.
WE JUST USE SPORES, SEE?
LIKE THIS!
KID, WAIT, NO!
KOFF! KOFF KOFF KOFF!
DAMMIT, KID, NOW I'M SEEING... SEEING...
...THE SECRETS...OF SVARTALFHEIM...

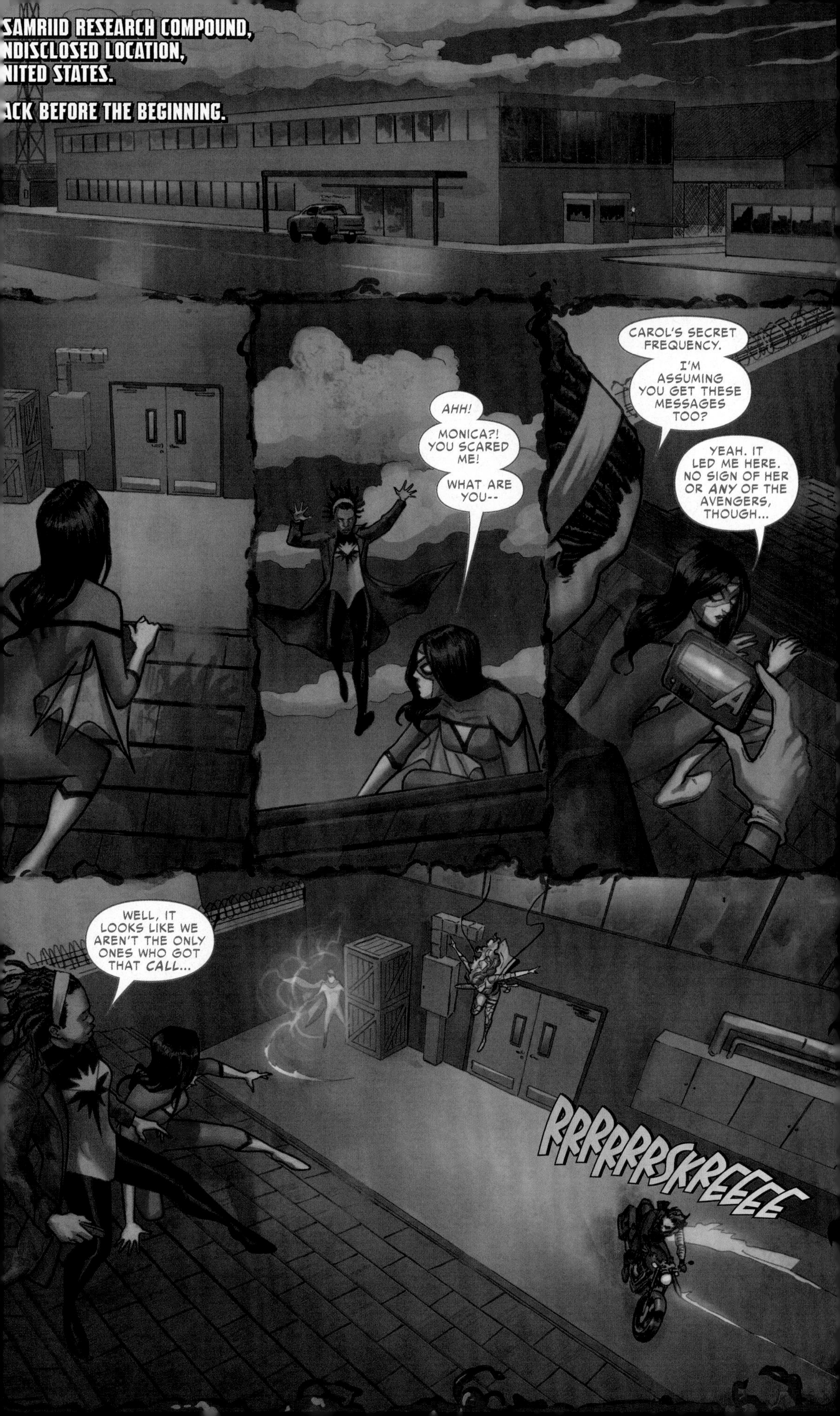
SAMRIID RESEARCH COMPOUND,
NDISCLOSED LOCATION,
NITED STATES.
ACK BEFORE THE BEGINNING.
AHH!
MONICA?! YOU SCARED ME!
WHAT ARE YOU--
CAROL'S SECRET FREQUENCY.
I'M ASSUMING YOU GET THESE MESSAGES TOO?
YEAH. IT LED ME HERE. NO SIGN OF HER OR ANY OF THE AVENGERS, THOUGH...
WELL, IT LOOKS LIKE WE AREN'T THE ONLY ONES WHO GOT THAT CALL...
RRRRRRSKREEEE

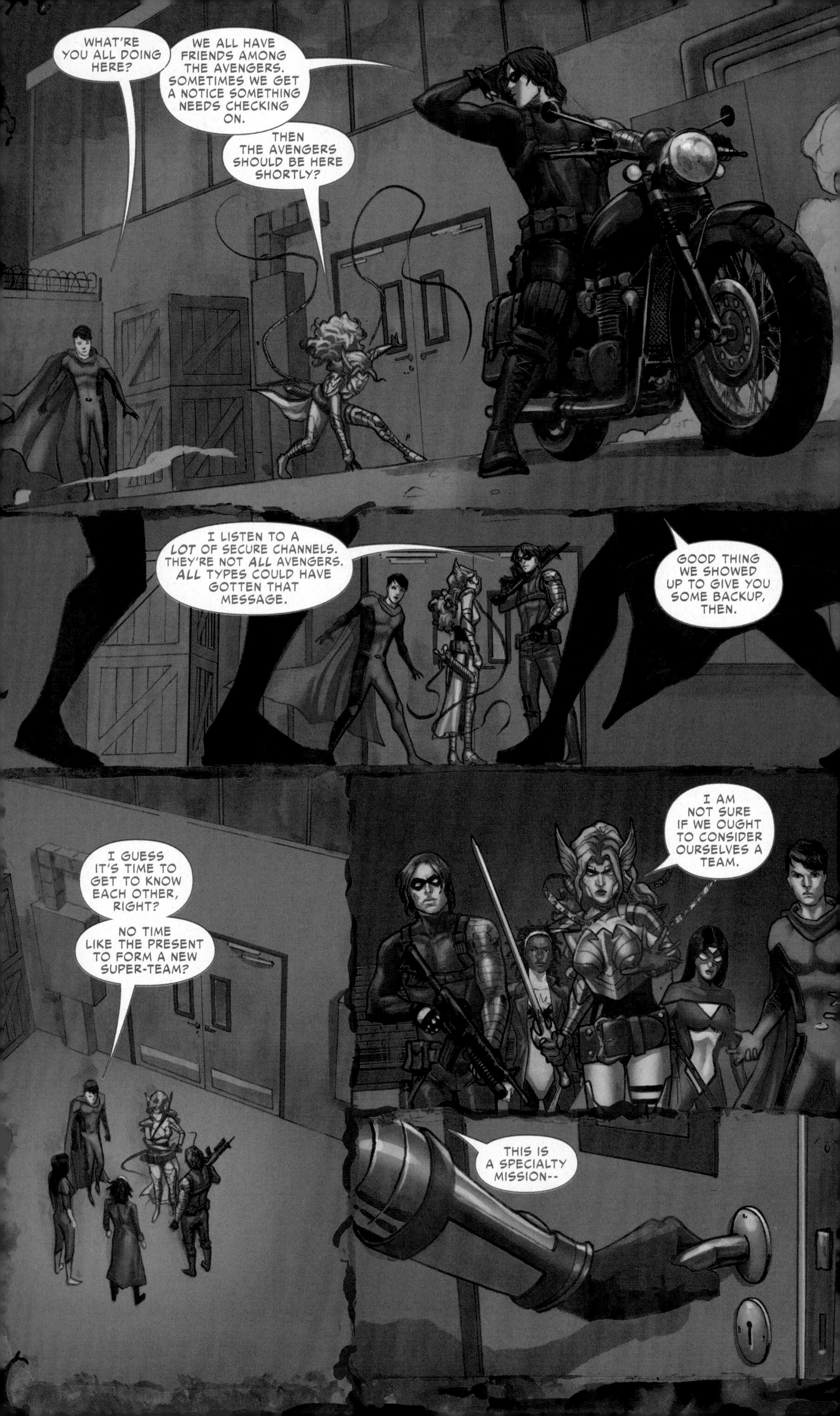
WHAT'RE YOU ALL DOING HERE?
WE ALL HAVE FRIENDS AMONG THE AVENGERS. SOMETIMES WE GET A NOTICE SOMETHING NEEDS CHECKING ON.
THEN THE AVENGERS SHOULD BE HERE SHORTLY?
I LISTEN TO A LOT OF SECURE CHANNELS. THEY'RE NOT ALL AVENGERS. ALL TYPES COULD HAVE GOTTEN THAT MESSAGE.
GOOD THING WE SHOWED UP TO GIVE YOU SOME BACKUP, THEN.
I GUESS IT'S TIME TO GET TO KNOW EACH OTHER, RIGHT?
NO TIME LIKE THE PRESENT TO FORM A NEW SUPER-TEAM?
I AM NOT SURE IF WE OUGHT TO CONSIDER OURSELVES A TEAM.
THIS IS A SPECIALTY MISSION--

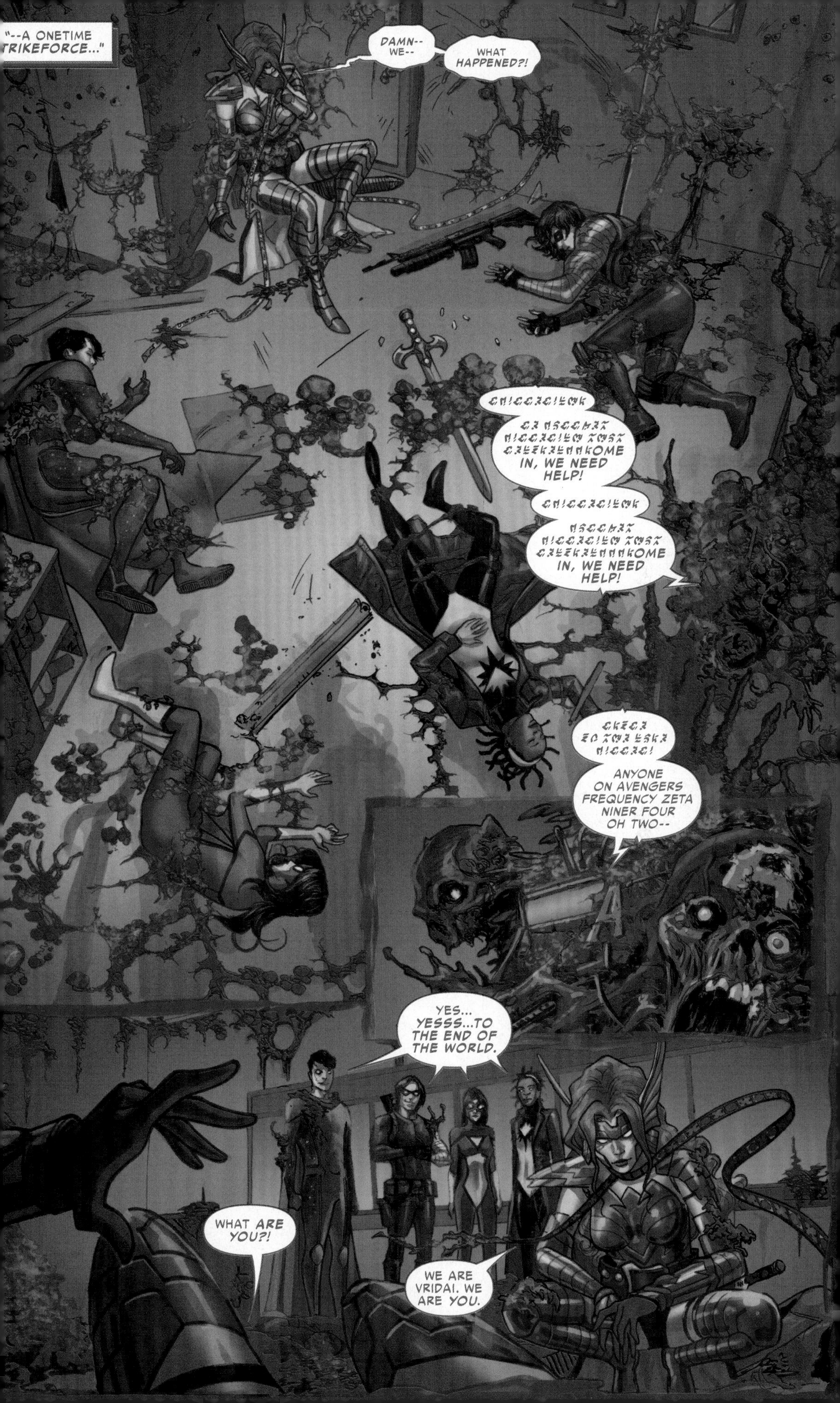
"--A ONETIME
TRIKEFORCE..."
DAMN-- WE--
WHAT HAPPENED?!
KOME IN, WE NEED HELP!
KOME IN, WE NEED HELP!
ANYONE ON AVENGERS FREQUENCY ZETA NINER FOUR OH TWO--
YES... YESSS...TO THE END OF THE WORLD.
WHAT ARE YOU?!
WE ARE VRIDAI. WE ARE YOU.

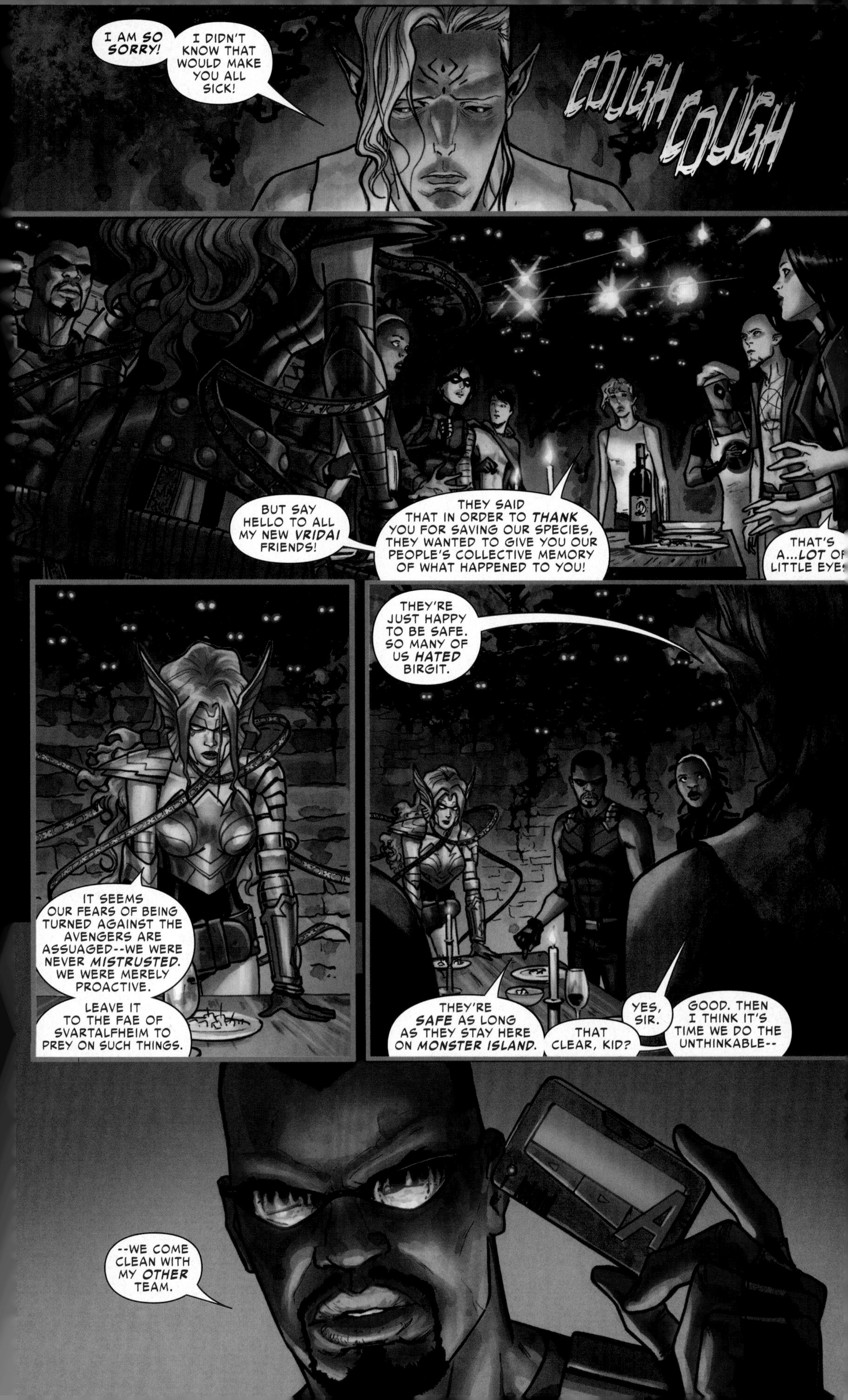
I AM SO SORRY!
I DIDN'T KNOW THAT WOULD MAKE YOU ALL SICK!
COUGH COUGH
BUT SAY HELLO TO ALL MY NEW VRIDAI FRIENDS!
THEY SAID THAT IN ORDER TO THANK YOU FOR SAVING OUR SPECIES, THEY WANTED TO GIVE YOU OUR PEOPLE'S COLLECTIVE MEMORY OF WHAT HAPPENED TO YOU!
THAT'S A...LOT OF LITTLE EYES
IT SEEMS OUR FEARS OF BEING TURNED AGAINST THE AVENGERS ARE ASSUAGED--WE WERE NEVER MISTRUSTED. WE WERE MERELY PROACTIVE.
LEAVE IT TO THE FAE OF SVARTALFHEIM TO PREY ON SUCH THINGS.
THEY'RE JUST HAPPY TO BE SAFE. SO MANY OF US HATED BIRGIT.
THEY'RE SAFE AS LONG AS THEY STAY HERE ON MONSTER ISLAND.
THAT CLEAR, KID?
YES, SIR.
GOOD. THEN I THINK IT'S TIME WE DO THE UNTHINKABLE--
--WE COME CLEAN WITH MY OTHER TEAM.

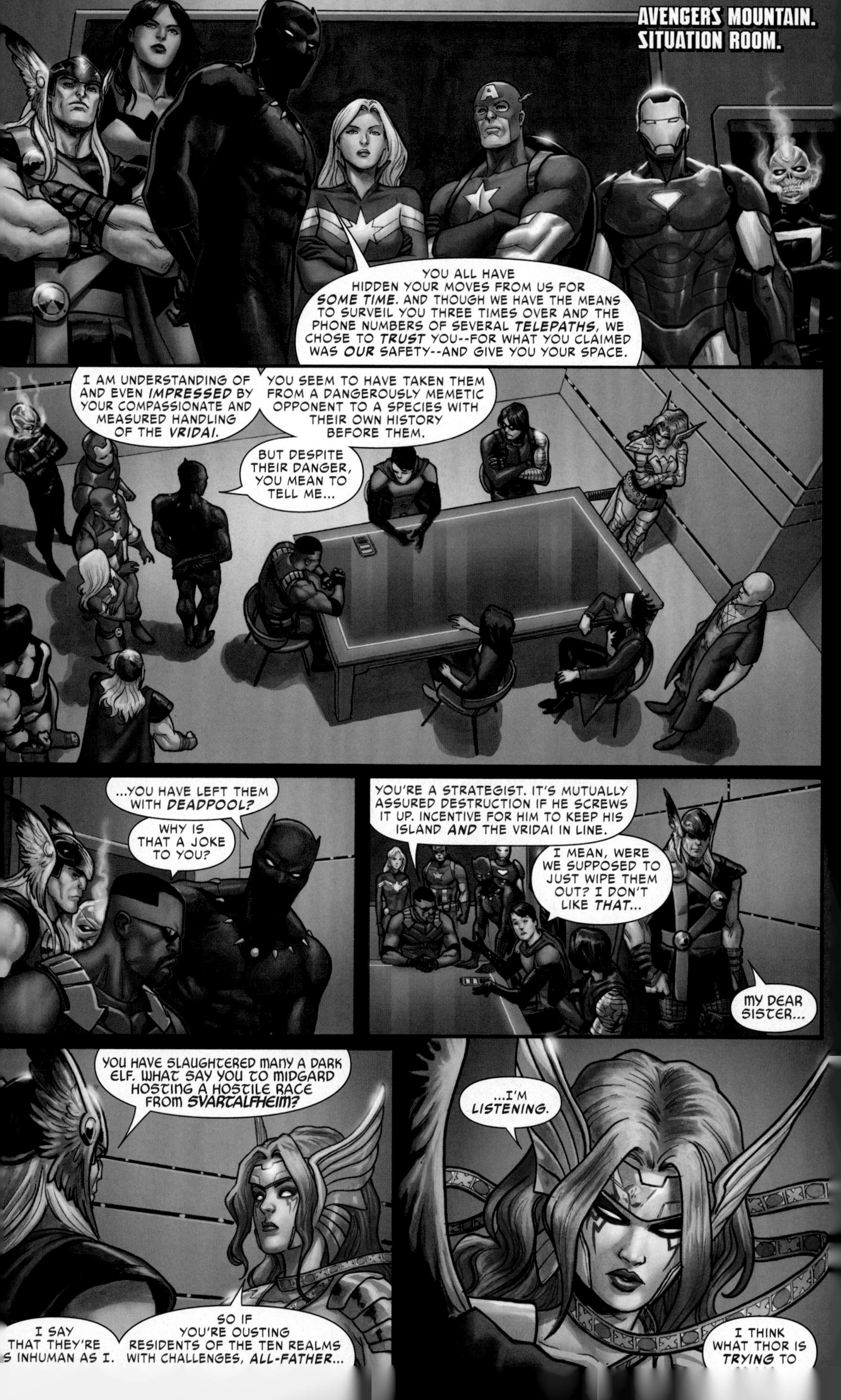

AVENGERS MOUNTAIN. SITUATION ROOM.
YOU ALL HAVE HIDDEN YOUR MOVES FROM US FOR SOME TIME. AND THOUGH WE HAVE THE MEANS TO SURVEIL YOU THREE TIMES OVER AND THE PHONE NUMBERS OF SEVERAL TELEPATHS, WE CHOSE TO TRUST YOU--FOR WHAT YOU CLAIMED WAS OUR SAFETY--AND GIVE YOU YOUR SPACE.
I AM UNDERSTANDING OF AND EVEN IMPRESSED BY YOUR COMPASSIONATE AND MEASURED HANDLING OF THE VRIDAI.
YOU SEEM TO HAVE TAKEN THEM FROM A DANGEROUSLY MEMETIC OPPONENT TO A SPECIES WITH THEIR OWN HISTORY BEFORE THEM.
BUT DESPITE THEIR DANGER, YOU MEAN TO TELL ME...
...YOU HAVE LEFT THEM WITH DEADPOOL?
WHY IS THAT A JOKE TO YOU?
YOU'RE A STRATEGIST. IT'S MUTUALLY ASSURED DESTRUCTION IF HE SCREWS IT UP. INCENTIVE FOR HIM TO KEEP HIS ISLAND AND THE VRIDAI IN LINE.
I MEAN, WERE WE SUPPOSED TO JUST WIPE THEM OUT? I DON'T LIKE THAT...
MY DEAR SISTER...
YOU HAVE SLAUGHTERED MANY A DARK ELF. WHAT SAY YOU TO MIDGARD HOSTING A HOSTILE RACE FROM SVARTALFHEIM?
I SAY THAT THEY'RE S INHUMAN AS I.
SO IF YOU'RE OUSTING RESIDENTS OF THE TEN REALMS WITH CHALLENGES, ALL-FATHER...
...I'M LISTENING.
I THINK WHAT THOR IS TRYING TO

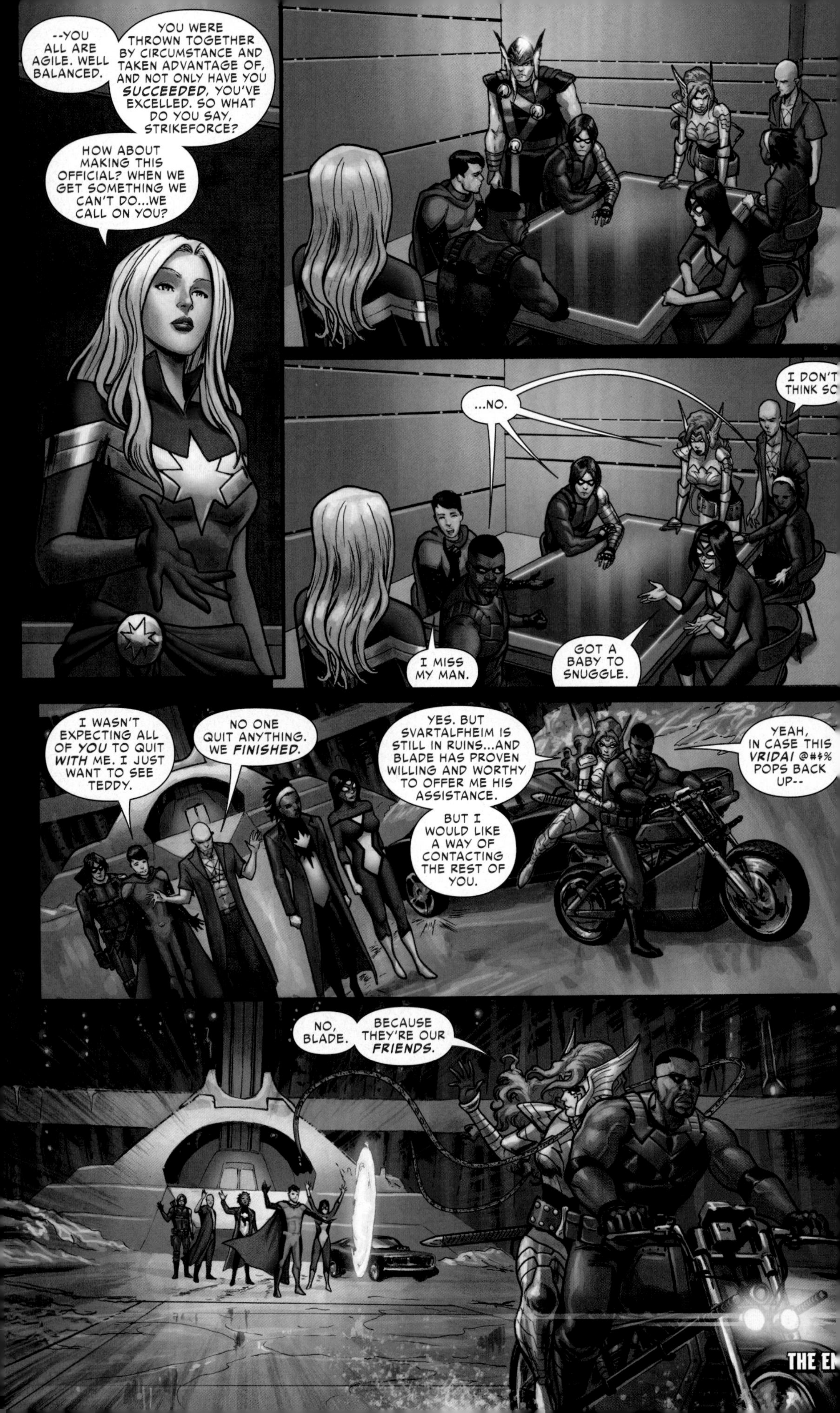
--YOU ALL ARE AGILE. WELL BALANCED.
YOU WERE THROWN TOGETHER BY CIRCUMSTANCE AND TAKEN ADVANTAGE OF, AND NOT ONLY HAVE YOU SUCCEEDED, YOU'VE EXCELLED. SO WHAT DO YOU SAY, STRIKEFORCE?
HOW ABOUT MAKING THIS OFFICIAL? WHEN WE GET SOMETHING WE CAN'T DO...WE CALL ON YOU?
...NO.
I DON'T THINK SO
I MISS MY MAN.
GOT A BABY TO SNUGGLE.
I WASN'T EXPECTING ALL OF YOU TO QUIT WITH ME. I JUST WANT TO SEE TEDDY.
NO ONE QUIT ANYTHING. WE FINISHED.
YES. BUT SVARTALFHEIM IS STILL IN RUINS...AND BLADE HAS PROVEN WILLING AND WORTHY TO OFFER ME HIS ASSISTANCE.
BUT I WOULD LIKE A WAY OF CONTACTING THE REST OF YOU.
YEAH, IN CASE THIS VRIDAI @#$% POPS BACK UP--
NO, BLADE.
BECAUSE THEY'RE OUR FRIENDS.
THE EN

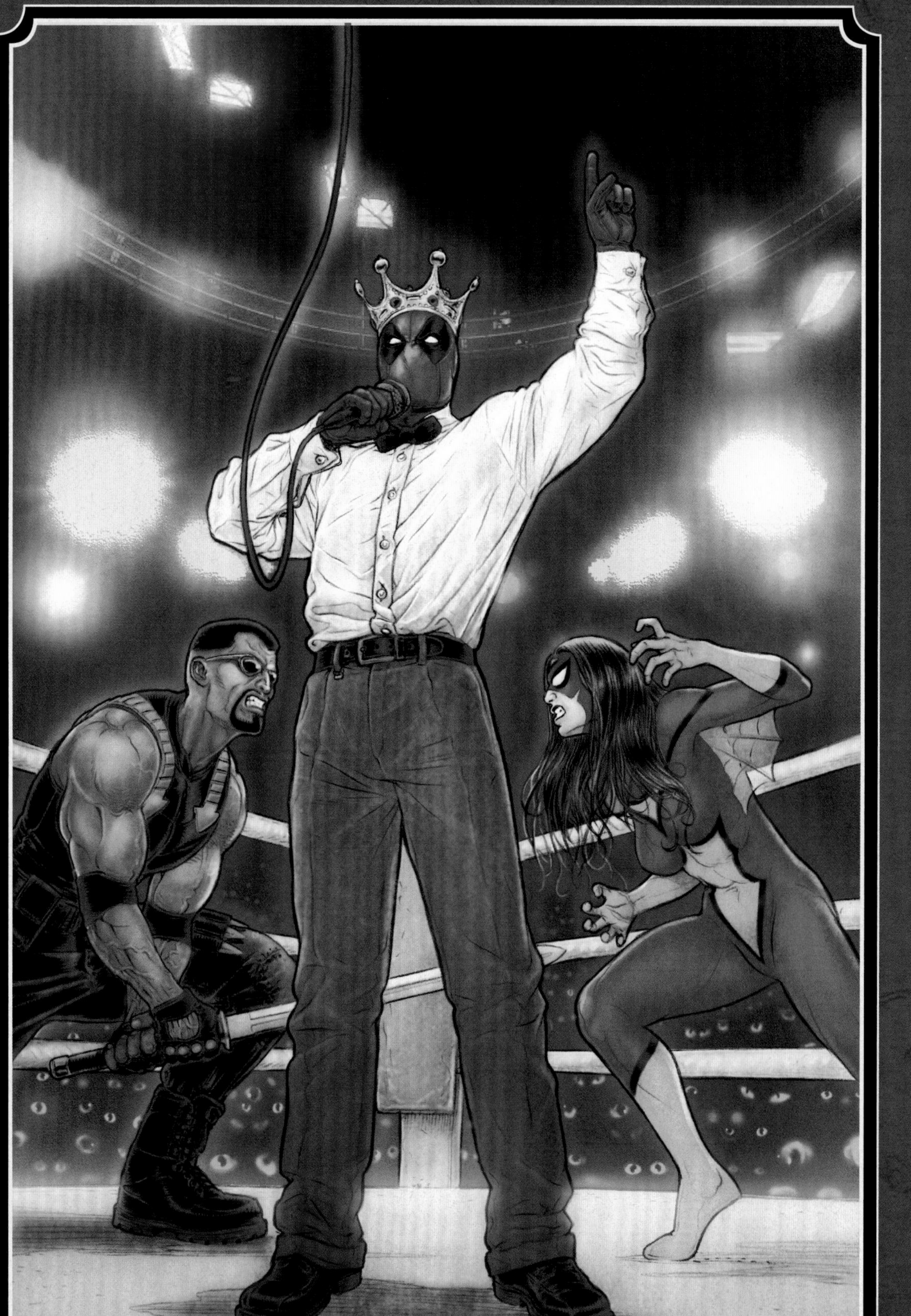

UNUSED COVER BY **DAN MORA** & **NOLAN WOODARD**

WAR OF THE REALMS STRIKEFORCE: THE DARK ELF REALM
AS THE DARK ELF MALEKITH WAGES HIS WAR ACROSS THE TEN REALMS,
THE PUNISHER LEADS THE CHARGE TO SHUT DOWN THE ENEMIES, BLACK BIFROST!

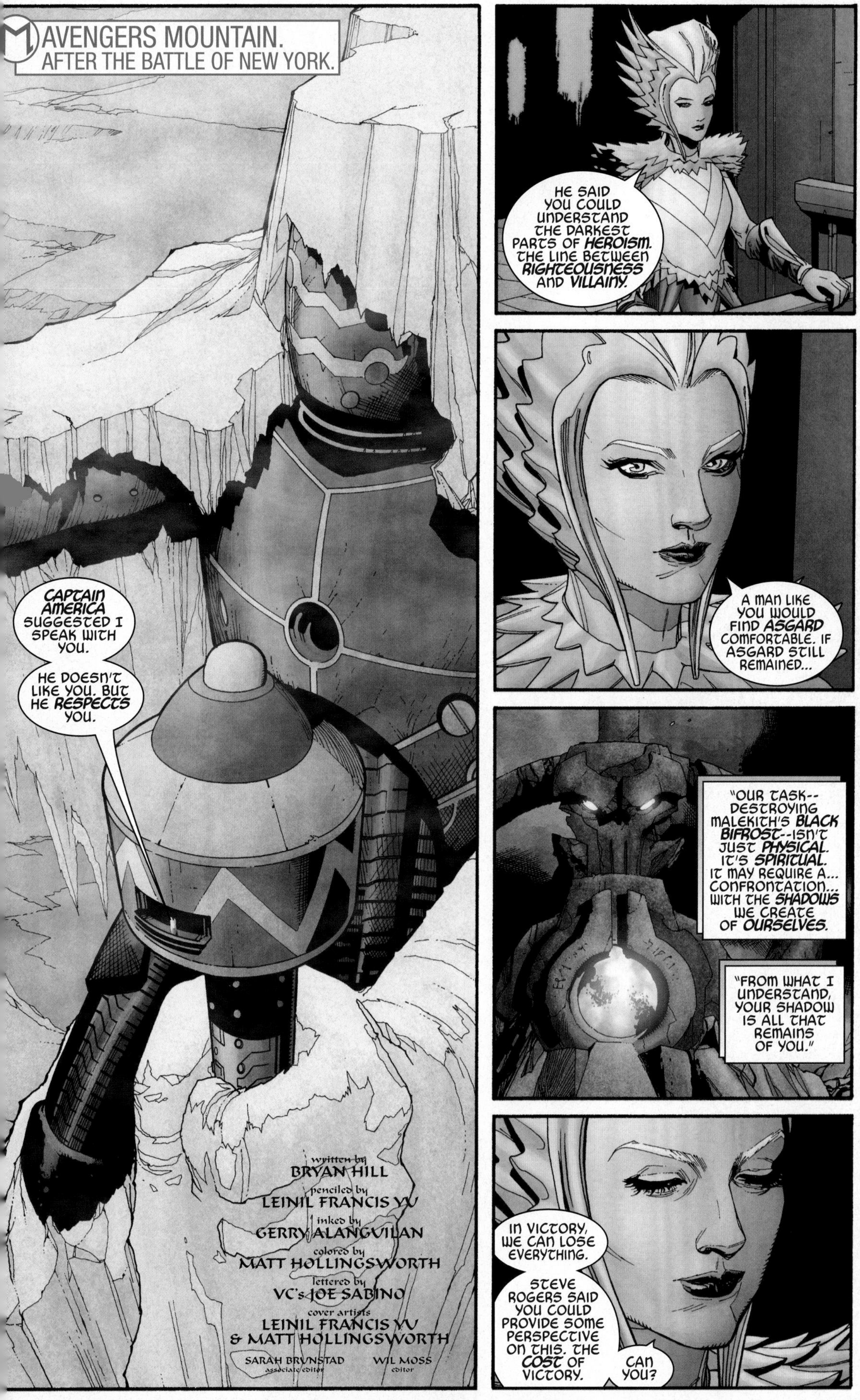
AVENGERS MOUNTAIN.
AFTER THE BATTLE OF NEW YORK.
CAPTAIN AMERICA SUGGESTED I SPEAK WITH YOU.
HE DOESN'T LIKE YOU. BUT HE RESPECTS YOU.
written by BRYAN HILL
penciled by LEINIL FRANCIS YU
inked by GERRY ALANGUILAN
colored by MATT HOLLINGSWORTH
lettered by VC's JOE SABINO
cover artists LEINIL FRANCIS YU & MATT HOLLINGSWORTH
SARAH BRUNSTAD associate editor
WIL MOSS editor
HE SAID YOU COULD UNDERSTAND THE DARKEST PARTS OF HEROISM. THE LINE BETWEEN RIGHTEOUSNESS AND VILLAINY.
A MAN LIKE YOU WOULD FIND ASGARD COMFORTABLE. IF ASGARD STILL REMAINED...
"OUR TASK--DESTROYING MALEKITH'S BLACK BIFROST--ISN'T JUST PHYSICAL. IT'S SPIRITUAL. IT MAY REQUIRE A... CONFRONTATION... WITH THE SHADOWS WE CREATE OF OURSELVES.
"FROM WHAT I UNDERSTAND, YOUR SHADOW IS ALL THAT REMAINS OF YOU."
IN VICTORY, WE CAN LOSE EVERYTHING.
STEVE ROGERS SAID YOU COULD PROVIDE SOME PERSPECTIVE ON THIS. THE COST OF VICTORY.
CAN YOU?

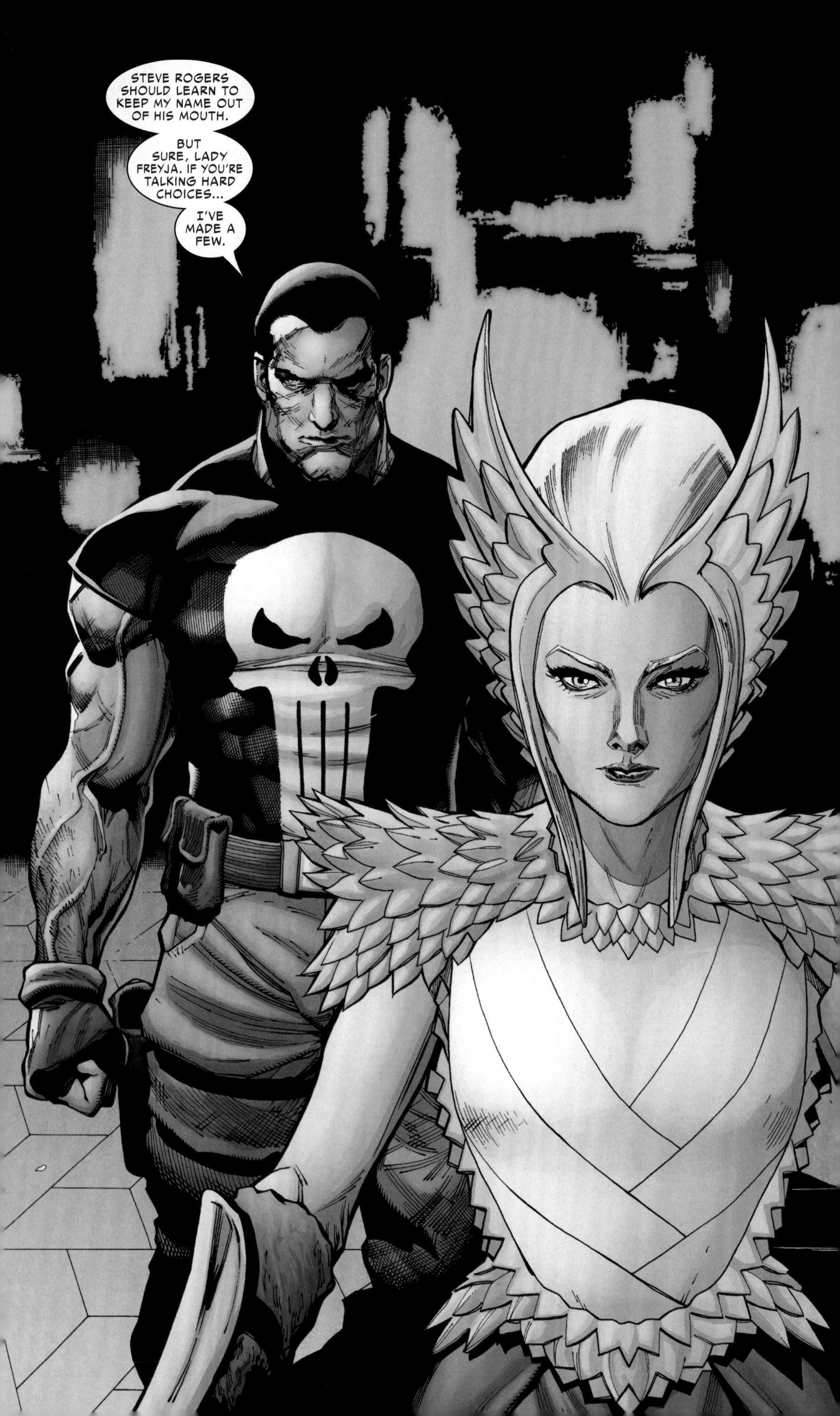
STEVE ROGERS SHOULD LEARN TO KEEP MY NAME OUT OF HIS MOUTH.
BUT SURE, LADY FREYJA. IF YOU'RE TALKING HARD CHOICES...
I'VE MADE A FEW.

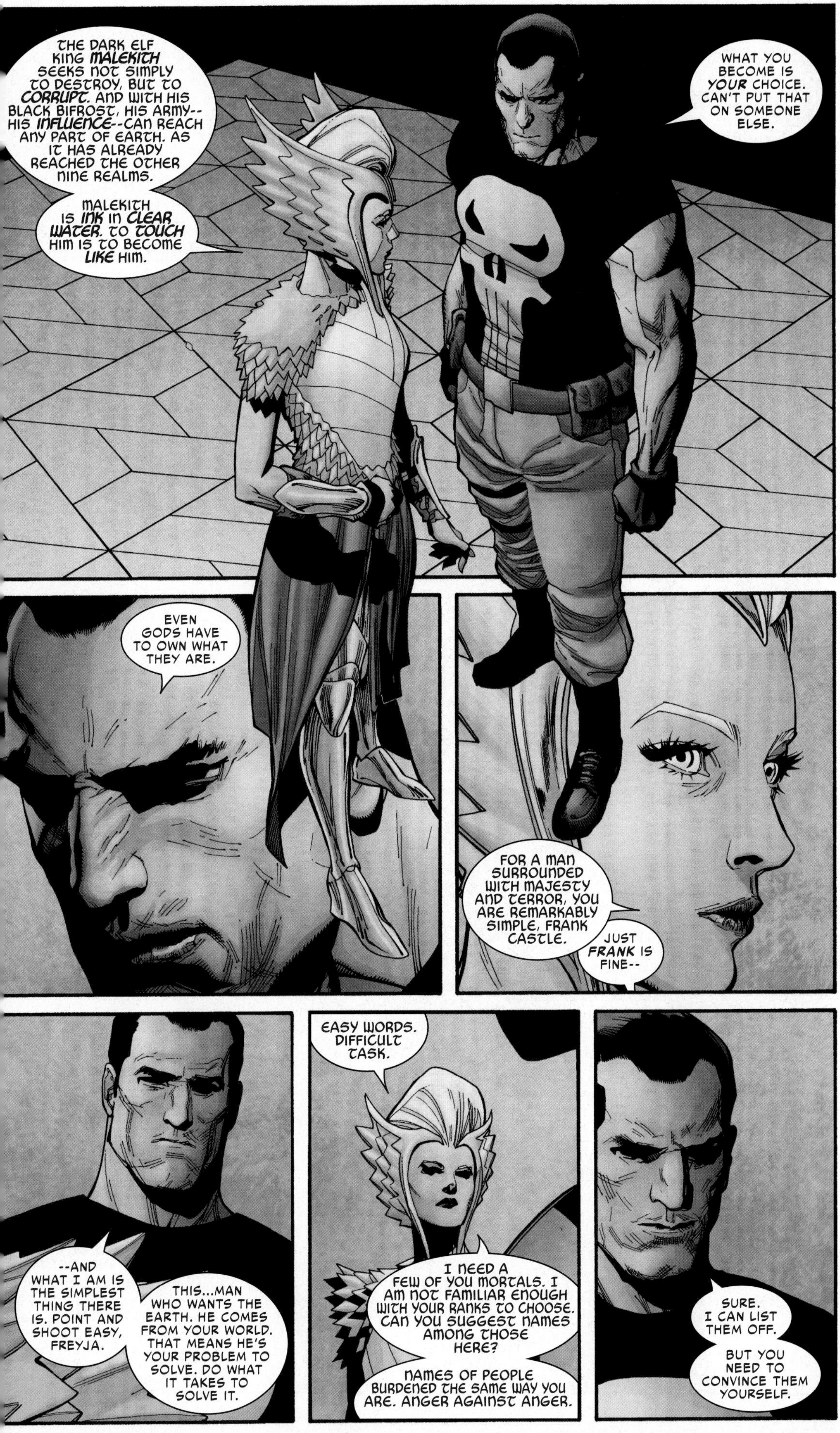

THE DARK ELF KING MALEKITH SEEKS NOT SIMPLY TO DESTROY, BUT TO CORRUPT. AND WITH HIS BLACK BIFROST, HIS ARMY--HIS INFLUENCE--CAN REACH ANY PART OF EARTH. AS IT HAS ALREADY REACHED THE OTHER NINE REALMS.
MALEKITH IS INK IN CLEAR WATER. TO TOUCH HIM IS TO BECOME LIKE HIM.
WHAT YOU BECOME IS YOUR CHOICE. CAN'T PUT THAT ON SOMEONE ELSE.
EVEN GODS HAVE TO OWN WHAT THEY ARE.
FOR A MAN SURROUNDED WITH MAJESTY AND TERROR, YOU ARE REMARKABLY SIMPLE, FRANK CASTLE.
JUST FRANK IS FINE--
--AND WHAT I AM IS THE SIMPLEST THING THERE IS. POINT AND SHOOT EASY, FREYJA.
THIS...MAN WHO WANTS THE EARTH. HE COMES FROM YOUR WORLD. THAT MEANS HE'S YOUR PROBLEM TO SOLVE. DO WHAT IT TAKES TO SOLVE IT.
EASY WORDS. DIFFICULT TASK.
I NEED A FEW OF YOU MORTALS. I AM NOT FAMILIAR ENOUGH WITH YOUR RANKS TO CHOOSE. CAN YOU SUGGEST NAMES AMONG THOSE HERE?
NAMES OF PEOPLE BURDENED THE SAME WAY YOU ARE. ANGER AGAINST ANGER.
SURE. I CAN LIST THEM OFF.
BUT YOU NEED TO CONVINCE THEM YOURSELF.

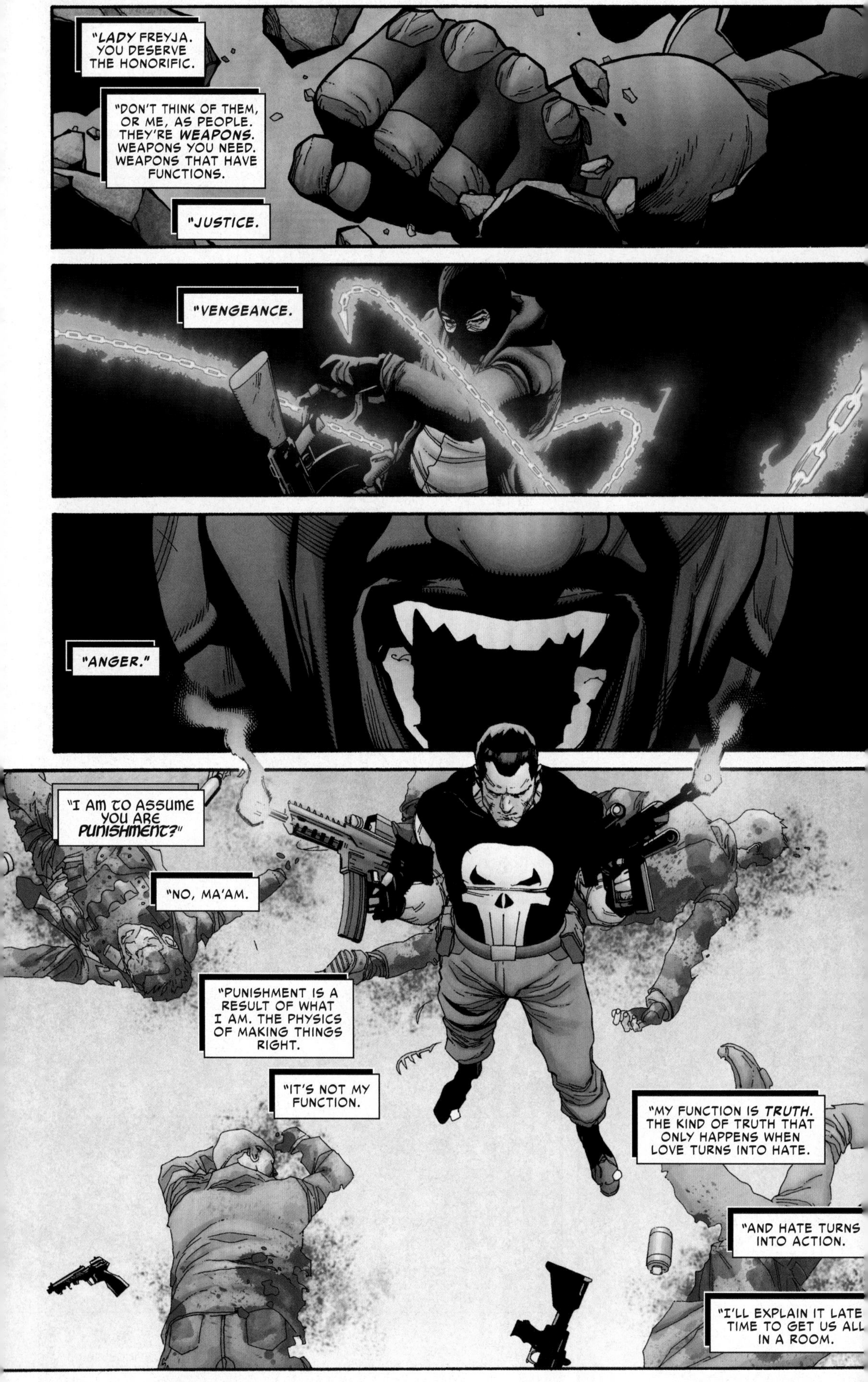
"LADY FREYJA. YOU DESERVE THE HONORIFIC.
"DON'T THINK OF THEM, OR ME, AS PEOPLE. THEY'RE WEAPONS. WEAPONS YOU NEED. WEAPONS THAT HAVE FUNCTIONS.
"JUSTICE.
"VENGEANCE.
"ANGER."
"I AM TO ASSUME YOU ARE PUNISHMENT?"
"NO, MA'AM.
"PUNISHMENT IS A RESULT OF WHAT I AM. THE PHYSICS OF MAKING THINGS RIGHT.
"IT'S NOT MY FUNCTION.
"MY FUNCTION IS TRUTH. THE KIND OF TRUTH THAT ONLY HAPPENS WHEN LOVE TURNS INTO HATE.
"AND HATE TURNS INTO ACTION.
"I'LL EXPLAIN IT LATE TIME TO GET US ALL IN A ROOM.

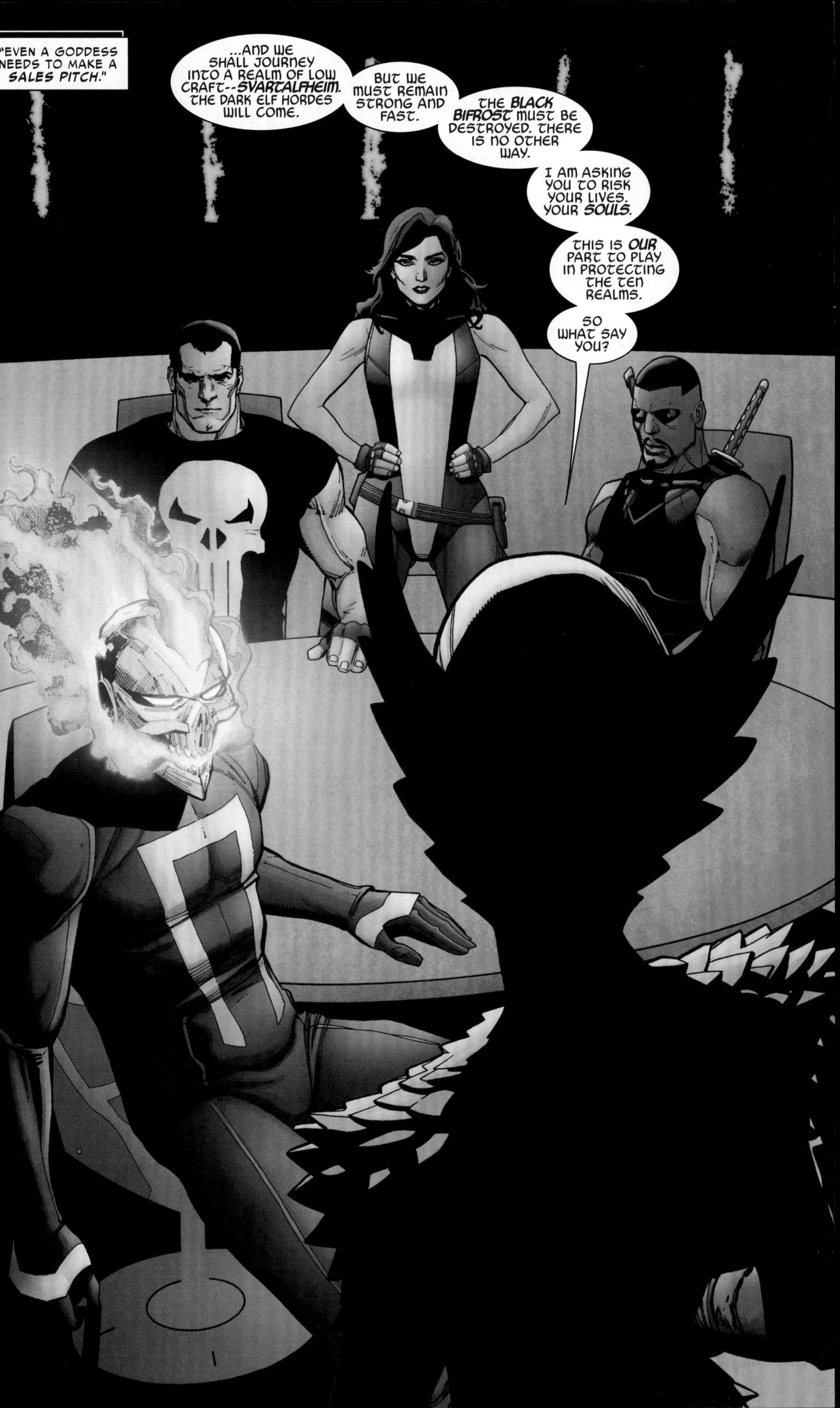
"EVEN A GODDESS NEEDS TO MAKE A SALES PITCH."
...AND WE SHALL JOURNEY INTO A REALM OF LOW CRAFT--SVARTALFHEIM. THE DARK ELF HORDES WILL COME.
BUT WE MUST REMAIN STRONG AND FAST.
THE BLACK BIFROST MUST BE DESTROYED. THERE IS NO OTHER WAY.
I AM ASKING YOU TO RISK YOUR LIVES. YOUR SOULS.
THIS IS OUR PART TO PLAY IN PROTECTING THE TEN REALMS.
SO WHAT SAY YOU?

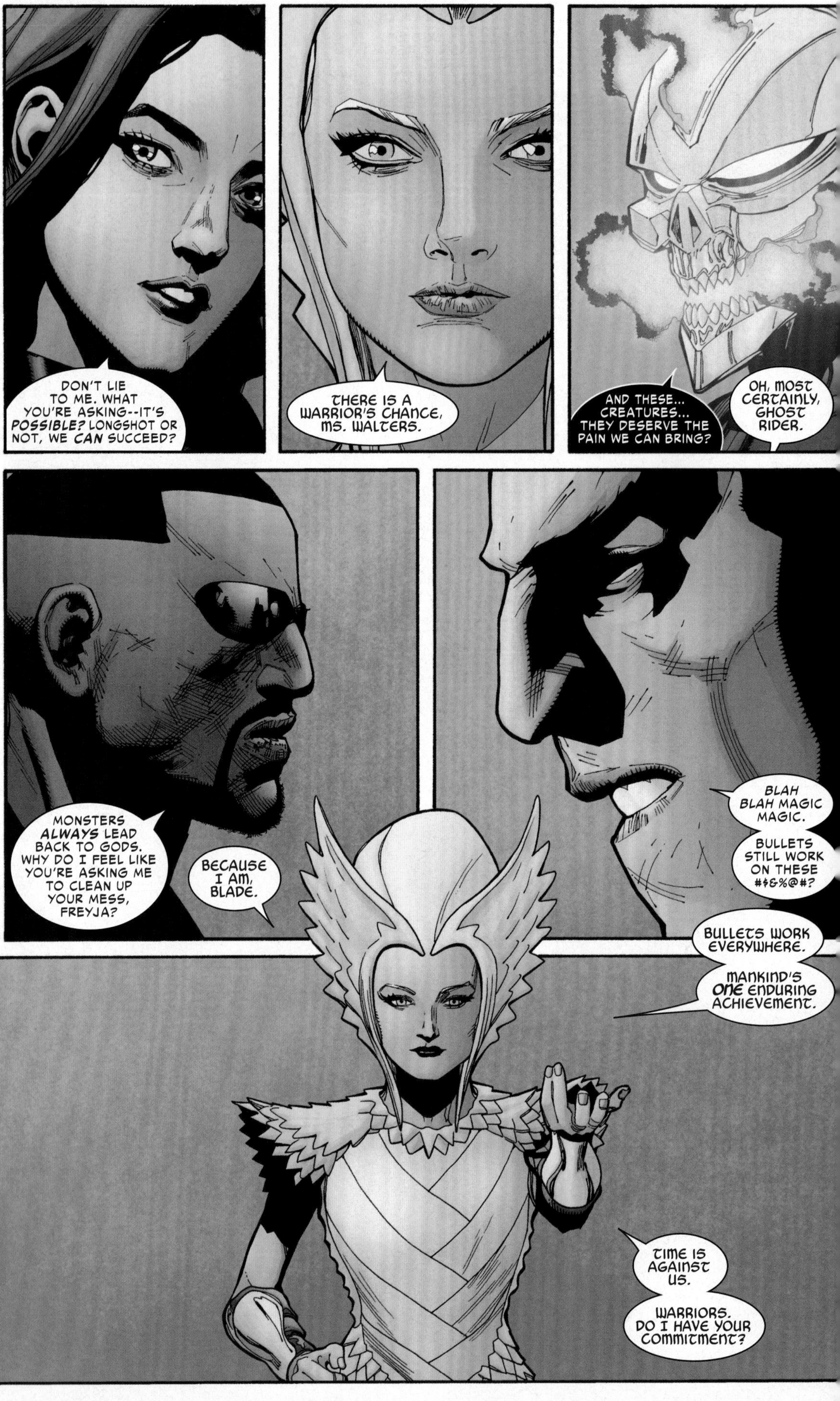
DON'T LIE TO ME. WHAT YOU'RE ASKING--IT'S POSSIBLE? LONGSHOT OR NOT, WE CAN SUCCEED?
THERE IS A WARRIOR'S CHANCE, MS. WALTERS.
AND THESE... CREATURES... THEY DESERVE THE PAIN WE CAN BRING?
OH, MOST CERTAINLY, GHOST RIDER.
MONSTERS ALWAYS LEAD BACK TO GODS. WHY DO I FEEL LIKE YOU'RE ASKING ME TO CLEAN UP YOUR MESS, FREYJA?
BECAUSE I AM, BLADE.
BLAH BLAH MAGIC MAGIC.
BULLETS STILL WORK ON THESE #$&%@#?
BULLETS WORK EVERYWHERE.
MANKIND'S ONE ENDURING ACHIEVEMENT.
TIME IS AGAINST US.
WARRIORS. DO I HAVE YOUR COMMITMENT?

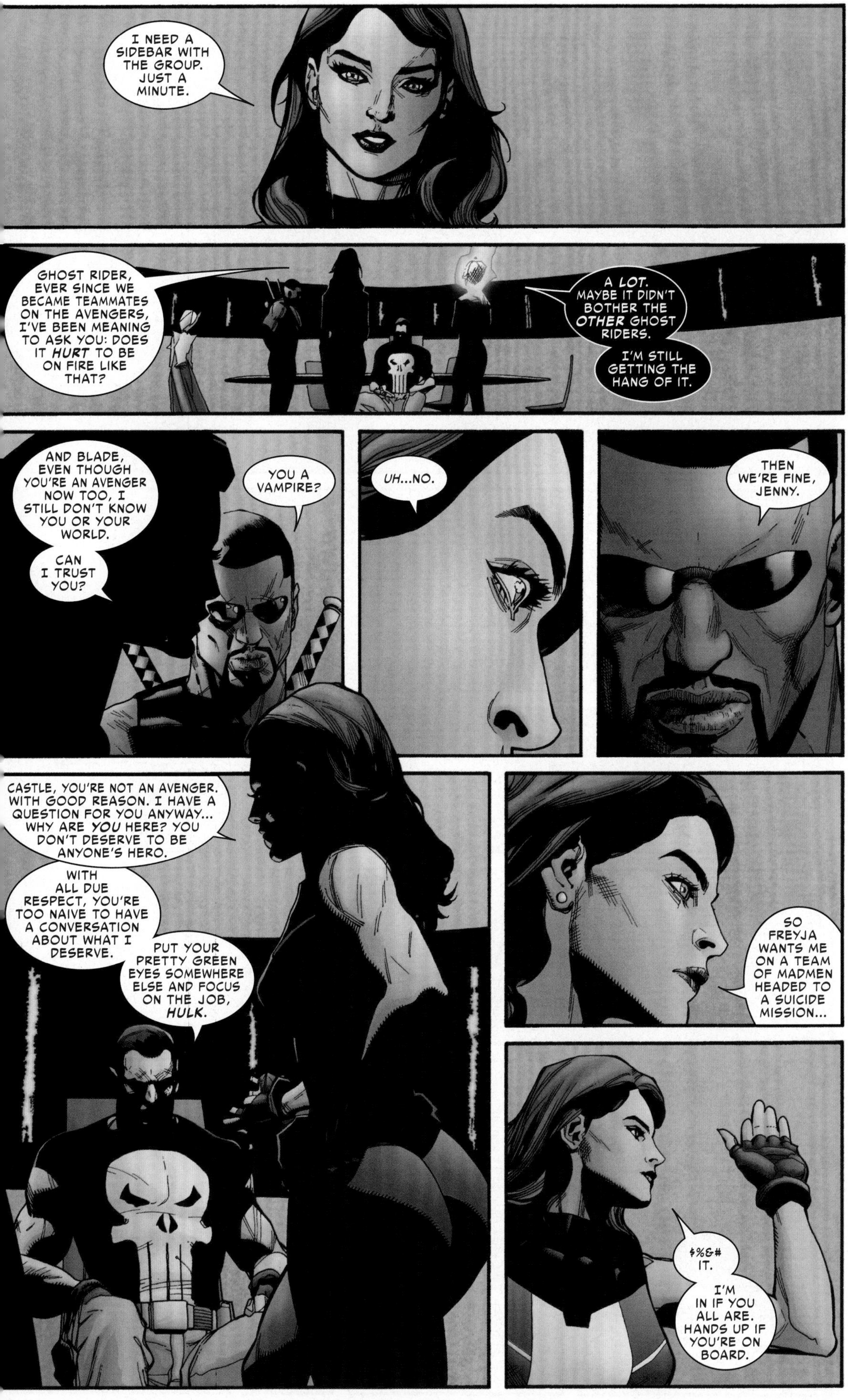
I NEED A SIDEBAR WITH THE GROUP. JUST A MINUTE.
GHOST RIDER, EVER SINCE WE BECAME TEAMMATES ON THE AVENGERS, I'VE BEEN MEANING TO ASK YOU: DOES IT *HURT* TO BE ON FIRE LIKE THAT?
A *LOT*. MAYBE IT DIDN'T BOTHER THE *OTHER* GHOST RIDERS.
I'M STILL GETTING THE HANG OF IT.
AND BLADE, EVEN THOUGH YOU'RE AN AVENGER NOW TOO, I STILL DON'T KNOW YOU OR YOUR WORLD.
CAN I TRUST YOU?
YOU A VAMPIRE?
UH...NO.
THEN WE'RE FINE, JENNY.
CASTLE, YOU'RE NOT AN AVENGER. WITH GOOD REASON. I HAVE A QUESTION FOR YOU ANYWAY... WHY ARE *YOU* HERE? YOU DON'T DESERVE TO BE ANYONE'S HERO.
WITH ALL DUE RESPECT, YOU'RE TOO NAIVE TO HAVE A CONVERSATION ABOUT WHAT I DESERVE.
PUT YOUR PRETTY GREEN EYES SOMEWHERE ELSE AND FOCUS ON THE JOB, *HULK*.
SO FREYJA WANTS ME ON A TEAM OF MADMEN HEADED TO A SUICIDE MISSION...
$%&# IT.
I'M IN IF YOU ALL ARE. HANDS UP IF YOU'RE ON BOARD.

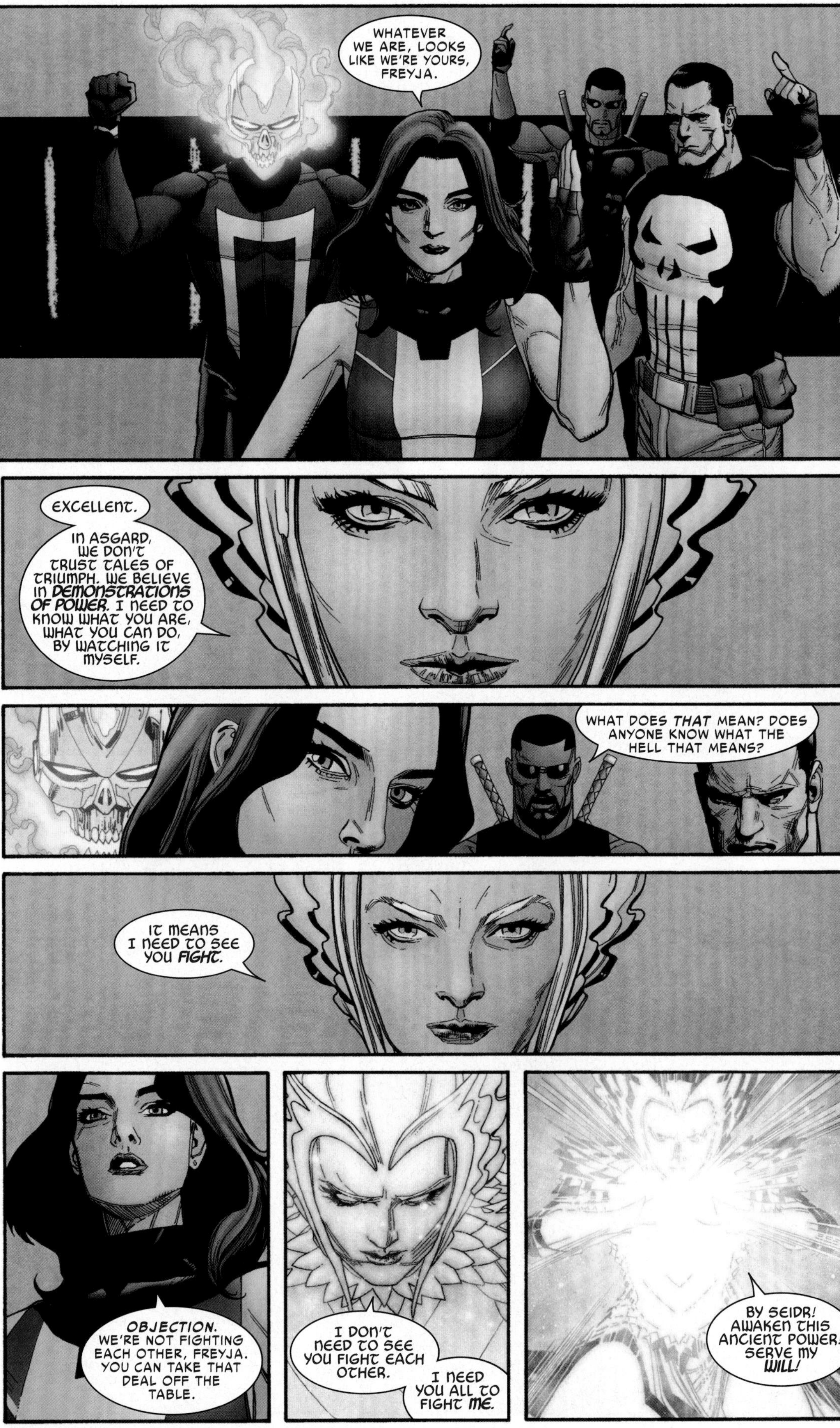
WHATEVER WE ARE, LOOKS LIKE WE'RE YOURS, FREYJA.
EXCELLENT.
IN ASGARD, WE DON'T TRUST TALES OF TRIUMPH. WE BELIEVE IN DEMONSTRATIONS OF POWER. I NEED TO KNOW WHAT YOU ARE, WHAT YOU CAN DO, BY WATCHING IT MYSELF.
WHAT DOES THAT MEAN? DOES ANYONE KNOW WHAT THE HELL THAT MEANS?
IT MEANS I NEED TO SEE YOU FIGHT.
OBJECTION. WE'RE NOT FIGHTING EACH OTHER, FREYJA. YOU CAN TAKE THAT DEAL OFF THE TABLE.
I DON'T NEED TO SEE YOU FIGHT EACH OTHER.
I NEED YOU ALL TO FIGHT ME.
BY SEIDR! AWAKEN THIS ANCIENT POWER! SERVE MY WILL!

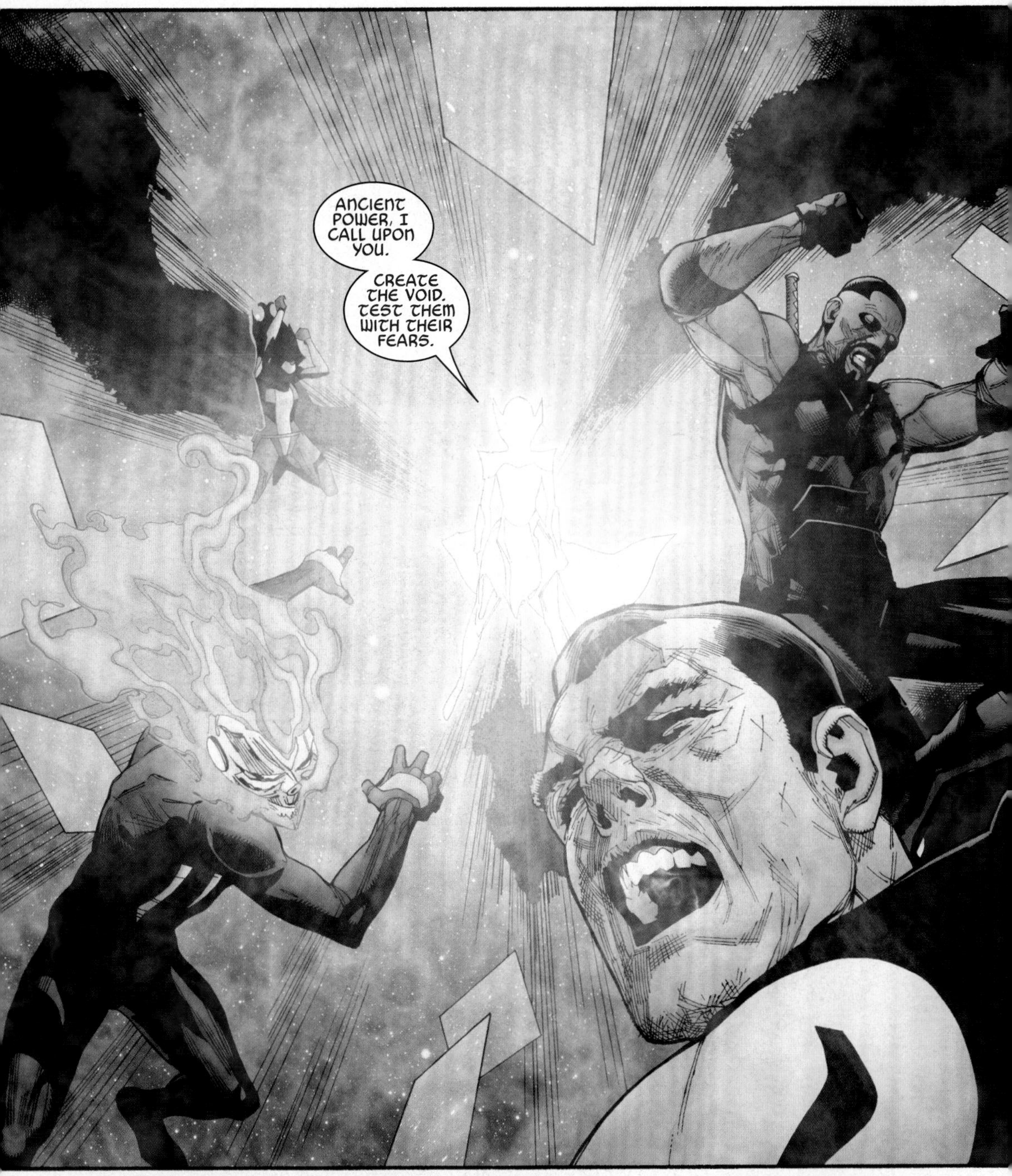
ANCIENT POWER, I CALL UPON YOU.
CREATE THE VOID. TEST THEM WITH THEIR FEARS.

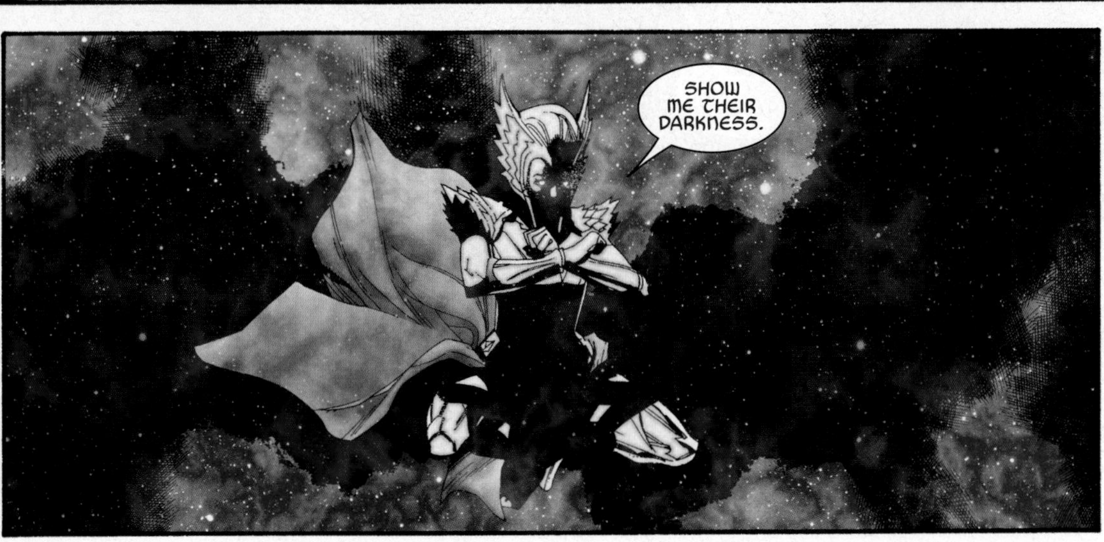
SHOW ME THEIR DARKNESS.

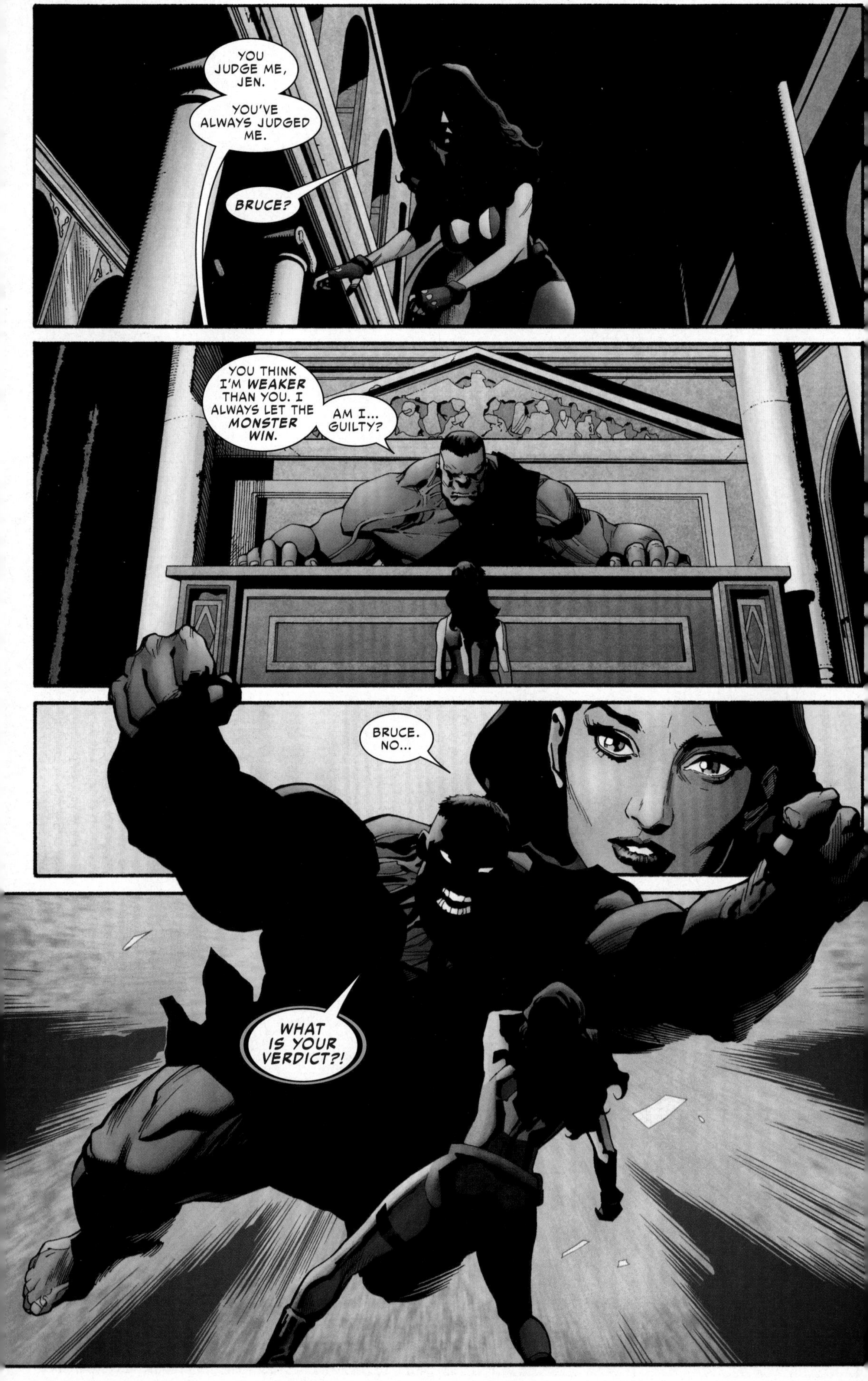

YOU JUDGE ME, JEN.
YOU'VE ALWAYS JUDGED ME.
BRUCE?
YOU THINK I'M WEAKER THAN YOU. I ALWAYS LET THE MONSTER WIN.
AM I... GUILTY?
BRUCE. NO...
WHAT IS YOUR VERDICT?!

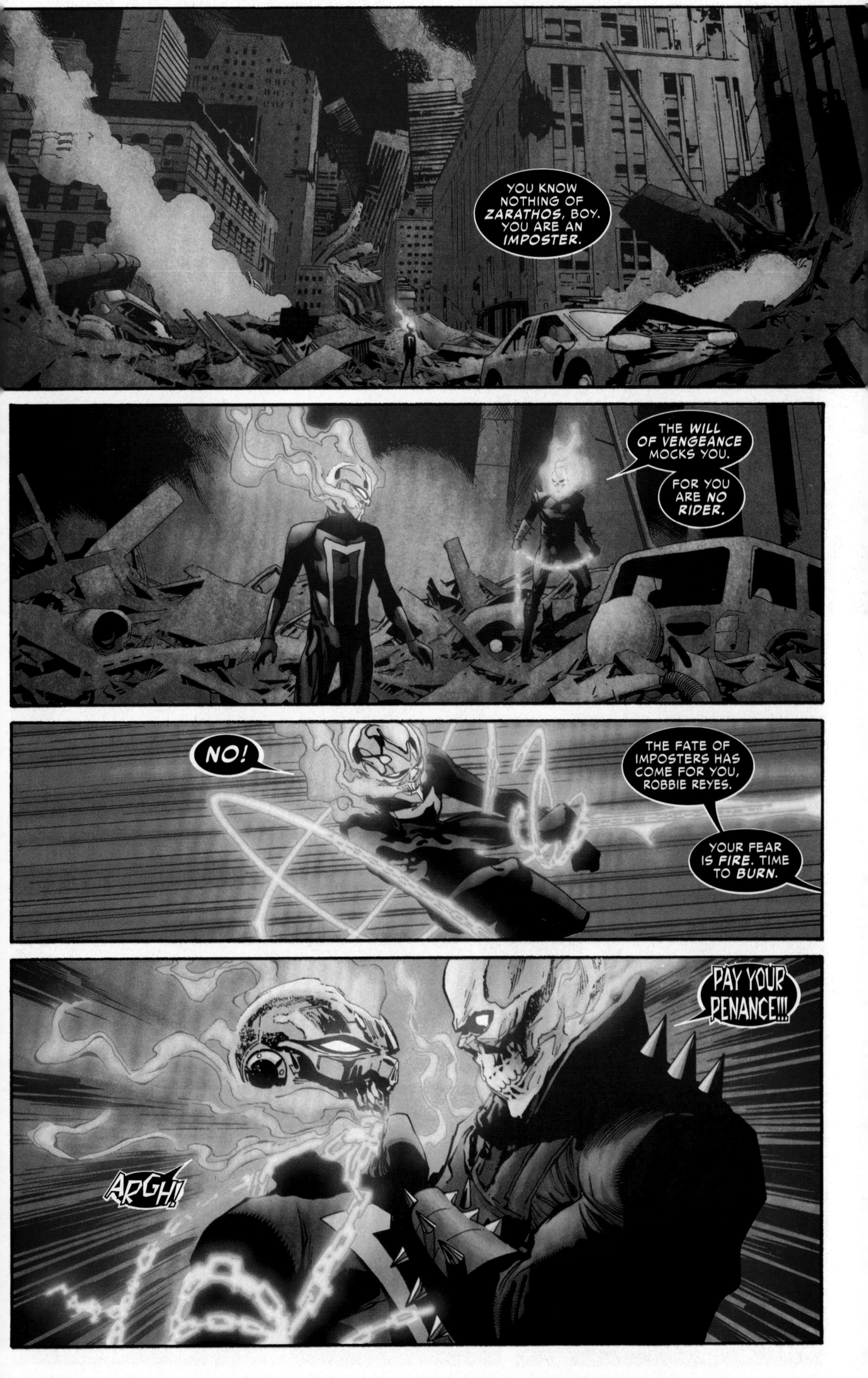
YOU KNOW NOTHING OF ZARATHOS, BOY. YOU ARE AN IMPOSTER.
THE WILL OF VENGEANCE MOCKS YOU.
FOR YOU ARE NO RIDER.
NO!
THE FATE OF IMPOSTERS HAS COME FOR YOU, ROBBIE REYES.
YOUR FEAR IS FIRE. TIME TO BURN.
PAY YOUR PENANCE!!!
ARGH!

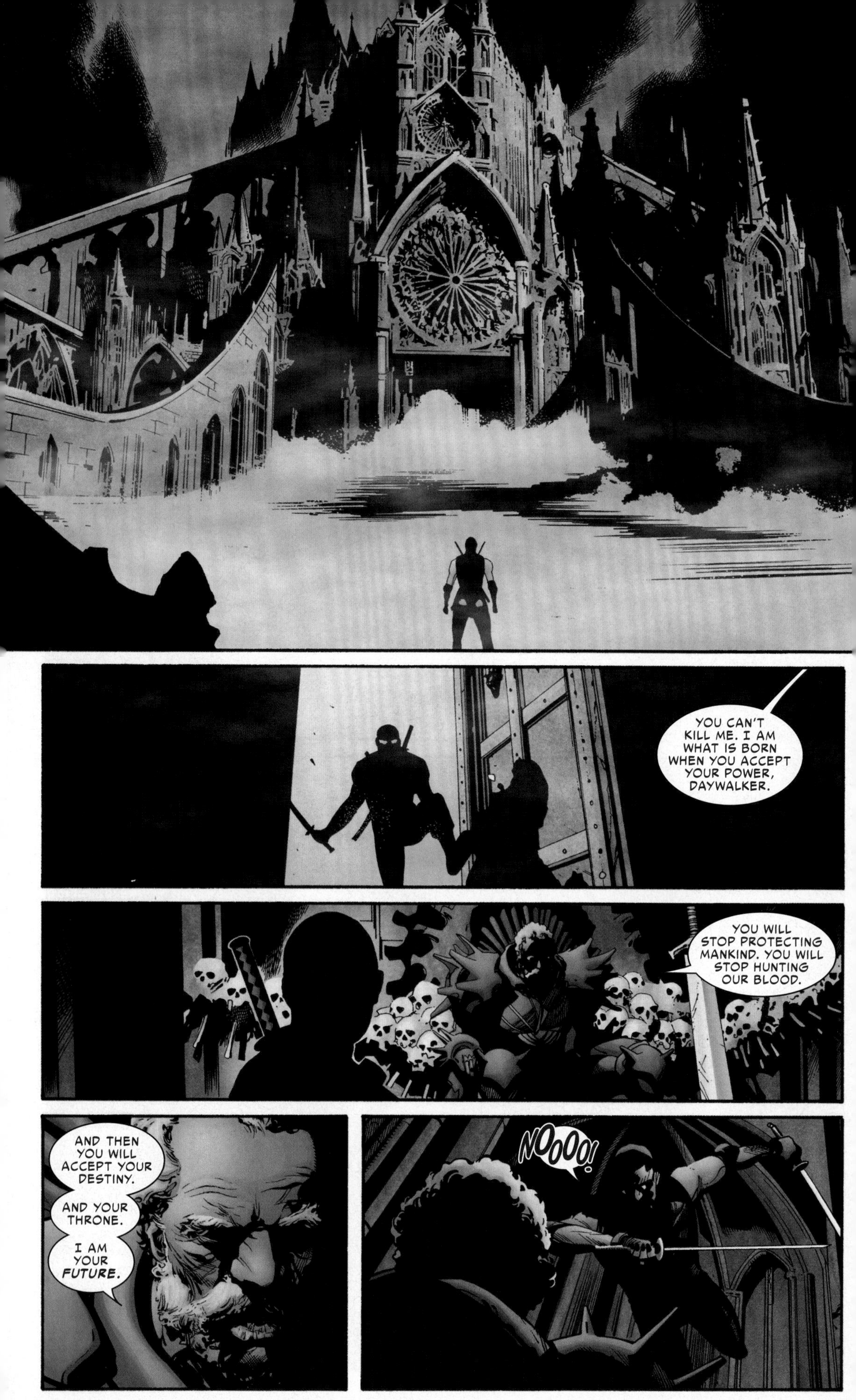
YOU CAN'T KILL ME. I AM WHAT IS BORN WHEN YOU ACCEPT YOUR POWER, DAYWALKER.
YOU WILL STOP PROTECTING MANKIND. YOU WILL STOP HUNTING OUR BLOOD.
AND THEN YOU WILL ACCEPT YOUR DESTINY.
AND YOUR THRONE.
I AM YOUR *FUTURE*.
NOOOO!

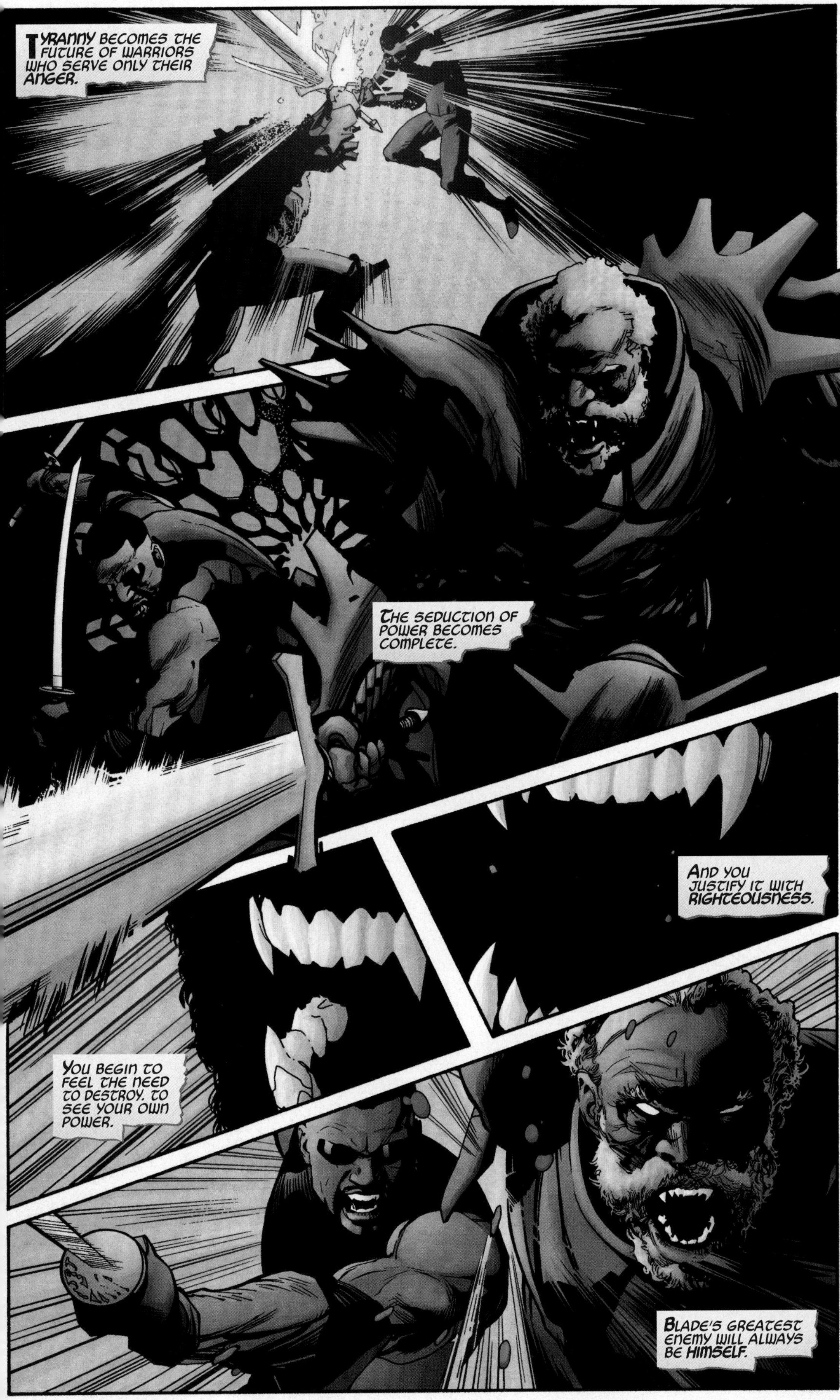
TYRANNY BECOMES THE FUTURE OF WARRIORS WHO SERVE ONLY THEIR ANGER.
THE SEDUCTION OF POWER BECOMES COMPLETE.
AND YOU JUSTIFY IT WITH RIGHTEOUSNESS.
YOU BEGIN TO FEEL THE NEED TO DESTROY. TO SEE YOUR OWN POWER.
BLADE'S GREATEST ENEMY WILL ALWAYS BE HIMSELF.

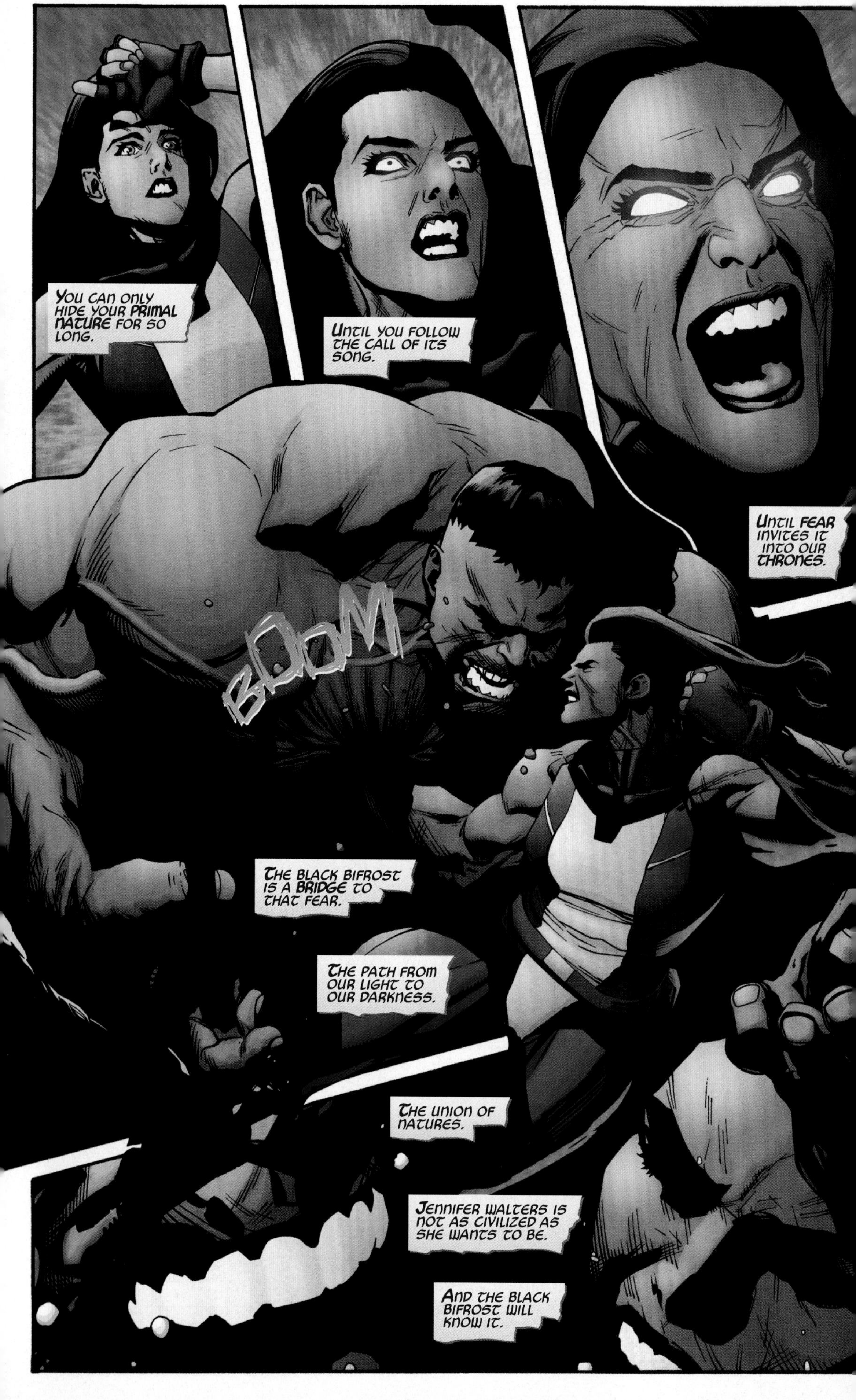

You can only hide your PRIMAL NATURE for so long.
Until you follow the call of its song.
Until FEAR invites it into our THRONES.
BOOM
The Black Bifrost is a BRIDGE to that fear.
The path from our light to our darkness.
The union of natures.
Jennifer Walters is not as civilized as she wants to be.
And the Black Bifrost will know it.

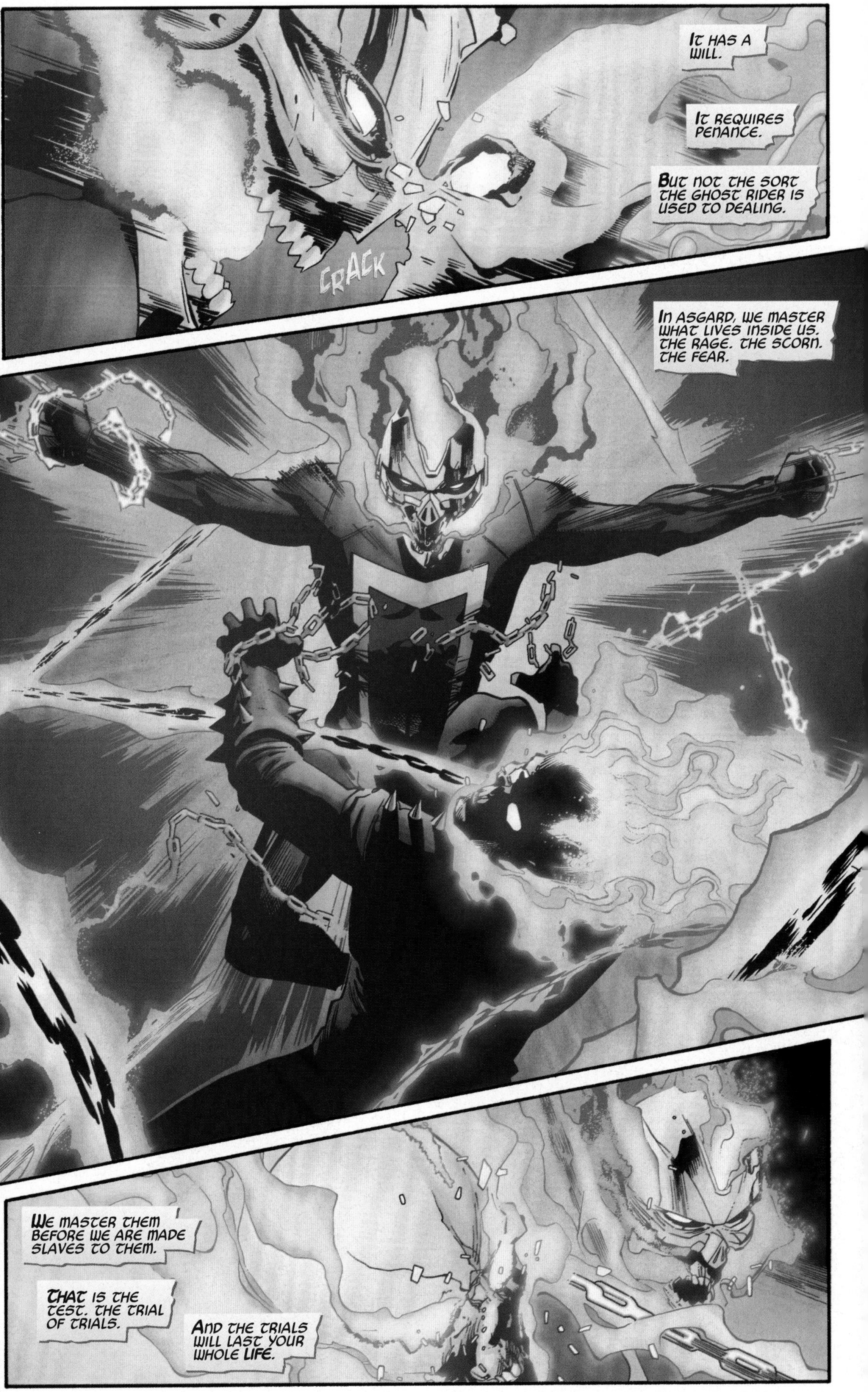
IT HAS A WILL.
IT REQUIRES PENANCE.
BUT NOT THE SORT THE GHOST RIDER IS USED TO DEALING.
CRACK
IN ASGARD, WE MASTER WHAT LIVES INSIDE US. THE RAGE. THE SCORN. THE FEAR.
WE MASTER THEM BEFORE WE ARE MADE SLAVES TO THEM.
THAT IS THE TEST. THE TRIAL OF TRIALS.
AND THE TRIALS WILL LAST YOUR WHOLE LIFE.

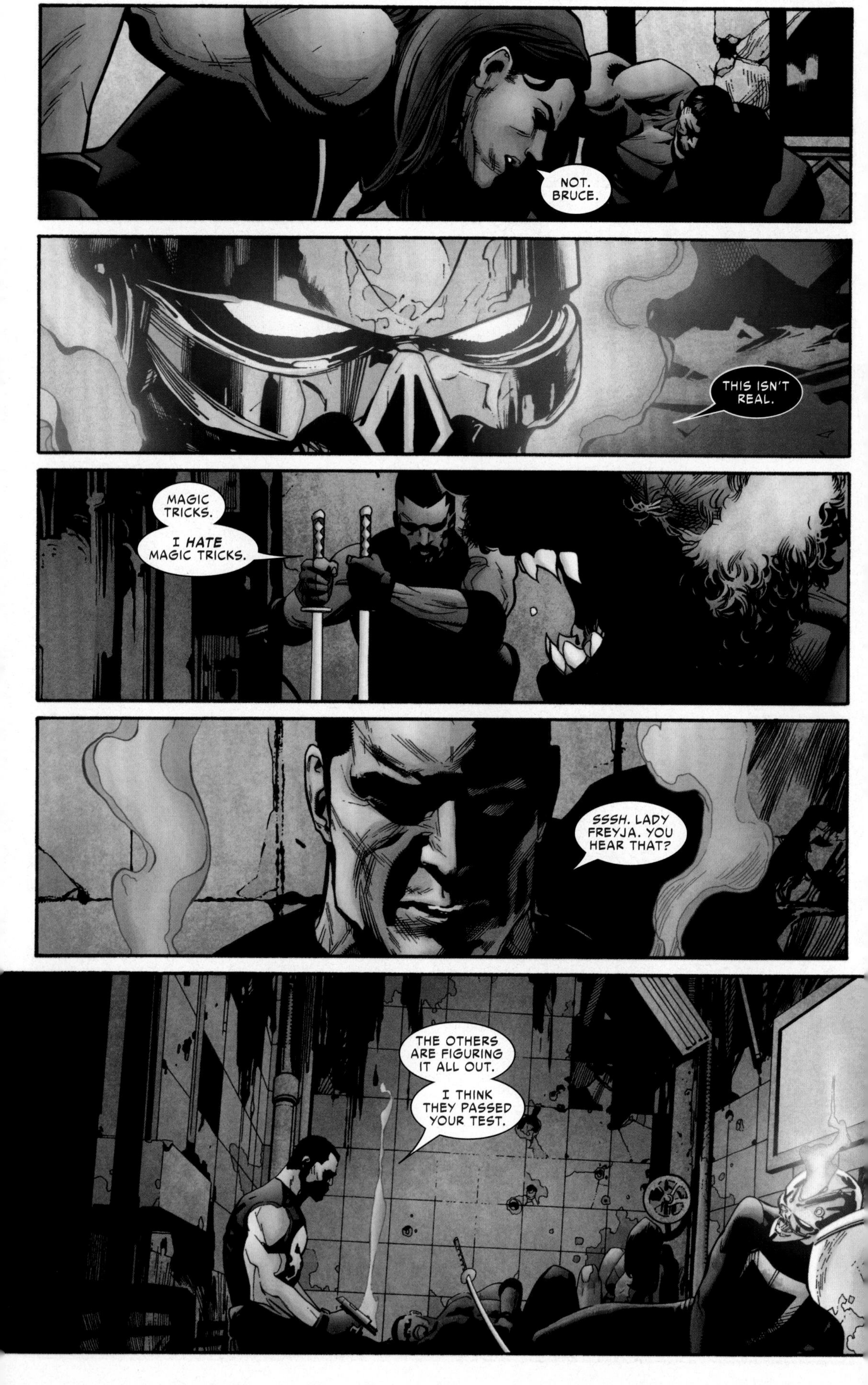
NOT. BRUCE.
THIS ISN'T REAL.
MAGIC TRICKS.
I *HATE* MAGIC TRICKS.
SSSH. LADY FREYJA. YOU HEAR THAT?
THE OTHERS ARE FIGURING IT ALL OUT.
I THINK THEY PASSED YOUR TEST.

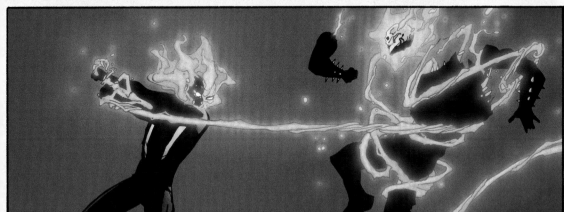

WELL DONE, WARRIORS. YOU HAVE FOUND YOUR SHADOWS.

NOW, COME FIND ME.

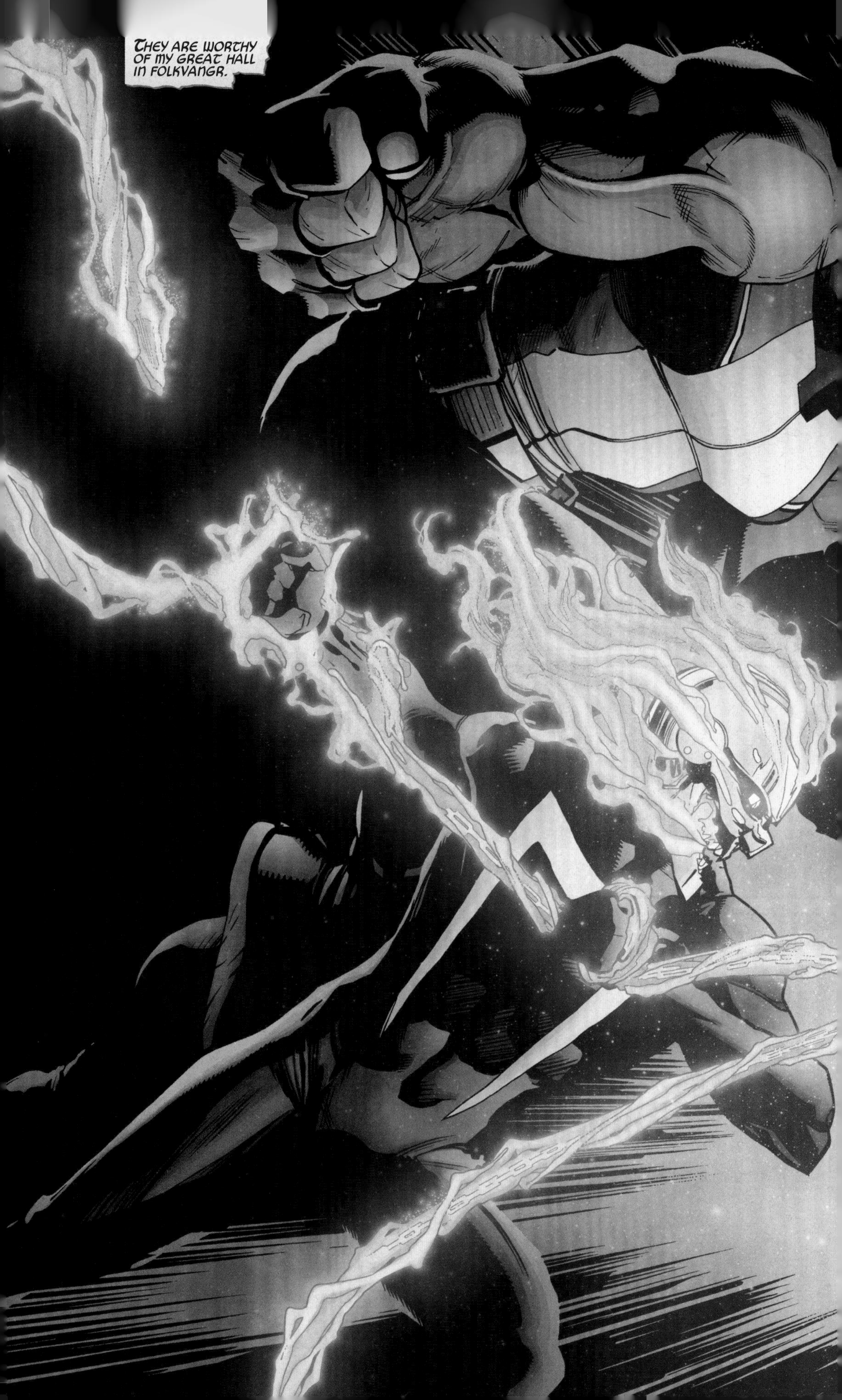
THEY ARE WORTHY OF MY GREAT HALL IN FOLKVANGR.

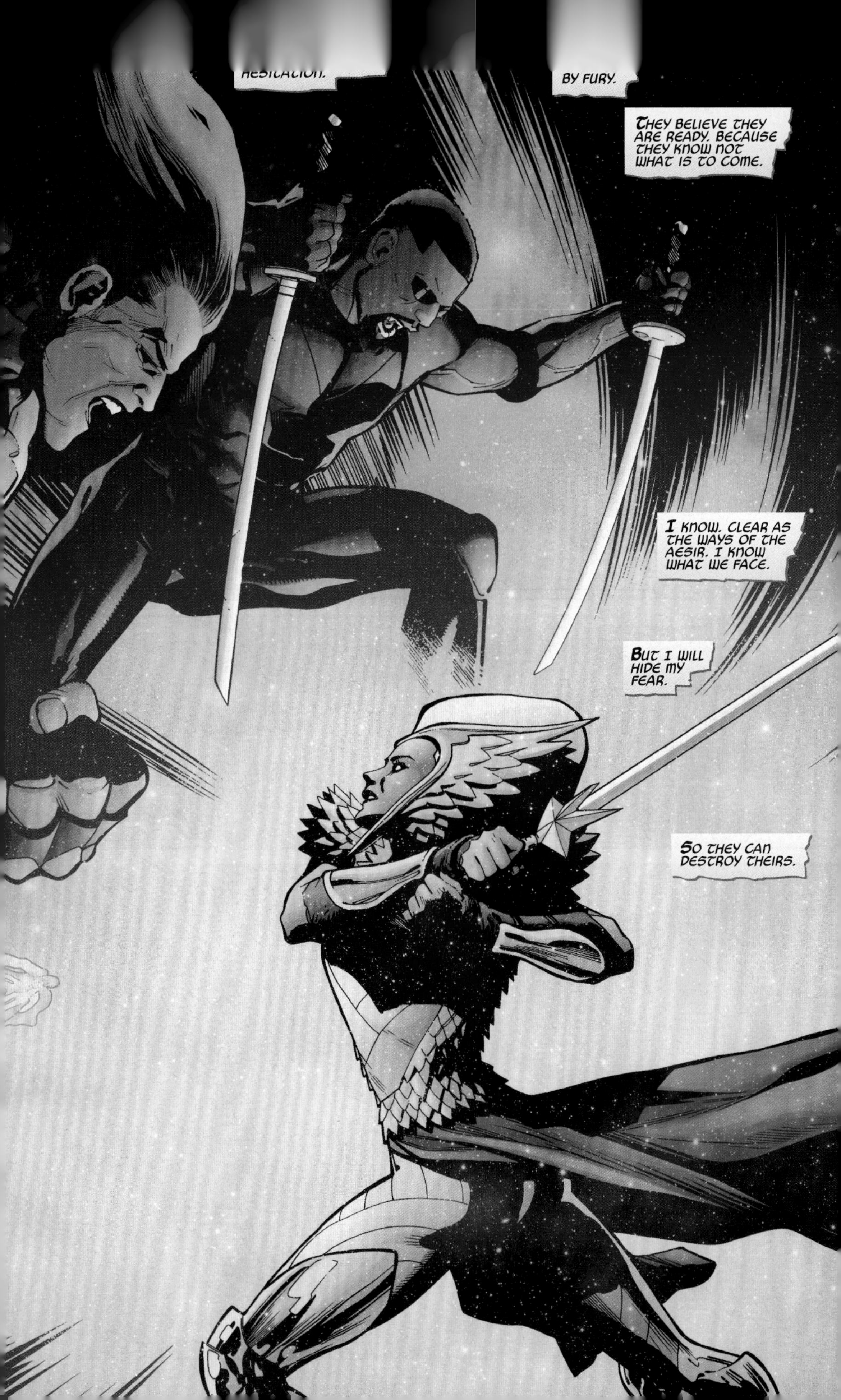
HESITATION.
BY FURY.
THEY BELIEVE THEY ARE READY. BECAUSE THEY KNOW NOT WHAT IS TO COME.
I KNOW. CLEAR AS THE WAYS OF THE AESIR. I KNOW WHAT WE FACE.
BUT I WILL HIDE MY FEAR.
SO THEY CAN DESTROY THEIRS.

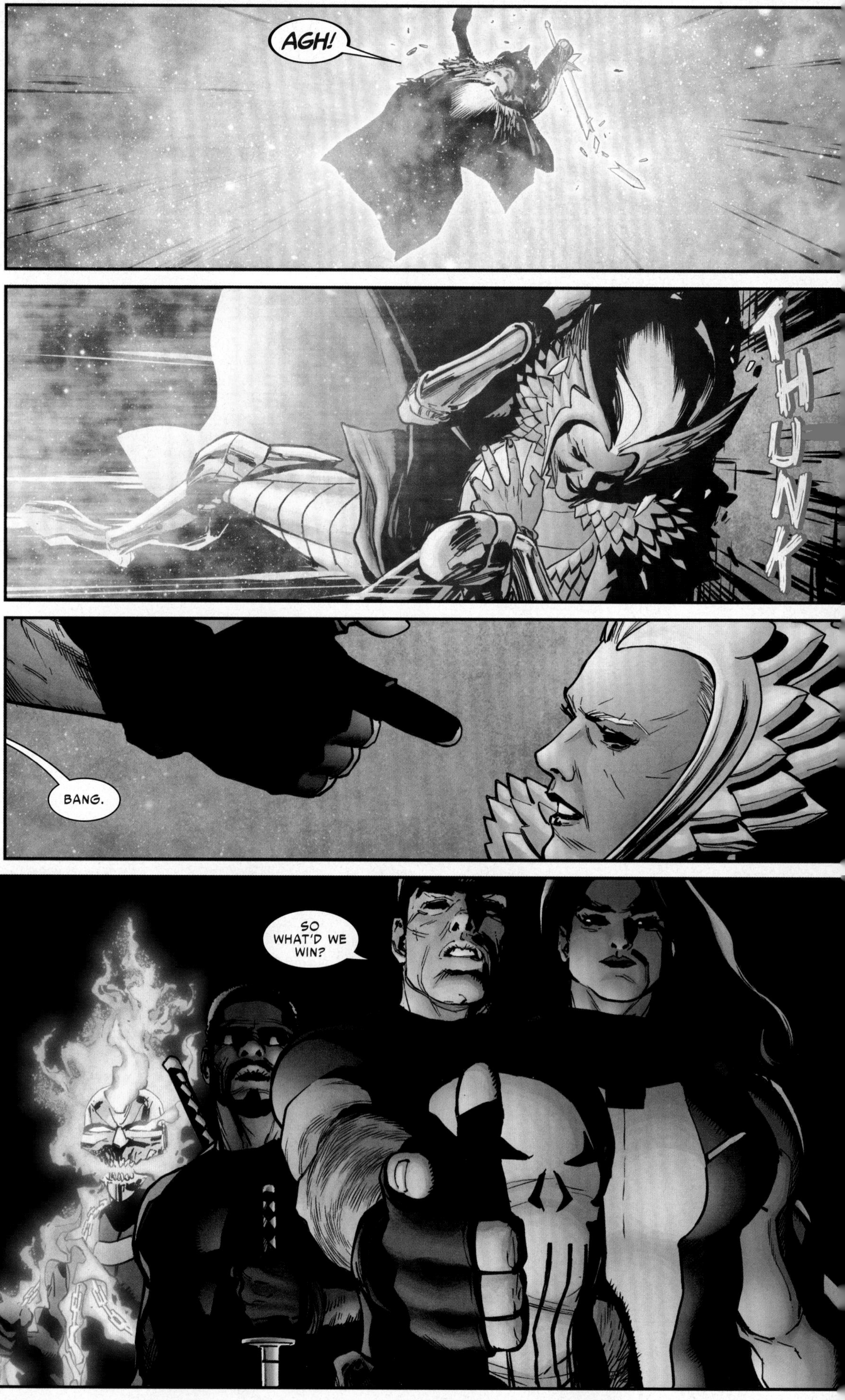
AGH!
THUNK
BANG.
SO WHAT'D WE WIN?

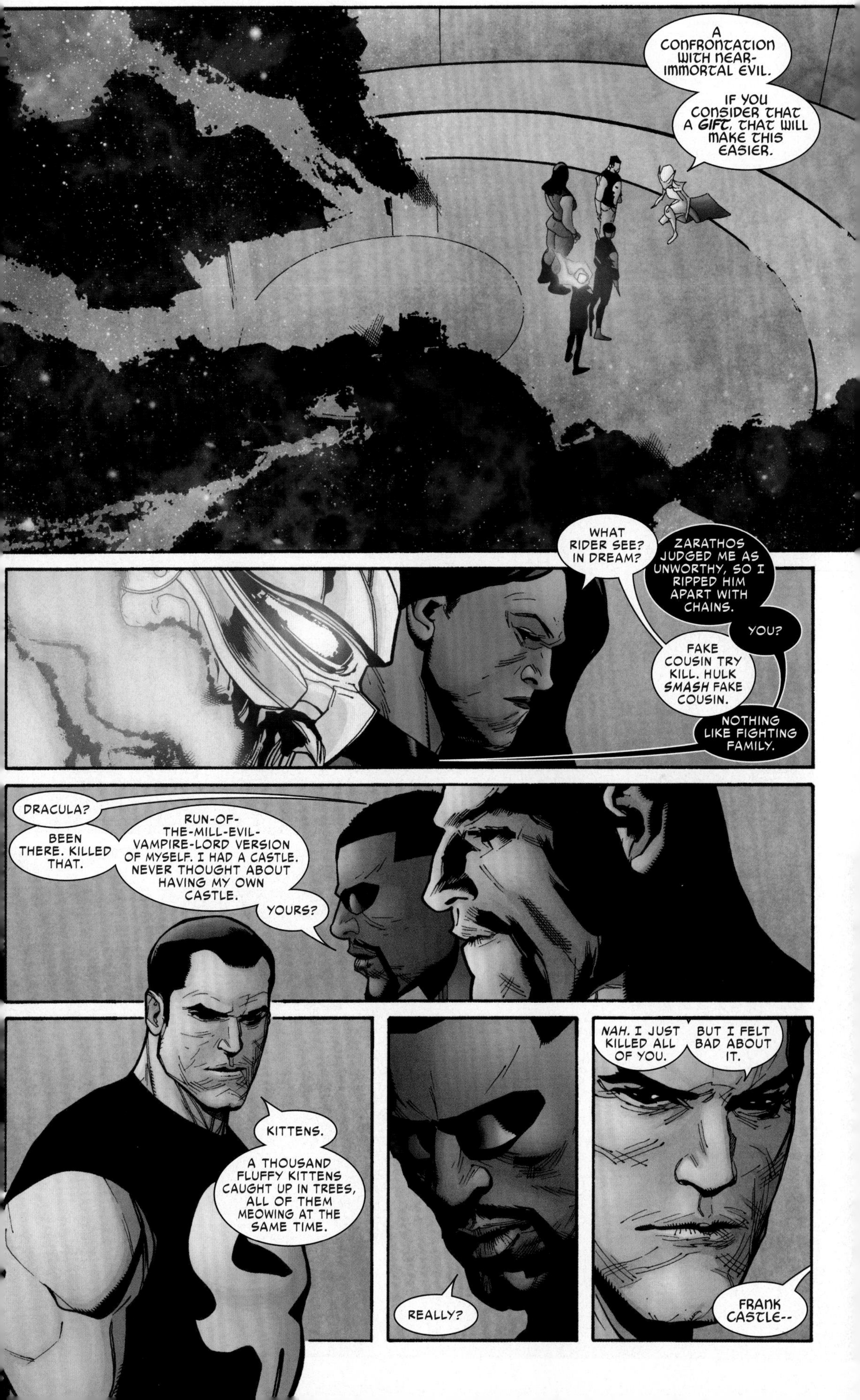
A CONFRONTATION WITH NEAR-IMMORTAL EVIL.
IF YOU CONSIDER THAT A GIFT, THAT WILL MAKE THIS EASIER.
WHAT RIDER SEE? IN DREAM?
ZARATHOS JUDGED ME AS UNWORTHY, SO I RIPPED HIM APART WITH CHAINS.
YOU?
FAKE COUSIN TRY KILL. HULK SMASH FAKE COUSIN.
NOTHING LIKE FIGHTING FAMILY.
DRACULA?
BEEN THERE. KILLED THAT.
RUN-OF-THE-MILL-EVIL-VAMPIRE-LORD VERSION OF MYSELF. I HAD A CASTLE. NEVER THOUGHT ABOUT HAVING MY OWN CASTLE.
YOURS?
KITTENS.
A THOUSAND FLUFFY KITTENS CAUGHT UP IN TREES, ALL OF THEM MEOWING AT THE SAME TIME.
REALLY?
NAH. I JUST KILLED ALL OF YOU.
BUT I FELT BAD ABOUT IT.
FRANK CASTLE--

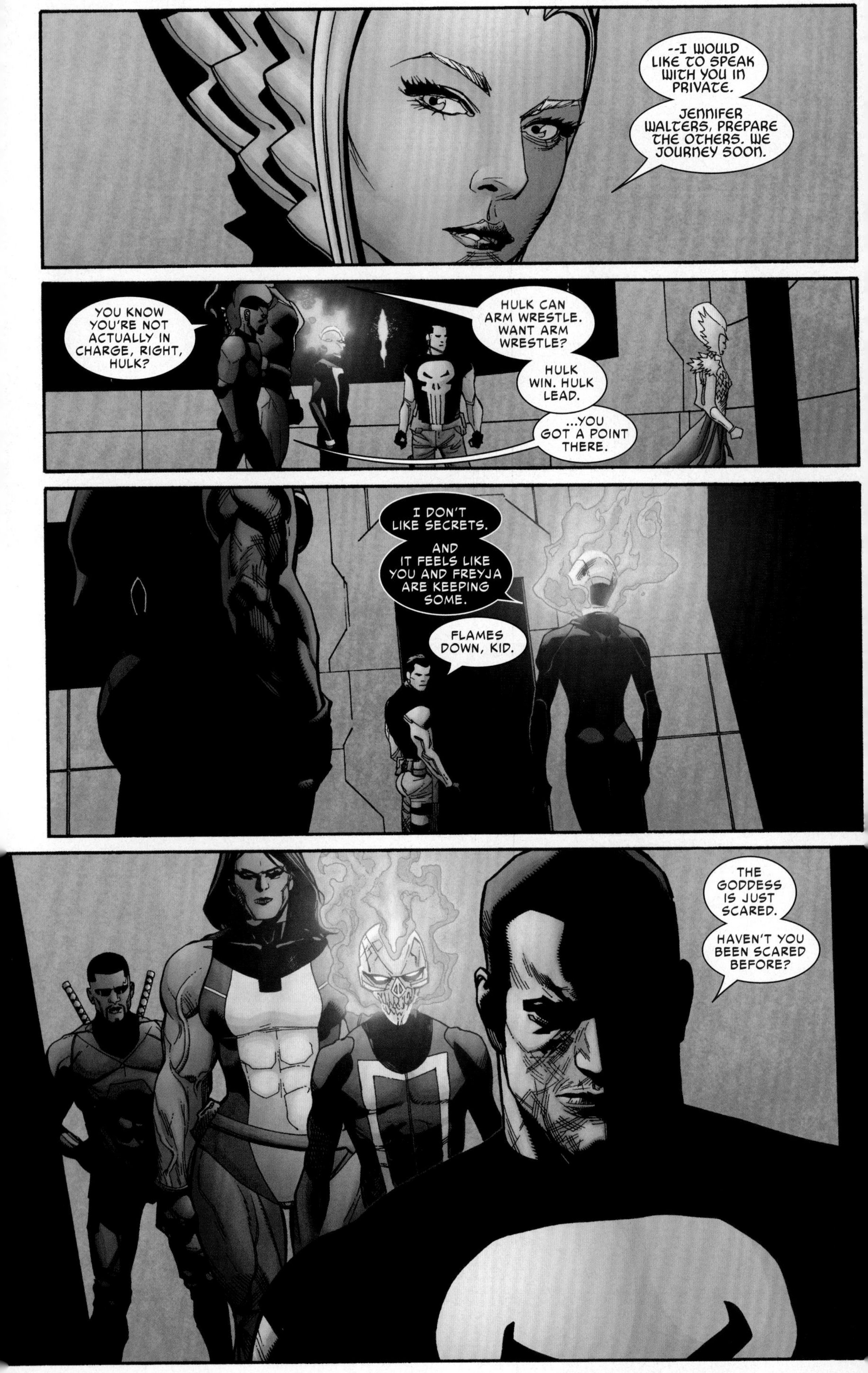
--I WOULD LIKE TO SPEAK WITH YOU IN PRIVATE.
JENNIFER WALTERS, PREPARE THE OTHERS. WE JOURNEY SOON.
YOU KNOW YOU'RE NOT ACTUALLY IN CHARGE, RIGHT, HULK?
HULK CAN ARM WRESTLE. WANT ARM WRESTLE?
HULK WIN. HULK LEAD.
...YOU GOT A POINT THERE.
I DON'T LIKE SECRETS.
AND IT FEELS LIKE YOU AND FREYJA ARE KEEPING SOME.
FLAMES DOWN, KID.
THE GODDESS IS JUST SCARED.
HAVEN'T YOU BEEN SCARED BEFORE?

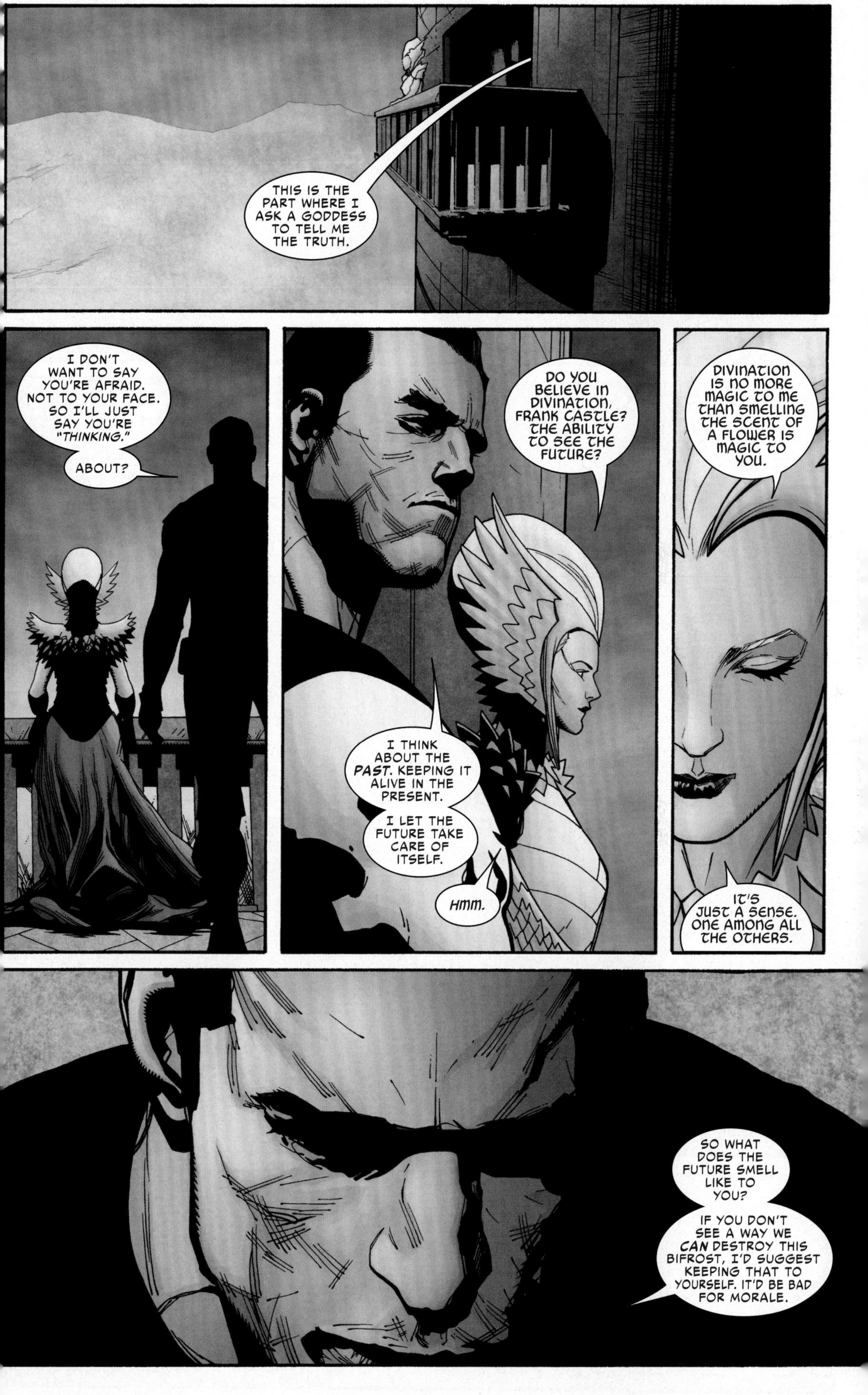
THIS IS THE PART WHERE I ASK A GODDESS TO TELL ME THE TRUTH.
I DON'T WANT TO SAY YOU'RE AFRAID. NOT TO YOUR FACE. SO I'LL JUST SAY YOU'RE "THINKING."
ABOUT?
DO YOU BELIEVE IN DIVINATION, FRANK CASTLE? THE ABILITY TO SEE THE FUTURE?
I THINK ABOUT THE *PAST*. KEEPING IT ALIVE IN THE PRESENT.
I LET THE FUTURE TAKE CARE OF ITSELF.
HMM.
DIVINATION IS NO MORE MAGIC TO ME THAN SMELLING THE SCENT OF A FLOWER IS MAGIC TO YOU.
IT'S JUST A SENSE. ONE AMONG ALL THE OTHERS.
SO WHAT DOES THE FUTURE SMELL LIKE TO YOU?
IF YOU DON'T SEE A WAY WE *CAN* DESTROY THIS BIFROST, I'D SUGGEST KEEPING THAT TO YOURSELF. IT'D BE BAD FOR MORALE.

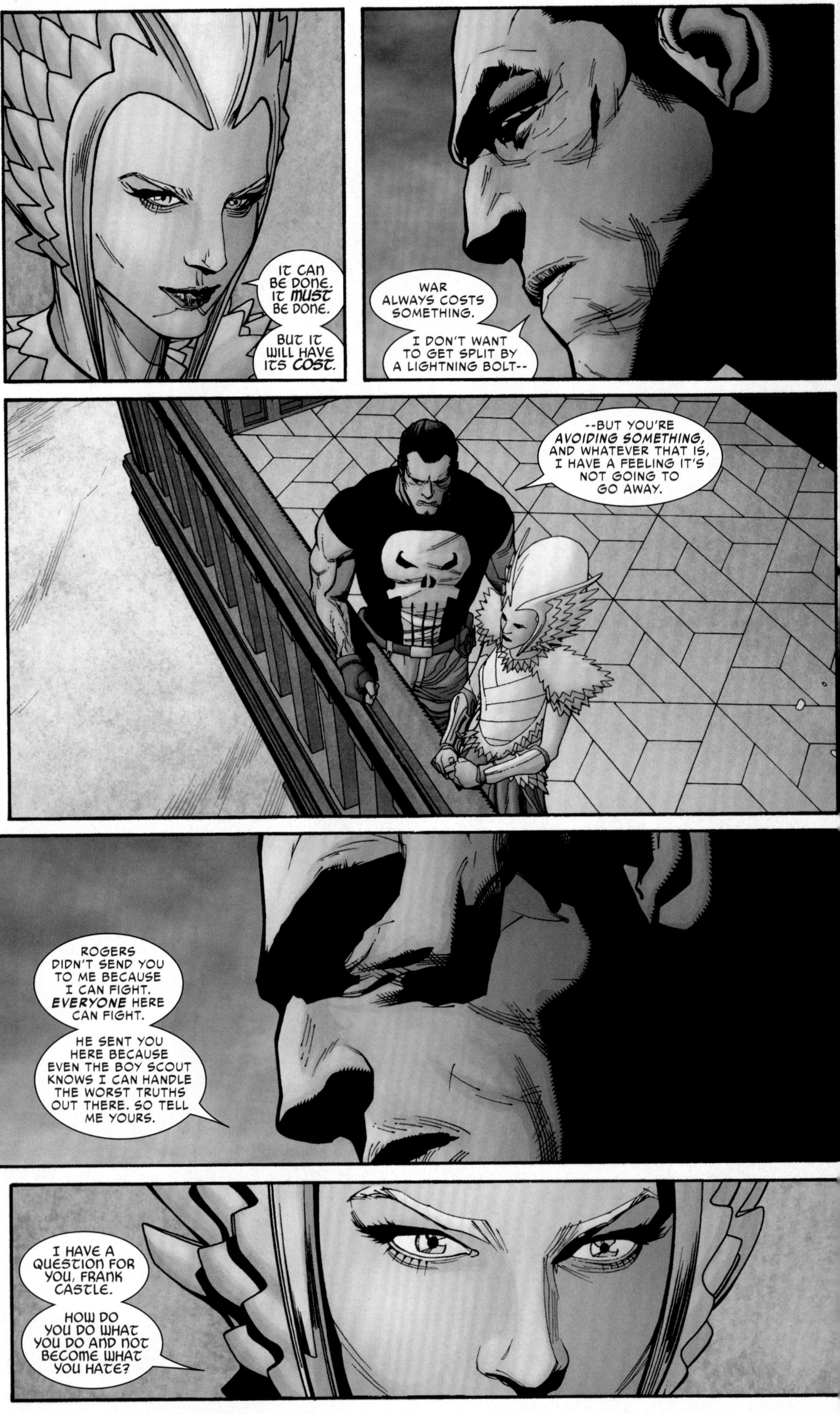
IT CAN BE DONE. IT MUST BE DONE.
BUT IT WILL HAVE ITS COST.
WAR ALWAYS COSTS SOMETHING.
I DON'T WANT TO GET SPLIT BY A LIGHTNING BOLT--
--BUT YOU'RE AVOIDING SOMETHING, AND WHATEVER THAT IS, I HAVE A FEELING IT'S NOT GOING TO GO AWAY.
ROGERS DIDN'T SEND YOU TO ME BECAUSE I CAN FIGHT. EVERYONE HERE CAN FIGHT.
HE SENT YOU HERE BECAUSE EVEN THE BOY SCOUT KNOWS I CAN HANDLE THE WORST TRUTHS OUT THERE. SO TELL ME YOURS.
I HAVE A QUESTION FOR YOU, FRANK CASTLE.
HOW DO YOU DO WHAT YOU DO AND NOT BECOME WHAT YOU HATE?

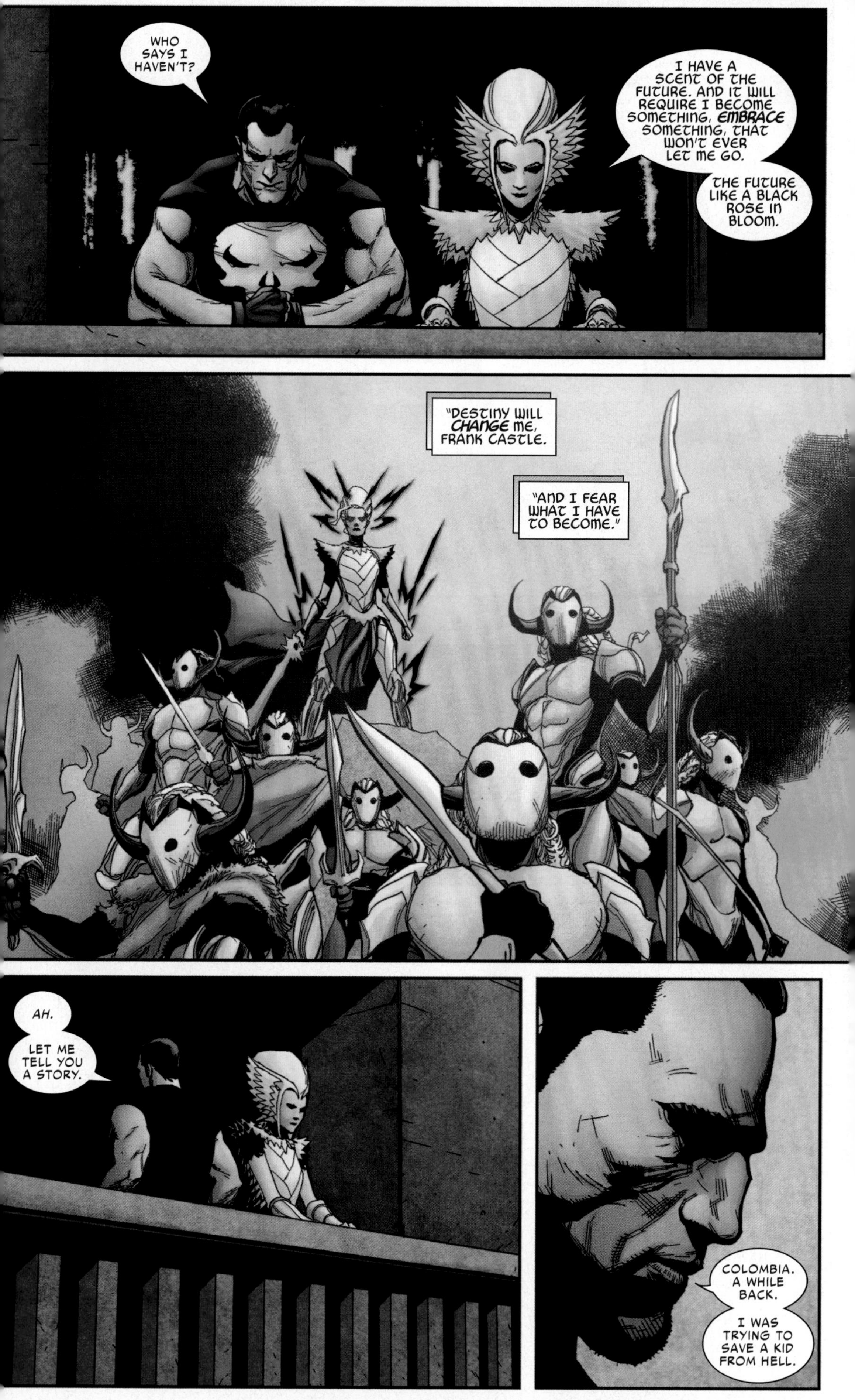
WHO SAYS I HAVEN'T?
I HAVE A SCENT OF THE FUTURE. AND IT WILL REQUIRE I BECOME SOMETHING, EMBRACE SOMETHING, THAT WON'T EVER LET ME GO.
THE FUTURE LIKE A BLACK ROSE IN BLOOM.
"DESTINY WILL CHANGE ME, FRANK CASTLE.
"AND I FEAR WHAT I HAVE TO BECOME."
AH.
LET ME TELL YOU A STORY.
COLOMBIA. A WHILE BACK.
I WAS TRYING TO SAVE A KID FROM HELL.

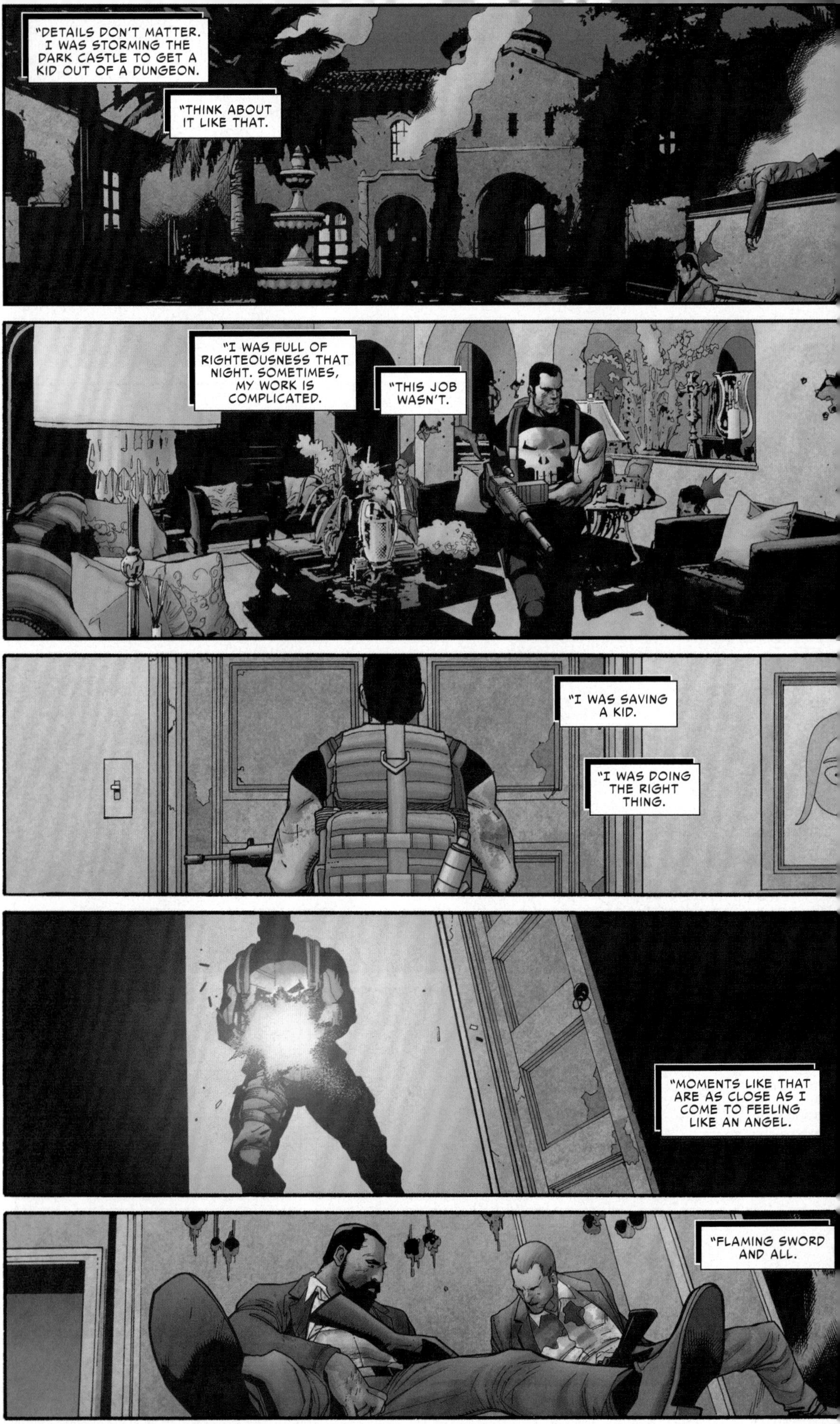
"DETAILS DON'T MATTER. I WAS STORMING THE DARK CASTLE TO GET A KID OUT OF A DUNGEON.
"THINK ABOUT IT LIKE THAT.
"I WAS FULL OF RIGHTEOUSNESS THAT NIGHT. SOMETIMES, MY WORK IS COMPLICATED.
"THIS JOB WASN'T.
"I WAS SAVING A KID.
"I WAS DOING THE RIGHT THING.
"MOMENTS LIKE THAT ARE AS CLOSE AS I COME TO FEELING LIKE AN ANGEL.
"FLAMING SWORD AND ALL.

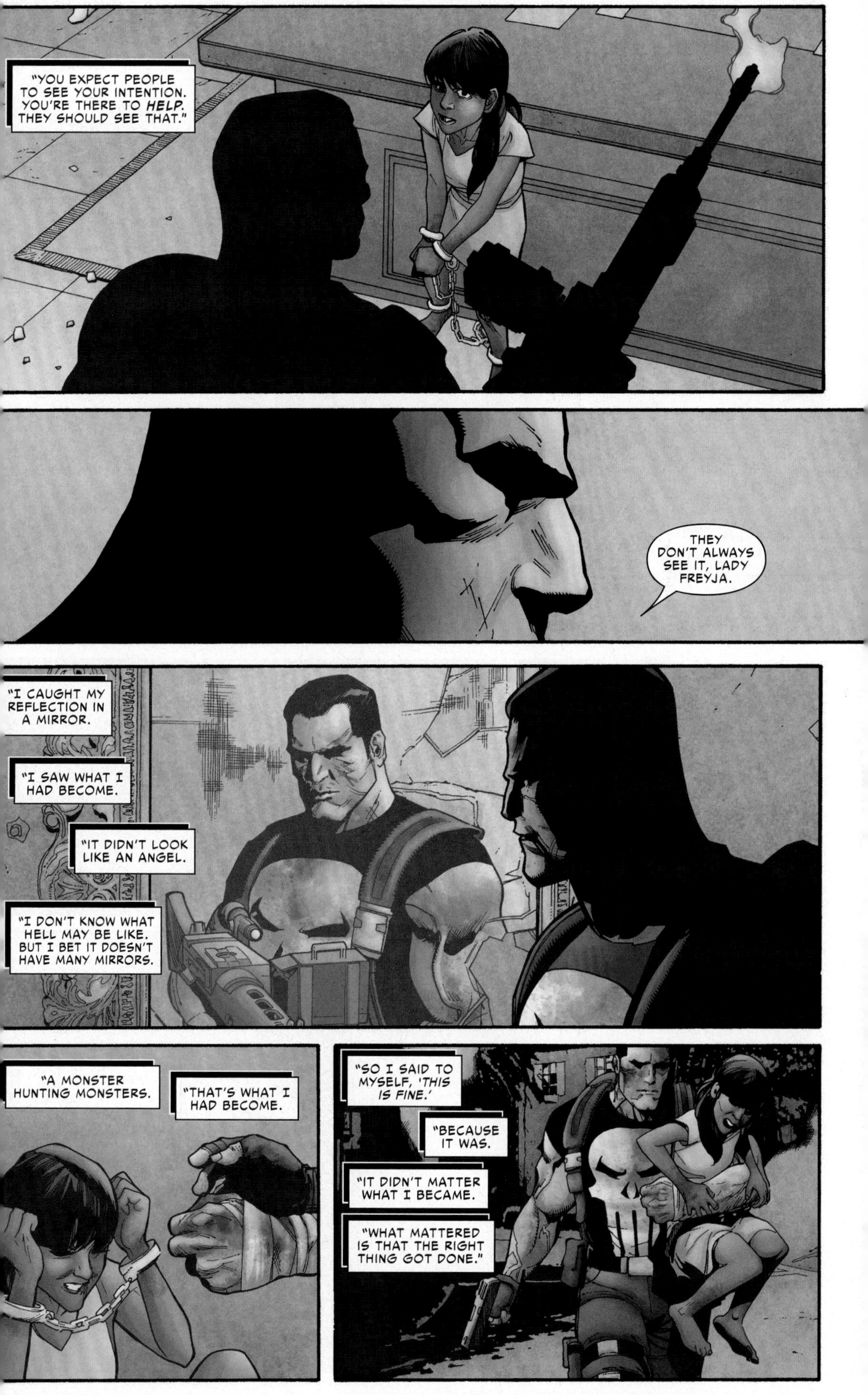
"YOU EXPECT PEOPLE TO SEE YOUR INTENTION. YOU'RE THERE TO *HELP*. THEY SHOULD SEE THAT."
THEY DON'T ALWAYS SEE IT, LADY FREYJA.
"I CAUGHT MY REFLECTION IN A MIRROR.
"I SAW WHAT I HAD BECOME.
"IT DIDN'T LOOK LIKE AN ANGEL.
"I DON'T KNOW WHAT HELL MAY BE LIKE. BUT I BET IT DOESN'T HAVE MANY MIRRORS.
"A MONSTER HUNTING MONSTERS.
"THAT'S WHAT I HAD BECOME.
"SO I SAID TO MYSELF, '*THIS IS FINE.*'
"BECAUSE IT WAS.
"IT DIDN'T MATTER WHAT I BECAME.
"WHAT MATTERED IS THAT THE RIGHT THING GOT DONE."

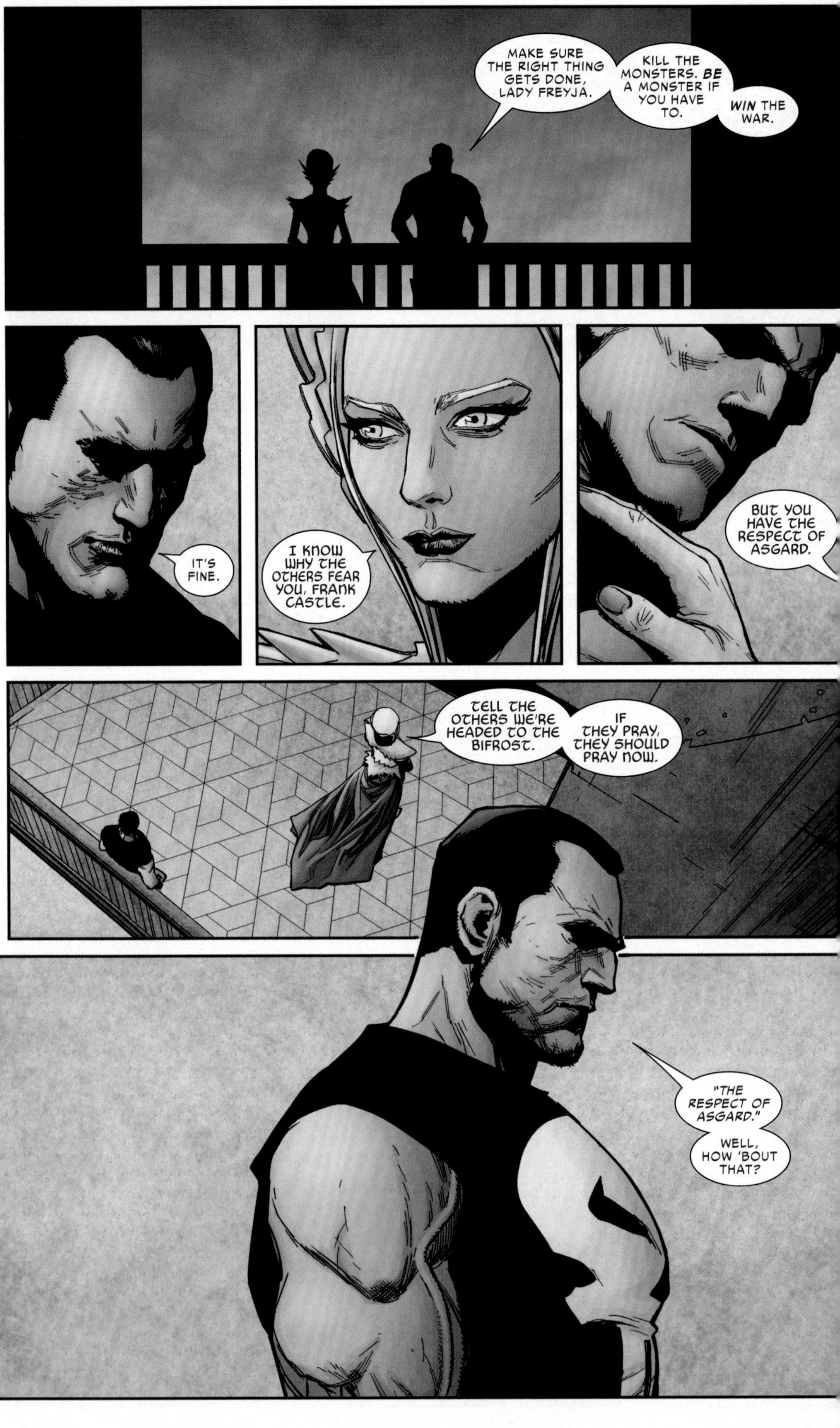
MAKE SURE THE RIGHT THING GETS DONE, LADY FREYJA.
KILL THE MONSTERS. BE A MONSTER IF YOU HAVE TO.
WIN THE WAR.
IT'S FINE.
I KNOW WHY THE OTHERS FEAR YOU, FRANK CASTLE.
BUT YOU HAVE THE RESPECT OF ASGARD.
TELL THE OTHERS WE'RE HEADED TO THE BIFROST.
IF THEY PRAY, THEY SHOULD PRAY NOW.
"THE RESPECT OF ASGARD."
WELL, HOW 'BOUT THAT?

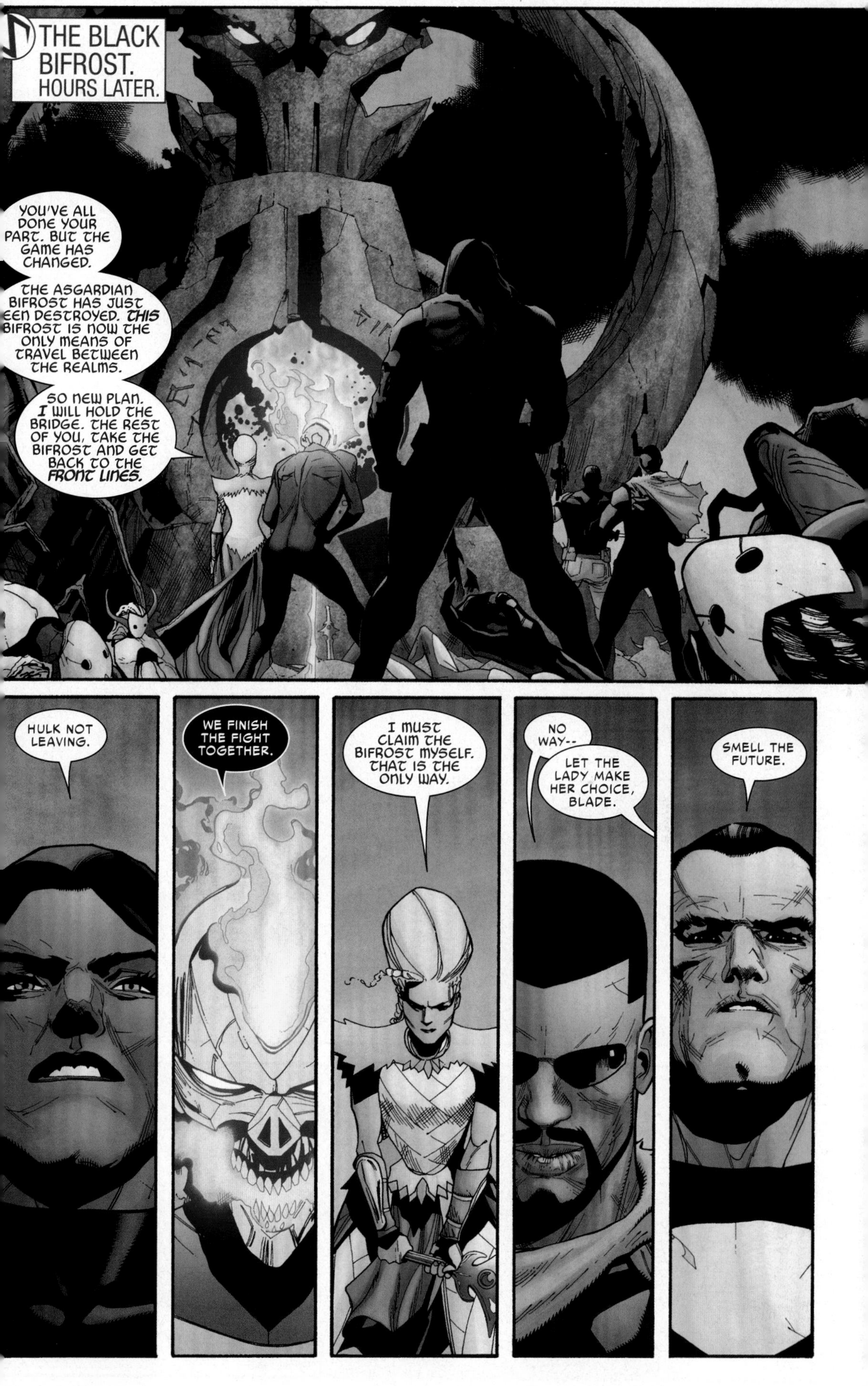

THE BLACK BIFROST. HOURS LATER.
YOU'VE ALL DONE YOUR PART. BUT THE GAME HAS CHANGED.
THE ASGARDIAN BIFROST HAS JUST EEN DESTROYED. THIS BIFROST IS NOW THE ONLY MEANS OF TRAVEL BETWEEN THE REALMS.
SO NEW PLAN. I WILL HOLD THE BRIDGE. THE REST OF YOU, TAKE THE BIFROST AND GET BACK TO THE FRONT LINES.
HULK NOT LEAVING.
WE FINISH THE FIGHT TOGETHER.
I MUST CLAIM THE BIFROST MYSELF. THAT IS THE ONLY WAY.
NO WAY--
LET THE LADY MAKE HER CHOICE, BLADE.
SMELL THE FUTURE.

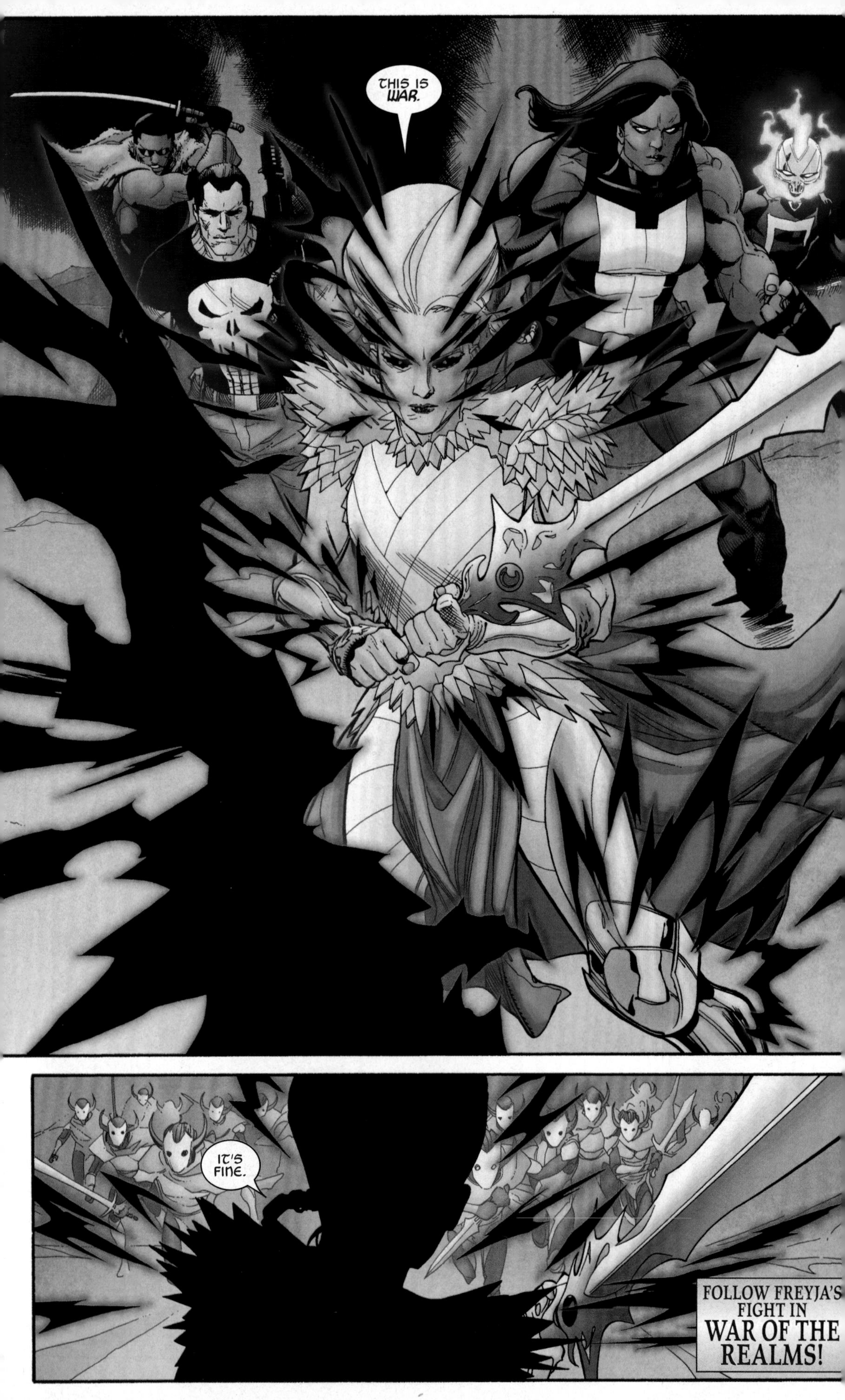
THIS IS WAR.
IT'S FINE.
FOLLOW FREYJA'S FIGHT IN WAR OF THE REALMS!